THE FRENCH REVOLUTION
EVENTS AND IDEAS

Michael Sonenscher
University of Cambridge

CAMBRIDGE
UNIVERSITY PRESS

Shaftesbury Road, Cambridge CB2 8EA, United Kingdom

One Liberty Plaza, 20th Floor, New York, NY 10006, USA

477 Williamstown Road, Port Melbourne, VIC 3207, Australia

314–321, 3rd Floor, Plot 3, Splendor Forum, Jasola District Centre,
New Delhi – 110025, India

Cambridge University Press is part of Cambridge University Press & Assessment,
a department of the University of Cambridge.

We share the University's mission to contribute to society through the pursuit of
education, learning and research at the highest international levels of excellence.

www.cambridge.org
Information on this title: www.cambridge.org/9781009463935

DOI: 10.1017/9781009463898

First published 2026

A catalogue record for this publication is available from the British Library

A Cataloging-in-Publication data record for this book is available from the Library of Congress

ISBN 978-1-009-46393-5 Hardback
ISBN 978-1-009-46390-4 Paperback

The French Revolution

Three questions have usually been asked about the French Revolution. Why did it happen? Why was it so violent? What was its legacy? These questions seem to beg other, more conceptually ambitious queries about causation, violence or legacies. This book aims to answer both sets of questions by bringing together events and ideas. Michael Sonenscher draws on neglected aspects of eighteenth-century intellectual and political life and thought to demonstrate the importance of ideas for making connections between historical explanation and historical narrative. Concisely synthesising a broad range of established scholarship, Sonenscher utilises new and fresh information to explore why using ideas as evidence adds a dimension of novelty, possibility, expectation and choice to the social, cultural and political history of the French Revolution. This is history about what was expected, but did not happen, and what was unexpected, but really did.

MICHAEL SONENSCHER is a fellow of King's College, University of Cambridge. He has written several books on the French Revolution, including *Before the Deluge* (2007) and *Sans-Culottes* (2009), as well as two broader studies in the history of political thought: *Capitalism: The Story behind the Word* (2022) and *After Kant: The Romans, the Germans and the Moderns in the History of Political Thought* (2023).

Contents

Acknowledgements   *page* vi

 1 Introduction: Ideas as Evidence   1
 2 Concepts of Revolution   24
 3 Causes and Causation   49
 4 Cutting the Cable: Rousseau, Sieyès and the Idea
    of a Representative System   72
 5 Public Debt as the Cement of Society   94
 6 Constituent Power and Political Power   116
 7 The Failure of the Feuillants   133
 8 The *Sans-Culottes*   159
 9 Robespierre and the Politics of the Terror   180
10 The War for the World: Social Science and Imperial Power   200
11 Conclusion: The Legacy   214

Index   227

Acknowledgements

I am grateful to the Provost, Fellows, librarians and members of the research committee of King's College, Cambridge, not only for practical support (books) but also for the kindness, commitment and hard work that I have always experienced from them. I am grateful too to many helpful people at the Cambridge University Library for reassurance that the once fabled information superhighway still has a residual presence. I have a broader and deeper debt to my wife, Elizabeth Allen, to her family and their several respective families. Knowing them all has helped me get through some of the more solitary or unhappy moments associated with this book. Sadly, and with apologies to Radegund Norbury, the phrase 'Guillotines and Cake' as a possible title of this book had to hit the cutting-room floor. I am particularly grateful for information, advice and encouragement to Michael Behrent, Rafe Blaufarb, Richard Bourke, Graham Clure, John Dunn, Olivier Higgins, Jo Innes, Charlotte Johann, Colin Jones, Béla Kapossy, Iain McDaniel, Jonathan Rée, Stephen Sawyer, Katie Scott, Gareth Stedman Jones, Sylvana Tomaselli, Charles Walton and Richard Whatmore. Thanks too to Glyn Baker for reminding me of the Diamond Necklace Affair and other things that I sometimes forget. I have a particular debt to Isaac Nakhimovsky, not only for reading the whole text but also for rereading the growing assortment of revisions, modifications and additions that I have intermittently inflicted upon him. The same applies to Colin Jones, the most conscientious and constructive of readers, and Duncan Kelly, the editor of the series in which this book appears. Nobody could have asked for a better combination of knowledge, patience, criticism and insight than those that he has supplied, always in full and always on time. I owe a great deal to Liz Friend Smith, Rosanna Barraclough and Ruth Boyes at the Cambridge University Press, not only for their willingness to accommodate the size of this book but also for turning it into something worth looking at, both outside and in. Thanks too to Sajukrishnan Balakrishnan and to Ayesha Fahima Arshad Hussain for bringing a complex editorial process to its final destination and to Lucian Robinson for checking the results. I am grateful, finally, to the large number of students of both the French Revolution and the history of political thought whom I have met and talked with over the years. This book is as much a record of that longer time of learning and thinking as of the relatively shorter time that it has taken me to write and rewrite it. Credit for what I have learnt goes to them. Responsibility for what I have got wrong is mine.

CHAPTER ONE

Introduction: Ideas as Evidence

Three questions have usually been asked about the French Revolution: why did it happen?; why was it so violent?; and what was its legacy? At first sight all three questions seem to beg other, more conceptually ambitious questions, whether about causation, violence or legacies. The aim of this short book is to answer both sets of questions by bringing together events with ideas. Combining the two actually helps to make the answers to the second, more conceptually oriented set of questions more historically and analytically focussed. It does so because the French Revolution owes much of its complexity to ideas and, more particularly, to the range and multiplicity of appearances and temporalities that ideas can lend to events. Complexity, not only in France and not only at the time of the French Revolution, is more than an effect of large numbers of people living in different circumstances with different, sometimes antagonistic, interests. It is also an effect of the range of occasionally compelling, but occasionally competing, emotional responses, moral evaluations and causal assessments made by, or of, people living in similar circumstances with similar, overlapping or complementary interests. Complexity, in short, has as much to do with interpretation and context as with multiplicity and diversity because descriptions, as is well known, can be either thick or thin, and evaluations in their turn can have as much to do with empathy, identity and distinction as with measurement, comparison and analysis. Physiology, it is said, cannot identify the difference between a tic and a wink.[1] The world, it is also said, can be seen

---

[1] On thick description, see, famously, Clifford Geertz, *The Interpretation of Cultures* (New York, 1973), 15–42, and, on distinction, Pierre Bourdieu, *Distinction* [1979] (London, 1984). 'The difference between the Parthenon and the World Trade Center, between a French wine glass and a German beer mug, between Bach and

either through rose-tinted spectacles or through a glass darkly. It will be the same world but it will, nonetheless, look different. The same set of people can, in a similar sense, be described as flourishing or failing, equal or unequal, subject or free, just as praying while smoking differs from smoking while praying, and lives, like glasses of water, seem to have different prospects if they are said to be half full or half empty. Appearances, it seems, count, but not only – or not really – because of the appearances themselves.

Appearances do, however, capture something distinctive about events, whether, in the first instance, as a simple set of names, dates, times and places or, in something nearer to the last instance, as an intricate combination of actions, intentions, causes and meanings that, conceptually and symbolically, anchor appearances to history and give them what has sometimes been called their historicity, or the qualities of singularity and particularity that, more fundamentally, make them what they were. The French Revolution, from this perspective, was one of many revolutions but it was also, nonetheless, *the* French Revolution. Appearances are, therefore, both a starting point and an end point. They form a link between the idea of the beginning of a sequence and the idea of a completed whole, or between what could be called serial time and affective time. The resulting combination of unity and multiplicity seems to mean that appearances have an ability to make events and ideas add up to something historically distinct or, as it has sometimes been called, a totality.[2] Writing at the time when the French Revolution had run much of its course, the German philosopher Georg Wilhelm Friedrich Hegel gave the name of phenomenology to this way of thinking about appearances and set out to show how something envisaged as both a sequence and a whole (*Ganze*) could enable events and ideas to cohere.[3] As he set out to show, the flexibility that comes with language and

John Philip Souza, between Sophocles and Shakespeare, between a bicycle and a horse, though explicable by historical moment, necessity, and destiny, is before all a difference of imagination.' Guy Davenport, *The Geography of the Imagination* (San Francisco, 1981), 1.

[2] For a helpful overview, see John E Grumley, *History and Totality. Radical Historicism from Hegel to Foucault* (London, 1989) and, earlier, Martin Jay, *Marxism and Totality* (Cambridge, 1984).

[3] For an initial indication of Hegel's conceptual vocabulary in his treatment of wholeness, see Shterna Friedman, 'Freedom and Totality: How Hegel Became

thinking not only helps to explain how something can be made up of many things but also how both aspects of this fusion of unity and multiplicity can remain conceptually distinct. Many minutes, for example, make up a day, but Tuesday is still different from Wednesday. Many years later, a more context-oriented version of the same approach was given the name of 'thick description' by the British philosopher Gilbert Ryle and, in this guise, the concept was taken over to become one of the keys to the interpretation of cultures in the works of the American anthropologist Clifford Geertz.[4] A brief account of the origins and significance of this two-sided approach to appearances, centred particularly on the events of the French Revolution, can be found towards the end of this book. Here, however, it is important to begin with appearances in their initial, more straightforward sense, as the names, dates, times and places that, cumulatively, made up the sequence of events that became the French Revolution.

That sequence began on 20 August 1786 with a memorandum to France's king Louis XVI drafted by his controller-general of finances, Charles-Alexandre de Calonne. In it, Calonne indicated that projected royal expenditure in 1787 was likely to exceed projected royal income by some 115 million livres (at that time forty French livres were equivalent to some three English pounds). The point of the memorandum was to set out an agenda for an assembly of the kingdom's most notable subjects which, accordingly, was summoned by Louis XVI to meet on 22 February 1787 to address the problem of the deficit. Its immediate brief was to discuss and, Calonne hoped, to endorse a substantial package of fiscal, financial and institutional reforms. On the fiscal side, Calonne proposed the creation of a land tax, to be paid in kind, not cash, and at rates that were calibrated to four different levels of fertility of cultivated land. On the institutional side, there would be a network of elected provincial assemblies whose members would be drawn from a broad cross section of property owners rather than from the three separate French estates of the clergy, nobility and commoners. The responsibilities

Hegel', *History of Political Thought*, 45 (2024), 124–56. See more fully Jean Hyppolite, *Logique et existence* (Paris, 1952), 7–26.

[4] Gilbert Ryle, 'Thinking and Reflecting' [1966], in his *Collected Papers*, 2 vols. (London, 1971), 2, 465–79.

of these provincial assemblies would include the administration of tax assessments and the collection of tax revenue, a proposal indicating the likely abolition of the many existing offices, including the various royal tax farmers and the thousands of others that could be bought and sold, bequeathed or inherited, adding up to a total of some 60,000 venal offices in all. Finally, on the financial side, a public bank was to be established, internal customs barriers were to be removed, restrictions on the grain trade were to be lifted, forced labour was to be replaced by a monetary tax and the duty raised on salt was to be standardised throughout the kingdom.

Calonne's proposals were rejected by the Assembly of Notables and, on 8 April 1787, he was dismissed. After a short interlude, his successor, the archbishop of Toulouse, Etienne Loménie de Brienne, dissolved the Assembly of Notables on 25 May 1787 and, over the course of that year and the next, tried to persuade, then force, the thirteen French high courts of appeal, or Parlements, to adopt much the same set of reforms. In addition to being high courts of appeal in civil and criminal legal matters, the Parlements also had a long-standing, if somewhat indeterminate, right to object to – or remonstrate on – projected royal legislation, usually by invoking some – equally indeterminate – interpretation of the fundamental laws of the monarchy, or the kingdom or, sometimes, both. In keeping with this tradition, the several hundred law officers, or magistrates, of the Parlements flatly refused to endorse Brienne's proposals. As their opposition became firmer, the stage seemed set for a replay of events that had unfolded in France in 1771 and 1772 when, in what was called the Maupeou coup, the French royal army had been used to dissolve all thirteen Parlements, enabling the government of Louis XVI's grandfather, Louis XV, to impose a new set of legal institutions on the kingdom. Although Louis XVI reinstated the Parlements when he became king in 1774, something similar to the Maupeou coup seemed likely to recur when, some sixteen years later on 8 May 1788, a royal edict established a plenary court and stripped the Parlements of their status as high courts of appeal. But, by the late summer of 1788, in the wake of open resistance from the Parlements, notably from the Parlement of the province of the Dauphiné situated in the southern French city of Grenoble, conditions began to change. The royal government began to backtrack, and on 8 August 1788, Louis XVI issued an invitation to his subjects to discuss the composition of a meeting of the Estates-General of the whole kingdom. The meeting was set initially to take place several years in the future but, as the problem of the deficit became more acute, it was brought forward to begin in May 1789. Before it began to meet, the king's subjects were invited to discuss a number of preliminary questions about its composition, procedures and powers.

The initial question that they were expected to address was whether the Estates-General should meet as it had done when it had last been convened almost 175 years earlier in 1614, with three separate sets of delegates representing the first, second and third estates, or the clergy, nobility and commoners, each elected by separate electoral assemblies in every province, bailiwick, town and parish. This initial question about the scale and level of continuity between 1614 and 1789 was, in reality, made up of three further and more substantive questions. The first was a question about the respective size of each delegation, particularly in the light of the increase in size of the third estate and the urban population of France since 1614. The second was a more difficult question about whether the representatives of the three estates should meet separately, but with a requirement to reconcile their respective views under ministerial guidance or supervision, as had been the case when the Estates-General were last summoned to deliberate on the grievances (*doléances*) of the assorted orders, provinces, corporations and estates of the kingdom. The third question arose directly from the second and was a large, composite and potentially intractable question about the rights, powers, offices, procedures, responsibilities and obligations of the Estates-General if, unprecedentedly, it was to deliberate and decide as a single body.

On 16 August 1788, however, before any of these questions could be answered, the royal treasury suspended cash payments on bills presented for financial settlement and began to issue promissory paper notes to cover the deficit. A week later, on 24 August, Brienne resigned and was replaced two days later by Jacques Necker, a Swiss banker who had held the office of director general of finance between 1776 and 1783 when France had intervened in support of American independence in the war between Britain and the nascent United States. The meeting of the Estates-General was now brought forwards to 5 May 1789. The period before it met was filled by an immense number of local and provincial meetings and electoral assemblies where grievances were drafted, delegates were elected and mandated powers were discussed and defined. When, however, the meeting began, it quickly became deadlocked on the three questions that had arisen over its composition, procedures and powers. The deadlock paralysed the Estates-General and seeped into the royal ministry, the royal court and the royal family, with different ministers and rival clients of the king and queen advocating competing policies or incompatible measures to move ahead. As the deadlock continued into the early summer, and despite a unilateral declaration by the representatives of the Third Estate on 17 June 1789 proclaiming themselves to be a National Assembly, it was still possible to think that decisive royal action would deliver a replay of the Maupeou coup of 1771–72. When, finally, the expected show of force seemed about to appear, with news of the abrupt dismissal of Jacques Necker on 11 July 1789 and the simultaneous appointment of a new, reputedly hard-line ministry, continuing high-level wrangling and ministerial hesitation allowed large swathes of the population of Paris to take to the streets in search of arms to counter the anticipated royal coup. The search for arms gave rise to a siege of the royal fortress known as the Bastille on the eastern side of Paris and, as the crowd grew in size over the three following days, sheer force of numbers blocked the long-anticipated recourse to force. Faced with the prospect of carnage, the army high command did not act and, on 14 July 1789, the Bastille fell. After its fall, the short-lived ministry appointed by Louis XVI after Necker's dismissal was given the derisive name of the Ministry of the Hundred Hours.

The most obvious and immediate question arising from this sequence of events is how to explain why the deficit that was predicted in the autumn of 1786 gave rise to the French Revolution and, more specifically, to the armed insurrection that began in Paris on 11 July 1789 and culminated on 14 July 1789 with the fall of the Bastille, the event still commemorated in France over 200 years later. This initial question is connected, equally obviously, to a further set of questions centred on explaining why, after the Bastille fell, a further seven Parisian insurrections and intermittent outbursts of street fighting – on 5–6 October 1789, 17 July 1791, 20 June 1792, 10 August 1792, 31 May–2 June 1793, 5 September 1793 and 27 July 1794 – gave rise to, or helped to produce, the various, sometimes deliberately orchestrated political turning points and organised acts of retribution that came to be known generically as the Terror. By the time of the Terror, starting in the spring of 1793 and continuing into the summer of 1794, France had become a republic, loudly proclaimed soon after the Parisian insurrection of 10 August 1792. In place of the old French monarchy, this first French republic was governed by a combination of an elected constitutional Convention, a name that echoed the one given to its counterpart in the United States, and its two great Committees of Public Safety and General Security established in the spring of 1793. In conjunction with the Convention and its committees, the republic was also governed less formally by the purely voluntary membership of a network of political clubs headed, famously, by the Jacobin club of Paris. It is not clear how or why a voluntary association like the Jacobin club, initially one of many societies established in 1789 or 1790 and modelled on the earlier English Society for Constitutional Information established in 1780, could turn into something like a virtual government and become the power base of Maximilien Robespierre, Louis-Antoine Saint-Just, Georges Couthon and their political allies until they were overthrown on 27 July 1794 (or 9 Thermidor Year II according to the new French republican calendar) by a Parisian insurrection initiated by dissident members of the Convention. Nor, finally, is it clear why the political upheaval in France gave rise to a huge European war, beginning on 20 April 1792 and ending only twenty three years later with the final defeat of Napoleon's army at the battle of Waterloo, long after a military coup in 1799 brought the French republic to an end and replaced it, first by the French Consulate and then, in 1804, by the first French Empire.

Deficits usually cause tax rises, expenditure cuts or a mixture of both, not revolutions or major wars. Nor have many revolutions given rise to new territorial and administrative divisions, a new calendar, new weights and measures, a new currency, a new religion and a proliferation of new or replacement names – such as 'Brumaire', 'Germinal', 'Anaxagoras', 'Anacharsis' and 'Commune-Affranchie' instead, for example, of 'Marie', 'Joseph', 'Louis', 'Saint' or 'Lyon'– for people, places, months or years. There was a *levée en masse* in France in 1793 followed by more-or-less permanent mass conscription until the end of the Napoleonic wars in 1815. In 1792 and 1793, there were also *armées révolutionnaires*, or revolutionary militias, established not to fight at the fronts, but to promote the virtues of patriotism and cement allegiance to the republic in face of the adverse economic, political and military conditions generated by war and civil war. At different times, particularly in 1792–93 and 1795, the new French paper currency (named the *assignat*) lost its purchasing power at frightening speed and the prices of cereals and other basic subsistence goods rose equally alarmingly. In 1793 and 1794, an administratively enforced maximum was imposed on prices and wages but revoked when, after Robespierre's fall, the Committees of Public Safety and General Security were stripped of their powers and the Jacobin club was closed down. There was a Cult of Reason during the French Revolution, but there was also a Cult of the Supreme Being, as well as something called 'Theophilanthropy'. There was a Jacobin club, but also a Cordeliers club, a Social Circle, a Society of Friends of the Blacks, a Fraternal Society of the Two Sexes and many other lesser-known voluntary associations, some associated with people called *sans-culottes* and others with those named *bonnets de laine* (flat caps), *hommes à piques* (pikemen) or, sometimes, *hommes à moustaches* (men with a moustache). Breeches or their absence, along with red caps of liberty, the *Marseillaise* and the still intellectually and hermeneutically challenging paintings of Jacques-Louis David and Jacques Réattu were as much a part of the French Revolution as were open-air guillotines and women knitting when the blade fell. As these particularities indicate, quite a lot more is required to explain why the deficit that Calonne forecast in 1786 gave rise to the type of revolution that the French Revolution became.

This is why ideas matter. The claim should not be taken to mean that ideas have some special causal power, as would be the case if such concepts as language, discourse, symbols, culture or ideology are taken to be more like historical agents than analytical distinctions and exposed, consequently, to much the same charge of circularity that once used to be made to what was called the social interpretation of the French Revolution.[5] Ideas, instead, are best seen as simply part of human life, like food or song or sex or work, with as much or as little causal power as any of the rest. The aim of this book is, accordingly, to use ideas as evidence, just as social, political, economic or cultural historians use other types of evidence to make the historical interpretations or explanations that they make. Importantly, however, using ideas as evidence

---

[5] Alfred Cobban, *The Social Interpretation of the French Revolution* (Cambridge, 1964).

means doing something significantly different from using other forms of historical evidence, whether economic, military, religious, cultural, demographic or biographical. Most historical evidence is largely retrospective in character and firmly part of a time and place. Ideas, however, can have a prospective quality that is unavailable in other types of historical evidence because ideas can address the future as well as the past. They can, inversely, also remain long buried before being brought back to life, sometimes in a new or unexpected guise. In either sense, ideas can have a synthetic quality that can straddle the boundaries of time and place. Something about Oliver Cromwell and George Washington, for example, made both significant figures in the politics of the French Revolution even though the first had been dead for over a century, while the second was living several thousands of kilometres away from France. Although neither was actually there, both Cromwell and Washington still had a presence in the French Revolution.

As these examples suggest, ideas can refer to what might have been, but never was, while other types of historical evidence usually have a more unambiguously positive and finite quality. Using ideas as evidence can involve reconstructing forgotten visions of the future, piecing together frustrated expectations of change or working out the point of past precepts that, in fact, were never practically applied. Investigating ideas sometimes calls, therefore, for finding out more about what once seemed possible but never became actual. This, it should be emphasised, does not mean that using ideas as evidence is like doing what is sometimes called counterfactual or virtual history because, unlike something counterfactual (such as a French victory at the Battle of Waterloo or a successful escape from Paris by Louis XVI in 1791), ideas really did exist and can still be objects of historical inquiry. The past might well be another country but it is usually easier to identify and describe than the future because the future, by definition, does not exist. It can, of course, be guessed at, speculated about, predicted and sometimes even prophesied but it can, nonetheless, never actually happen. The past, however, really did.

There is, however, still a residual gap between the factual existence of the past and its frequently different factual presence. One description of what this difference could mean was set out famously some two generations after the French Revolution by Karl Marx. 'Tradition', he wrote, from all the dead generations weighs like a nightmare on the brain of the living. And, just when they appear to be revolutionising themselves and their circumstances in creating something unprecedented, in just such moments of revolutionary crisis, that is when they nervously summon up the spirits of the past, borrowing from them their names, marching orders and uniforms in order to enact new scenes in world history, but in this time-honoured guise and with this borrowed language.[6]

This gap between the factual past and its factual presence is another reason why ideas matter. It is not necessary to be a follower of Martin Heidegger to register that historicity and creativity are quite closely connected and that quite a lot is involved in explaining how and why something living can be distinguished from something dead and made available for extraction in some mysteriously more than purely factual sense from the long kaleidoscope of the past.[7] Something distinctive in the history and politics of the French Revolution occurred for example when, early in May 1793, François-Noel Babeuf changed his name to Gracchus Babeuf. The point was not only the change of name but also the change of values that the change was intended to signify. It was a change designed to bring together past and future in some quite strongly moral sense and to refer as much to present injustice as to the potential for justice of future possibilities. In this case, the change of name changed little else but, after Babeuf's trial and execution in 1797, his name was revived in the 1820s to become a symbol of the many questions about property, community and citizenship that, in the context of the arguments over restitution and retribution that developed after 1815, came to be associated with the French Revolution. As this example indicates, the several different temporal dimensions involved in using ideas as evidence add something extra to historical explanation. Explaining how and why a potentially large number of initial possibilities crystallised into a more specific set of historical actualities means that this type of historical

---

[6]   Karl Marx, The Eighteenth Brumaire of Louis Bonaparte [1852], in Karl Marx, Later Political Writings, ed. Terrell Carver (Cambridge, 1996), 32.

[7]   Martin Heidegger, Qu'est-ce que la métaphysique? [1929], translated by Henry Corbin [1938], ed. Marc Froment-Meurice (Paris, 1985), particularly pp. 48–50. For a helpful way in, see Leslie Paul Thiele, 'Heidegger, History, and Hermeneutics', Journal of Modern History, 69 (1997), 534–56.

explanation calls for dealing with two questions rather than one: both about what did not happen and about what really did. From this perspective, explanations using ideas as evidence do not have to be seen as alternatives to social, political, economic, cultural or biographical explanations. They can, instead, make the explanations more precise.[8]

Using ideas as evidence on the basis of this dual set of perspectives makes it possible to identify something about the gaps between causation and creation that sometimes open up in historical explanation. Filling in the gaps seems sometimes to call for investigating lateral thinking, joining up the dots or seeing around the corners, but seems at other times to call for recovering brilliant insights, capturing moments of inspiration, identifying flashes of genius or explaining sudden improvisation because both types of occurrence can be parts of what ideas can do. But, whether the ideas in question occurred suddenly or slowly, finding out what they once meant, how they were thought to be connected and why they came to matter is where studying history comes in. Some of the ideas available in late eighteenth-century France may have been more accessible than others, or at least more familiar. Some may have been more original than others, or at least more striking. Some looked forwards, but others looked backwards, not only for precepts or precedents but also for reasons to transpose recognised examples or established insights into new or unknown settings. Some of the resulting moves were connected to events that actually happened, while others turned out to be no more than idle speculation or wishful thinking. But since, for identifiable historical reasons, some ideas could make things look different, either morally or causally, and could do so in imaginative, emotional, intentional and interactive ways, finding out how they arose and what they could do makes it possible to add a level of contingency and choice to the arguments and conflicts of the period of the French Revolution that would not otherwise be there.

In setting out to meet this brief, I have tried to integrate information about institutions, individuals, dates and events into what, I hope, is a fairly straightforward historical and chronological narrative about the relationship between ideas that, looking forwards, once seemed to matter

---

[8] For a suggestive starting point, see David Bell and Colin Jones (eds.), *French Revolutionary Lives* (New York, 2024).

but, looking backwards, turned out to have fallen by the wayside to become curiosities.[9] Inversely, however, I have also tried to show that ideas that look as if they belonged quite strongly to one side or another of a straightforward binary divide (between, for example, belief and unbelief, religion and enlightenment, authority and community) will start, instead, to look less strongly differentiated when positioned more fully in the historical contexts in which they were first considered, thought, formulated, created, adapted, established, used, interpreted, applied or appropriated. Using ideas as evidence calls, consequently, for finding out more about contexts because a difference in context can sometimes make a difference to evidence or its significance. In this sense, the history of the French Revolution involves comparison between many different, sometimes overlapping, contexts – some old, others new – but all related to what happened before and after 1789.

The point was first made by the Italian philosopher and historian Benedetto Croce with his assertion that 'all true history is contemporary history'. Subsequently, its meaning began to get lost when later historians dropped the most important of Croce's adjectives from his nouns.[10]

---

[9] For comprehensive initial guidance to institutions, individuals, dates and events, see Colin Jones, *The Longman Companion to the French Revolution* (London, 1988). For alternative overviews, see William Doyle, *The French Revolution: A Very Short Introduction* [2001] (Oxford, 2019) and Hervé Leuwers, *La révolution française: une histoire occidentale* (Paris, 2025) and, for a collection of texts in translation, Laura Mason and Tracey Rizzo (eds.), *The French Revolution: A Document Collection* (Indianapolis, 2023). For earlier discussion, see Michael Sonenscher, *Before the Deluge: Public Debt, Inequality and the Intellectual Origins of the French Revolution* (Princeton, 2007) and *Sans-Culottes: An Eighteenth-Century Emblem in the French Revolution* (Princeton, 2008).

[10] Benedetto Croce, 'History, Chronicle, and Pseudo-History' [1930], in his *Philosophy, Poetry, History*, ed. Cecil Sprigge (London, 1966), 497–508 (at p. 498). Compare to E. H. Carr: 'All history is "contemporary history" declared Croce, meaning that history consists essentially in seeing the past through the eyes of the present and in the light of its problems and that the main work of the historian is not to record, but to evaluate; for, if he does not evaluate, how can he know what is worth recording?' Edward Hallett Carr, *What Is History?* [1961], ed. Richard Evans (London, 2001), 17. Carr's simplification was taken a step further in 1997 by his future editor, Richard Evans: 'All history', according to Evans, 'was written, consciously or unconsciously, from the perspective of the present': Richard Evans, *In Defence of History* (London, 1997), 30–31. Comparison, in this rendition, simply disappeared. For a fine recent example of Croce's approach,

Putting them back by reinstating Croce's emphasis on both the true (in the sense of genuine or authentic, rather than simply objective or neutral) and the contemporary (in the full range of meanings of both now and then) makes it clear that 'true history' is not only contemporary history but also comparative history because the difference between the one and the other is not as clear-cut as it seems. Heidegger, in his 1935–36 lecture course on 'What Is a Thing?' made a distinction between the *historical* and the *historial* to try to capture the difference.[11] Both apply to things, but the first is generic, while the second is specific. The opportunity for comparison supplied by the resulting combination makes it possible to use the two overlapping temporal perspectives – one now, the other then – and the two corresponding sets of ideas as evidence to address the initial questions about causation, violence and legacies associated with the French Revolution to produce something nearer to the type of historical examination that Croce had in mind. Part of the evidence consists of things that were expected but did not happen. Other parts consist of ideas or arrangements that were long forgotten and could then look brand new. Comparison throws more light on both and, with this addition, comparison makes it possible to tell a fuller story.

Comparison was as much a part of eighteenth-century French thought as of how French history has come to be written. There were, in the first place, assessments of France and events in France made concurrently by contemporaries. They, in the second place, were matched by assessments of the initial assessments made either by contemporaries or posterity. These, in the third place, were followed by assessments of both sets of earlier assessments made in more recent times. Comparison applied, for example, to the French monarchy and the question of whether its most appropriate counterpart was a Roman Caesar, a medieval ruler, a divine-right sovereign, an Oriental despot, a British king or a pyramidal hierarchy of ranks. It applied to the French nobility and the question of whether a comparable equivalent could be found in military chivalry, feudal justice, a landed aristocracy, a centralised court, a Venetian oligarchy or the

this time centred on the work of the French historian Marc Bloch and his famous study of the royal touch, *Les rois thaumaturges*, of 1924, see Carlo Ginzburg, *Dialogue avec Marc Bloch* (Lyon, 2025).

11 Martin Heidegger, *Qu'est-ce qu'une chose? [1971]* (Paris, 2023), 49–53, 61.

British peerage. It applied also to the French church and the question of whether its head was best seen as human or divine, Roman or French, single or conciliar and to the further question of whether its clergy were elected or appointed, members of a community or officials in an organisation and, finally, whether it was the owner, beneficiary or trustee of the property it possessed. Comparison applied most comprehensively to France itself and to the many questions about whether, fundamentally, it was urban or rural, maritime or territorial, agricultural or commercial, growing or shrinking, Northern or Southern in origin and Atlantic or Mediterranean in orientation, and in light of the many possible answers that could be given to questions like these, whether they amounted to a plausible evaluation of how France was situated in space and time.

Comparison also has a particular salience to the relationship between the French Revolution and the transformation of the many eighteenth-century concepts of enlightenment into a single concept called The Enlightenment. Comparison makes it easier to see that the transformation had more to do with failure and attempts to explain failure than with projects and attempts to realise a project. Until it was given the definite article in the nineteenth century, there was never a single eighteenth-century concept of enlightenment. Nor was there any unequivocal opposition between enlightenment and, for example, superstition, enthusiasm, inspiration, idolatry, fetichism, fanaticism or religion; still less between enlightenment and the more recent concepts of either a counter-Enlightenment or a radical Enlightenment. There were, instead, at least four different eighteenth-century concepts of enlightenment, each with different historical origins, conceptual contents, moral connotations, directions of travel and potential final outcomes.[12] At one conceptual pole, there was the somewhat specialised concept of a *prisca theologia*, meaning, more straightforwardly, an original body of true knowledge such as that

---

[12] For an initial way to these concepts, see Michael Sonenscher, 'The Age of Melancholy: The Imagination in the History of Modern Political Thought', *Polity*, 57 (2025), 6–28, and, more broadly, Vincenzo Ferrone, *The Politics of Enlightenment: Constitutionalism, Republicanism, and the Rights of Man in Gaetano Filangieri*, trans. Sophus A. Reinert (London, 2014); John Robertson, *The Enlightenment: A Very Short Introduction* (Oxford, 2015); Nicholas Cronk and Elisabeth Décultot (eds.), *Inventions of Enlightenment since 1800: Concepts of Lumières, Enlightenment and Aufklärung* (Liverpool, 2023).

bestowed by God on Adam and Eve. This was the knowledge given to the first couple to establish and maintain their integrity and, because it was a purely human endowment and capacity, was knowledge that had nothing to do with dogma, worship or confessional allegiance. Enlightenment, from this perspective, belonged to the past and was lost at the Fall. In the eighteenth century, as before, belief in the existence of this lost enlightenment gave rise to a huge range of attempts to recover part of that original endowment whether by means of comparative mythology, scholarly philology, imaginative numerology, ancient hieroglyphics or, simply, creative speculation. Its most widespread eighteenth-century manifestation was the Europe-wide vogue for freemasonry with its focus on something other than confessional dogma or allegiance and its emphasis on esoteric ceremony and ritual as a means both to identify and keep these vestiges of the creation more firmly in place. In France, this version of enlightenment was associated largely with the thought of a heterodox early eighteenth-century French bishop named François de Salignac de la Mothe-Fénelon and his even more heterodox follower, a Scottish Catholic exile named Andrew Michael Ramsay. It was still alive and significant at the time of the French Revolution, not only in France and other parts of Europe but also in the United States, where it came to be known, appropriately, as Universalism.

At something like the opposite pole to this concept of enlightenment was a concept of enlightenment associated with the thought of Jean-Jacques Rousseau and Immanuel Kant. The key component of this concept was what Rousseau called *perfectibilité*. Literally, the term looks as if it could be translated by the word perfectibility, but the meaning of Rousseau's coinage was more equivocal and could be translated as much by ingenuity, creativity or adaptability as by perfectibility. The last of these terms does, however, indicate something more like a result (rather than simply the means to produce a result) and, in this sense, Rousseau's concept captured something substantive in the human capacity to acquire new capacities. Perfectibility meant substituting a growing range of human capacities for the solitary, sentient, silent creatures dispersed across the landscape of what, in his famous *Discourse on the Origin of Inequality* of 1755, Rousseau called the first times. It meant substituting culture for nature, love for sex, language for silence, melody for harmony and, ultimately, states, laws and governments for strength, cunning and force. It also, however, meant substituting fight for flight, armies for weapons and war for violence. In this rendition, enlightenment was an attribute of the future rather than a vestige of the past. But, as was apparent from the Janus-faced history that Rousseau described and that Kant went on to amplify, enlightenment also had as much to do with what to avoid as with what to achieve.

Two further concepts of enlightenment can be positioned roughly midway between those associated with Fénelon on one side and Rousseau on the other. One was the work of one of Rousseau's contemporaries, the abbé Etienne Bonnot de Condillac, while the other was the work of one of Rousseau's early friends and later enemies, Denis Diderot, backed up by ideas from members of the large network of Diderot's collaborators and allies, starting with someone named Nicolas-Antoine Boulanger and going on to include Jean Le Rond d'Alembert, Claude-Adrien Helvétius, Pierre-Paul Thiry, baron d'Holbach and the abbé Guillaume-Thomas Raynal. The concepts of enlightenment produced by Condillac and Diderot could also look either backwards or forwards, but did not do so as strongly as those used either by Fénelon or Rousseau. In Condillac's case, the concept of enlightenment was connected to what he, picking up a term from the German philosopher Gottfried Wilhelm Leibniz, called *realisation*, meaning the mind's propensity to turn abstract concepts like a state, a country, freedom or justice into more like real things. From this perspective, what began as a sign of a thing could subsequently become an object of allegiance or an item of affection in their own right and this, Condillac emphasised, was the basis of the divisions and conflicts that scarred human history. The key to this concept of enlightenment was, therefore, analysis. Going back to identify the original primary components of abstract concepts to explain how errors and illusions had come into being was the means to recover and reinstate some of the more fundamental human qualities of need, understanding and affection. Unmasking the illusions inherited from the past turned, during the period of the French Revolution, into what came to be called ideology or the study of the origins of, and differences between, true and false ideas.

As was the case with Condillac, Diderot's concept of enlightenment also involved the elimination of error and illusion but his version of the concept called for accumulating more knowledge rather than using more analysis. In this sense, Diderot's concept of enlightenment was more future-oriented than Condillac's but was also more materially based than Rousseau's and, in keeping with the earlier criticism of Rousseau's attenuated concept of sociability made by Claude-Adrien Helvétius, relied on a more utility-based and socially generalisable concept of morality than Rousseau had done.[13] The starting point of this concept of enlightenment was the human vulnerability to natural disasters like fires, floods or famines, coupled with the propensity of early societies to attribute these catastrophes to supernatural powers like gods, spirits or daemons, whose behaviour then had to be managed, propitiated or appeased by means of worship, ritual and sacrifice. On this supposition, superstition and priestcraft were the other sides, but possibly also the true face, of religion. The solution, accordingly, relied on more knowledge and better understanding of the natural world and how to predict and control its behaviour. Agriculture, industry, trade and finance could all play a part but what mattered more fundamentally was the power that could be given to human life by physics, chemistry, biology, mathematics and engineering. More understanding of nature offered the prospect of more control over natural powers and more insight into the social qualities generated by, and required for, living under conditions of natural adversity. Humans might originally have had limited moral or social qualities, as both Rousseau and Condillac had claimed, but dealing with famines, fires or floods provided an education not only in natural philosophy but also in the social virtues. In this sense, Diderot's moral theory overlapped with that of Helvétius to become the conceptual core of what Jeremy Bentham was to call utilitarianism. Although there were still significant differences between their respective theories, knowing more and acting well complemented each other more firmly and durably than, it seemed, Rousseau was willing to concede. If the initial response to catastrophe was *sauve qui peut* (save yourself), the more considered and successful response was social cooperation and shared responsibility because earthquakes, fires and floods could not be countered by individual panache or heroic action. True virtues, Diderot insisted, were collective, consistent and durable, not individual feats of heroism, striking gestures of chivalry or the narrow range of qualities required for war. In the long run, the virtues

---

[13] On Rousseau and Helvétius, see Sonenscher, *Before the Deluge*, 266–81.

of propriety outweighed the martial virtues just as bourgeois virtues would one day eclipse the virtues of nobility.[14]

All four of these concepts of enlightenment supplied a fuller, more continuous and potentially more cohesive set of moral qualities than those to be found in the more sceptical examinations of history, morality and politics published mainly in the first half of the eighteenth century by two of France's most famous enlightened thinkers, Charles Louis de Secondat, baron de Montesquieu, and François Arouet de Voltaire. In different ways, the four concepts of enlightenment formed a historical and analytical bridge between the thought of Montesquieu and Voltaire in the eighteenth century and the accounts of human nature set out in the great treatises of the laws of nature and nations published by Grotius, Hobbes, Pufendorf and Locke in the largely Protestant countries of Northern Europe in the seventeenth century because of the emphasis on cultural acquisition and historical development that the former supplied to the latter. In this sense, each of the four concepts of enlightenment set out here was an outcome of the eighteenth century's re-engagement with the seventeenth century in the wake of the works of Montesquieu and Voltaire and in the light of the significantly more considerable historical dimension that their work added to earlier conceptions of human nature in the natural jurisprudence of the seventeenth century.

Something about the fissures that occurred during the French Revolution gave rise to a stronger and more polemical range of evaluations of these different concepts of enlightenment. As the evaluations became more polarised, the differences between the concepts became flatter and the concepts themselves were narrowed down to a more sharply opposed set of binary choices. In themselves, all four of these concepts of enlightenment were described, discussed, debated or dismissed in many parts of Europe and the Americas in the second half of the eighteenth century. None, however, had anything like the presence that they came to have in France during the French Revolution. There was no festival of the Supreme Being in the United States and, notwithstanding some similarities to other publications, there were no English, German or Italian equivalents of the abbé Augustin Barruel's *Memoirs of*

---

[14] On propriety, see Duncan Kelly, *The Propriety of Liberty: Persons, Passions and Judgement in Modern Political Thought* (Princeton, 2010).

the History of Jacobinism. Cumulatively, over the course of the French Revolution, the several different concepts of enlightenment turned into the Enlightenment. They did so, however, for reasons that, at least in the first instance, were not connected to the four initial concepts of enlightenment themselves but were connected instead to the more volatile and complicated combination of events that were expected but did not happen and ideas that were forgotten but could then look brand new that made the French Revolution what it was.[15]

One ingredient of this volatile mixture of the expected and the unexpected was a voluntary royal debt default or state bankruptcy. A second ingredient was a recently resuscitated medieval right known as a *droit de commune*, meaning the right to be a commune or to be a corporate institution able to manage its common affairs as if it was a person. A third component of the mixture began as a now largely overlooked English-language concept of constituent power, understood both in relation to the subjects of public credit and public debt and, more surprisingly, to what was called the religion of the magistrate, meaning a relatively neutral form of public worship that was separate from private judgement, private belief or private worship. A fourth was a concept of a republic that was once taken to exist among the Hebrew people but, subsequently, had been given a new lease of life, notably by Montesquieu, in a now largely overlooked cluster of eighteenth-century French discussions of the problematic nature of monarchy. As one late eighteenth-century French commentator put it flatly: 'Holy Scripture proscribes royal government.'[16] The two subjects of constituent power and the Hebrew republic were closely connected to a fifth ingredient formed by the intellectual legacy of the seventeenth-century English republican James

---

[15] Compare Jonathan Israel, *Radical Enlightenment: Philosophy and the Making of Modernity, 1650–1750* (Oxford, 2001); *Enlightenment Contested: Philosophy, Modernity and the Emancipation of Man, 1670–1752* (Oxford, 2006); *Democratic Enlightenment: Philosophy, Revolution, and Human Rights 1750–1790* (Oxford, 2016); *The Enlightenment that Failed: Ideas, Revolution and Democratic Defeat 1748–1830* (Oxford, 2019) to Peter Gay, *The Enlightenment*, 2 vols. (London, 1967–70) and, more recently, William Max Nelson, *The Time of Enlightenment: Constructing the Future in France, 1750 to Year One* (Toronto, 2020). For a different approach, see Keith Michael Baker, *Inventing the French Revolution* (Cambridge, 1990).

[16] Jean-Henri Bancal, *Du Nouvel Ordre Social fondé sur la Religion* (Paris, 1797), 1.

Harrington. A sixth and further ingredient was a salon-society joke centred on the subjects of women, breeches and patronage that was rehearsed recurrently in the seventeenth and eighteenth centuries. It was then turned into a more pointed joke about France's queen, Marie Antoinette, and, finally, into a popular political movement associated with the name of *sans-culottes*, or men without breeches. A seventh ingredient was a now-forgotten endorsement of civil war made recurrently in the decades preceding 1789 by a number of still relatively well-known French political commentators. A final set of ingredients centred on the subject of democracy, here understood as a provisional system of government that enabled many citizens to rule until, as a sovereign, they had ratified the constitution of their republic. These, largely, are the ingredients of this book. Fuller details will all be supplied later. At this stage, it is enough to emphasise that there was no necessary or immediate connection between any or all of them, still less to the range of different concepts of enlightenment already in existence in eighteenth-century France. Cumulatively and incrementally, however, connections came to be made and, as the similarities and differences crystallised into more visible, pronounced and contentious divisions, these became fresh sources of the recurrent interplay between events that were expected but did not happen and ideas that had been forgotten but could then look brand new. This is what this book is about. By combining ideas with events, its aim is to set out a history of the French Revolution that contains enough causal, conceptual and imaginative space to make room for the politics too.

The combination also has the broader effect of changing the historical significance of even some of the best-known events of the French Revolution. Here, at the end of this introduction, it is enough to single out four: the fall of the Bastille on 14 July 1789, the flight to Varennes of 20–21 June 1791, the insurrection of 10 August 1792 and the trial and execution of Louis XVI on 21 January 1793. The fall of the Bastille is arguably the best-known event of them all. Setting it alongside the resuscitation of the concept of the *droit de commune* not only adds a measure of organised agency and concerted reaction to news of Necker's dismissal on 11 July 1789 as a possible harbinger of a royal debt default but also gives a new significance to the formation of the French national guard and the largely unexplored subject of the problematic presence of an organised militia in the politics of the French Revolution. The second event is less well known. This was the flight to Varennes, or the event that took place on the night of 20–21 June 1791 when Louis XVI and Marie Antoinette secretly left Paris but were then arrested in the little town of Varennes and brought back in virtual captivity to the French capital. Although it is usual to see the flight to Varennes as a turning point in the French Revolution because it discredited the monarchy, it is less usual to see that it was also connected to something expected that did not happen as well as something unexpected that really did. In this case, what was expected, but did not happen, was a royal coup with a constitutional outcome. It was designed, by those who came to be known as Feuillants, to follow on from the abolition of noble titles that had occurred exactly a year earlier on 20 June 1790 and which eliminated the problem of trying to establish a moderating second chamber, analogous to the American Senate, on the basis of the huge existing French nobility. Without a nobility, the way was potentially clear to establish a revising second chamber made up either of appointed life peers, retired former legislators or elected former mayors. What, in short, was expected but did not happen was something like the Maupeou coup of 1771, but with a clearer and more durable constitutional outcome. What, instead, was unexpected, but really did occur was the emergence in the aftermath of the flight to Varennes of the political force known as the *sans-culottes*.

Usually, the *sans-culottes* are associated with the events of 1793 and 1794 and the politics of Robespierre, Saint-Just and their Jacobin allies. In fact, the *sans-culottes* were a Girondin creation and became a political force over a year earlier, in 1791 and 1792. Getting the chronology right throws a different light on the third of the four events; the Parisian insurrection of 10 August 1792, meaning the event that overturned the new French constitution of 1791, brought down the Bourbon monarchy and gave rise to the proclamation of the first French republic. Here too what was expected did not happen, but what was unexpected really did. What was expected, from a Girondin perspective, was a replay of the British Glorious Revolution of 1688, with a discredited king dismissed by a determined legislature. What was unexpected was violent conflict between the king's Swiss guards and insurgent members of the National Guard, the proclamation of a republic and the unforeseen problem of establishing a republican form of government without a republican constitution. This unexpected cluster of events helps, in turn, to throw fresh light on the fourth and final component of the initial list. This was the trial and execution of Louis XVI on 21 January 1793. Here too combining ideas with events throws a different light on the event itself. In this case, the event that took place was a substitute for one that did not. Instead of a repetition of the Glorious Revolution of 1688, Louis XVI was tried and executed. Instead of a determined legislature sweeping out its former monarch, there was a divided republic with no legislature, no constitution and no constitutional government, facing heated elections, a contentious decision about the king and queen and the far from favourable conditions of a global war.

In these conditions, as many historians have claimed, circumstances can count. So too, however, can ideas. They supplied the means to convict the king without having to refer his status or conduct to the judgement of the nation, the people, the *sans-culottes* or, still less, the largely unknown membership of French rural society. The ideas in question were brought back into circulation well before the insurrection of 10 August 1792 mainly by the political figures now usually labelled Feuillants or Girondins and were applied initially, in 1791 and 1792, to the twin problems of the French Empire and the French emigration. In the context of the first French republic, however, they allowed Robespierre and his Jacobin political allies to capture the political initiative from Brissot and his Girondin political allies and take the question of the king's trial from out of the hands of the nation and transfer it to the recently elected membership of the French republican Convention. The first of these ideas was a concept known as *lèse-nation*. It began to be used in the eighteenth century as a counterpart to the better-known concept of *lèse-majesté*. Where this latter concept referred to a crime (or lesion) perpetrated on the majesty of the king, the former concept referred to something analogous perpetrated on the unity, entitlements, integrity or rights of the nation. The second idea owed something to a passage from Montesquieu's *The Spirit of Laws* of 1748 in which he had written that in some dangerous circumstances it was necessary to draw a veil over the statue of liberty and temporarily suspend the rule of law. The third idea was more explicitly Roman in origin because it involved the Roman military concept of decimation, or the idea that, irrespective of innocence or guilt, one individual in ten would, in the French-language version the idea, be put to death *pour encourager les autres* and enforce the missing motivation. The fourth idea complemented the other three. It was centred on the concept of an outlaw or someone who was outside the law and was, therefore, beyond the formalities and procedures that made the law lawful. Together, they supplied much of the conceptual content of the legal, moral and political compound that came to be called the Terror.

As many of his contemporaries – and more of his enemies – were not slow to point out, Robespierre's politics were an unusual compound of Christianity, eighteenth-century conceptions of enlightenment and the politics of necessity.[17] In one sense, they brought together much of the mixture of what was expected but did not happen and what had been forgotten but could then look brand new that makes up much of the content of this book. In another sense, however, they had a logic and a purpose that were captured more specifically by the metaphor of the veiled Statue of Liberty, the Roman concept of decimation and the medieval concept of an outlaw. Each of these ingredients originated in other contexts but came, collectively, to inform the concept of a revolutionary government. This, in the first instance, is why the answers to the three initial questions about causation, violence and legacies raised at the beginning of this chapter have, in a real sense, to be historical answers. It is also, however, why the answers also have a political dimension that belongs more immediately to the time and place of their imaginative fusion. This, therefore, is a book about both.

---

[17] For a good example of how the compound was applied to Robespierre's politics, see Vincent René Barbet du Bertrand, *L'Ombre de Camille Desmoulins* (Arras, 1794).

CHAPTER TWO

Concepts of Revolution

According to a famous story published in 1830 in the memoirs of the comte de Montlosier and repeated a year later in a biography of the duc de la Rochefoucauld-Liancourt written by his son, Louis XVI was said to have asked the duke on 12 July 1789 whether the popular insurrection then underway in Paris was a revolt. 'No, sire', came the reply, 'it is a revolution'.[1] It is still usual to take the story to be indicative, first, of the categorical difference between a revolt and a revolution; second, of the new meaning imposed by the events of 1789 on earlier concepts of revolution; and third, of Louis XVI's characteristic failure to keep up, both with conceptual innovations and with events in France. Before the French Revolution, it is said, the concept of revolution meant something circular and referred standardly to a process closer to the literal meaning of a revolution. In this usage, a revolution meant reverting to origins, going back to first principles, reviving something original by, in keeping with the same metaphor, reforming root and branch or, more simply, doing something radical. After 1789, it is usually asserted, the concept became more future-oriented and, at its simplest, came to mean replacing what was old and bad by what was new and good.[2] Time, in this conception, brought history and morality together to move in

---

[1] François Dominique de Reynaud, comte de Montlosier, *Mémoires*, 2 vols. (Paris, 1830), 1: 210; Frédéric Gaëtan de la Rochefoucauld-Liancourt, *Vie du duc de la Rochefoucauld-Liancourt* (Paris, 1831), 26. On Montlosier, see Robert Casanova, *Montlosier et le parti prêtre* (Paris, 1970) and Joseph Brugerette, *Le comte de Montlosier et son temps* (Aurillac, 1931).

[2] See, helpfully, John Dunn, *Modern Revolutions: An Introduction to the Analysis of a Political Phenomenon* [1972], 2nd ed. (Cambridge, 1989), xv–xxix, and Jean Céard, 'Généalogies: jalons pour la préhistoire du mot de révolution', in Daniela Gallingani, Claude Leroy, André Magnan and Blandine Saint-Girons (eds.), *Révolutions du Moderne* (Paris, 2004), 129–32.

synchrony along the same linear path. Revolutions might, initially, be inseparable from crises, but the outcome of a crisis was now taken to be something more than the simple recovery of political health. A crisis could, instead, result in a whole new society for a whole new age.

On these premises, there seems to be something tautologous about the claim that the French Revolution changed the meaning of the concept of revolution. That, it could be said, is what revolutions do. Or, in the light of the difference between a revolt and a revolution captured by the story about Louis XVI, that by 1830 is what revolutions had come to be said to do. In this respect, the story about Louis XVI and whether the insurrection in Paris in 1789 was a revolt or a revolution is rather like the remark attributed to Marie Antoinette about letting the starving peasants eat cake. In that case, the remark initially had nothing to do with Marie Antoinette because it first appeared in 1783 in Jean-Jacques Rousseau's posthumously published *Confessions* where, long before it was associated with the French queen, Rousseau described 'a great princess' reacting to the news that 'the peasants had no bread' by saying 'let them eat cake', or, in the original, *qu'ils mangent de la brioche.*[3] Something about later interpretations of the French Revolution, however, caused the remark to be attributed to Marie Antoinette. Something similar caused the question about the difference between a revolt and a revolution to be attributed to Louis XVI. In both cases, however, the attributions were supplied by hindsight and, in this light, were used mainly to capture something putatively significant about the characters of the individuals to whom the attributions were applied (offensive ignorance or bewildered indecision, for example). This, plus hindsight, is perhaps what revolutions also can do. It is – less tendentiously – what stories about individuals and everyday life certainly can do. Hindsight and the presence of an author make both stories plausible. It is not clear, however, that history contains either.

The two retrospective attributions do, nonetheless, raise further questions. In one case, they raise questions about the events of the French Revolution and about how and why the subjects of cakes and starving peasants came to be associated so indelibly with Marie Antoinette. In the

---

[3] Jean-Jacques Rousseau, *Les Confessions [1783]*, 3 vols. (London, 1786), vol. 2, bk. 6, 296.

other case, however, they raise questions about the underlying concept of revolution and how and why something about the properties and nature of the French Revolution gave rise to a new and putatively clear distinction between a revolt and a revolution. In this latter case, the initial problem is how to avoid the tautology built into simply repeating the assertion that revolutions are different from revolts. Here, too, bringing the history of ideas into the picture can help because, before the French Revolution, the distinction underlying Louis XVI's question was considerably less clear-cut. A revolt was not necessarily something limited, small-scale or piecemeal, while a revolution was not necessarily something comprehensive, large-scale or transformative. In Christian doctrine, for example, the Fall was a revolt, not a revolution. It was, however, a revolt that was transformative because it had the connotations given both to the event and to the term in, for example, the many eighteenth-century French translations of John Milton's *Paradise Lost*.[4] As one of Milton's near contemporaries, a French Protestant pastor named Jean Claude, put it near the end of the seventeenth century, Christ's sufferings gave back their natural lustre to the sanctity and virtue lost by the revolt of the human race. In this context, revolt, not revolution, was what had effaced the human capacity for morality, while Christ's death made it possible to bring it back.

When, Claude explained, one or several individuals rise up successively in opposition to their duty, this could not be called 'a revolt *par excellence*' because it would be called a revolt *by* someone or so and so. In the case of the Fall, however, 'there would have to be a whole body or an entire society of men for it to be called *a revolt* in absolute terms' because, Claude continued, 'the term properly means an uprising by subjects against their

---

[4] For Milton in eighteenth-century France, see Honoré Gabriel Riqueti, comte de Mirabeau, *Théorie de la royauté d'après la doctrine de Milton* (1789) and, for commentary, Jean Gillet, *Le Paradis perdu dans la littérature française de Voltaire à Chateaubriand* (Paris, 1975); Tony Davies, 'Borrowed Language: Milton, Jefferson, Mirabeau', in David Armitage, Armand Himy and Quentin Skinner (eds.), *Milton and Republicanism* (Cambridge, 1989), 254–71. See more recently John T. Shawcross, 'A Reconsideration of Satan as Hero and Milton's Influence in the French Revolution', in Christophe Tornu and Neil Forsyth (eds.), *Milton, Rights and Liberties* (Berne, 2007), 417–45, and Christophe Tornu (ed.), *Milton in France* (Berne, 2008).

sovereign'. Much the same interpretation of the relationship between subjects and sovereigns was made by the French revolutionary leader the comte de Mirabeau in his Milton-inspired compilation *Théorie de la royauté d'après la doctrine de Milton* ('The Theory of Royalty According to the Doctrine of Milton') of 1789.[5] Revolts could entail ruin, but, as with the Fall, could entail recovery. Revolutions, like those of the stars, were more ordinary but less motivated or goal-oriented. When, in 1793, the Jacobin leader Maximilien Robespierre proposed the insertion of an additional article into the new Declaration of the Rights of Man of the first French Republic, he followed this earlier usage, although he applied the concept of revolt to a different group of subjects and a different type of sovereign. 'Kings, aristocrats and tyrants whoever they are', the article announced, were 'slaves in revolt (*révoltés*) against the sovereign of the earth, which is the human race, and against the legislator of the universe, that is nature'.[6]

On these premises, a revolution was not something with a being or an ontological status of its own because those categories were associated more readily with a revolt. Revolts were real turning points, but revolutions had many possible directions of travel. This was why, over the course of the eighteenth century, scores of books were published on the subject of revolutions. There was a history of the revolutions in the government of the ancient Roman republic, coupled with a cluster of further studies of the seventeenth-century revolutions in England, Sweden, Spain and Portugal, all written in the early eighteenth century by the abbé René de Vertot. Many more books were published during the eighteenth century on the revolutions in Sweden, Poland, the Netherlands, Corsica, Russia and Persia. There were revolutions in government, revolutions in finance, revolutions in warfare and revolutions in commerce. 'No event has proved so important to mankind in general, and to the nations of

---

[5] Jean Claude, *Oeuvres posthumes*, 5 vols. (Amsterdam, 1688), 3: 336, 498–99.

[6] For the text, see Maximilien Robespierre, *Oeuvres*, ed. Albert Laponneraye (Paris, 1840), 355; and Maximilien Robespierre, speech to the Convention, 24 April 1793, reprinted in his *Oeuvres*, 11 vols. (Paris, 1910–2007), eds. Victor Barbier, Marc Bouloiseau, Jean Dautry, Gustave Laurent, Georges Lefebvre, Georges Michon, Albert Soboul, Charles Vellay and Florence Gauthier, vol. 9, 469. On the differences between revolt, rebellion and revolution, but without the theological dimension, see Raymond Williams, *Keywords [1976]* (London, 2014), 265–70.

Europe in particular, as the discovery of the New World and the passage to the East Indies by the Cape of Good Hope', wrote the abbé Guillaume-Thomas Raynal in his *Philosophical and Political History of the Settlements and Trade of the Europeans in the East and West Indies* when it was published in English translation in 1782. 'That period gave rise to a revolution in commerce, in the power of nations, in the manners, industry and government of every people.'[7] The same term applied to the high-level intrigues and court politics that made the Danish revolution of 1772 look rather like the beginning of the French Revolution of 1789. In Denmark, as in France, there was a divided nobility, an unpopular queen, a ministerial favourite, rumours of sexual impropriety and a more radically indecisive king than even Louis XVI was able to be. When the explosion finally came, the favourite was executed and the king deposed, the result, as one political commentator put it, was 'surely one of the most rare revolutions that history can offer for our observation'.[8]

In this light, the question that Louis XVI was said to have asked presupposed an unequivocal answer to the more fundamental question of whether a revolt or a revolution was the more pivotal or transformative event. In older theological usage, the answer was clearly a revolt. In modern political usage, or at least by 1830, the answer, equally clearly, was a revolution. It is tempting, here, to invoke the assertion made in the 1920s by the famous future Nazi Carl Schmitt that modern political concepts are simply secularised versions of theological concepts. But the assertion begs more questions than it answers, both about the clarity and finality of the conceptual switch from revolt to revolution as the name of a transformative event and about why, in the light of the multiple meanings of eighteenth-century concepts of revolution, the concept of revolution as transformation came to be applied particularly to the *French* Revolution. These questions presuppose two further questions: first about how and why the concept of revolution as transformation first arose and, second, and in keeping with the putative switch from the theological to the political involved in the modern distinction between

---

[7] Guillaume-Thomas Raynal, *Philosophical and Political History of the Settlements and Trade of the Europeans in the East and West Indies*, 5 vols. (Edinburgh, 1782), I:1.3

[8] [Seneca Otto Falkenskjold], *Mémoires authentiques et intéressans, ou histoire des comtes Struensee et Brandt* (London, 1789), 142.

revolt and revolution, about how and why the transformation in question came to be said to be both catastrophic and ruinous but also redemptive and liberating. Answering these two questions calls for paying closer attention to a range of more clearly and narrowly delineated subjects than Carl Schmitt considered. Together, they form a context that helps to explain why the theme of ruin and recovery came to be transferred from the theological concept of revolt to the political concept of revolution. The first in this range was the subject of war and public debt and their joint relationship to what in the second half of the eighteenth century came to be called the mercantile system. The second was the subject of decline and fall, and the possibility that modern Europe's future might repeat ancient Rome's past. The third was the subject of crisis, understood as much in social as in medical terms, as a kind of turning-point poised, either in biological terms between life and death, or in social and political terms, between ruin and recovery. All three of these subjects predated the French Revolution by several decades, and all three were central to the transformation of earlier concepts of revolt into modern conceptions of revolution. Together, they gave rise to two different versions of political economy. While the first endorsed public debt, the second rejected public debt.

An initial indication of what this transformation involved can be found in a comment on the subject of revolution made by Victor Riqueti, marquis de Mirabeau (father of the Milton-admiring comte de Mirabeau and cofounder, as will be indicated shortly, of the ambitious French programme of political and economic reform known as Physiocracy) in a letter written in 1772 to a Swedish noble named Carl Fredrik Scheffer, shortly after Sweden's king Gustavus III had seized power in Stockholm in that year. 'The general clamour and my own reflections taught me, a long time ago, that we are living in the century of revolutions', Mirabeau wrote. The frequency of modern revolutions, he continued, 'have, more than anything else, bound me to the study of what I regard as the sole anchor yet able to moor a humanity adrift in a sea of opinion, fragmented, demoralised and exhausted by error'.[9] The anchor in question was Physiocracy, or the name given by its supporters to what they also identified as the new

---

[9] Osvald Siren, 'Ur Markis de Mirabeau's Brev till Greve Carl Fredrik Scheffer', *Lychnios* (1948–49), 51–84 (Mirabeau to Carl Fredrik Scheffer, 22 September 1772).

science of political economy. Physiocracy, according to Mirabeau, had made the Swedish revolution 'truly heroic' and a model of the type of revolution from above that he endorsed. Other versions of revolution, however, were more dangerous. 'We will see', Mirabeau wrote to his brother in 1779 at the beginning of French involvement in the American revolution, 'whether insurrection against divine or human hierarchies is of our vintage or whether, in the general, necessary and imminent revolution which threatens the whole of Europe, anyone else has shown how to put societies gently back on their natural base and prevent Europe from experiencing what happened to the kingdoms of Mithridates and Masaeniello'.[10]

Mirabeau died, somewhat symbolically, on 12 July 1789, leaving the rhetorical question that he had asked his brother in 1779 unanswered. But the question itself helps to throw new light on the change in the meaning of the concept of revolution. First, according to its underlying logic, there were crises and revolutions. Second, there was the application of a mechanism able to promote recovery and reform. Finally, there was an outcome that, as Mirabeau put it, put societies gently back on their natural base but at a higher level of prosperity and culture, or, to use a word that Mirabeau himself coined, 'civilisation'. [11] Mirabeau's version of the sequence was based on the sophisticated combination of political authority, free trade and a single tax that was given the name of Physiocracy. By 1789, however, others had adopted different versions of the sequence. But, irrespective of whether they chose Mirabeau's solution, they continued to describe the initial problem in much the same way as Mirabeau had done and, as he did too, began by predicting the likelihood of a revolution that would repeat the cycle of decline and fall that had brought the ancient world to an end and had ushered in a millennium of violence, death and darkness. On this basis, the events surrounding the fall of the Bastille had as much to do with fears that had been averted as with hopes that were realised and, similarly, as much to do

---

[10] Musée Arbaud (Aix-en-Provence), Fonds Mirabeau, 31, fol. 78, Mirabeau to the chevalier de Mirabeau, 28 August, 1779. The allusion was to two earlier revolts, one leading to the Mithridatic wars of 88-63BCE, and the other headed by the Neapolitan Tommaso Aniello (Maseniello) against Spanish rule in 1647.

[11] On Mirabeau and the concept of civilisation, see Sonenscher, *Before the Deluge*, 218–19.

with preventing catastrophe as with promoting freedom. As the apocryphal story about Louis XVI's struggles with the concept of revolution helps to show, contemporary characterisations of the French Revolution took over some of the connotations of a revolt and transferred them to the concept of a revolution. If, as William Wordsworth was to write in his autobiographical poem *The Prelude*, it was bliss in that dawn to be alive and to be young was very heaven, the emotions that he recalled had as much to do with catastrophe averted as with a future that now began to look golden. As Mirabeau's grim characterisation of the eighteenth century as an age of revolution helps to suggest, both sides of this political and emotional spectrum could be associated with the problem of the French deficit. It could threaten ruin, but could promise redemption. And this, at the outset, was what happened.

'Dined today', the English agricultural reformer and political commentator Arthur Young noted in Paris on 17 October 1787, 'with a party, whose conversation was entirely political'. The content of that conversation now looks unfamiliar, particularly when set alongside most modern accounts of the origins of the French Revolution. 'It is very remarkable', Young continued,

> that such conversation never occurs, but a bankruptcy is a topic; the curious question on which is, *would a bankruptcy occasion a civil war, and a total overthrow of the government?* The answers that I have received to this question appear to be just; such a measure, conducted by a man of abilities, vigour and firmness, would certainly not occasion either one or the other. But the same measure, attempted by a man of a different character, might possibly do both.[12]

From Young's perspective in the autumn of 1787, the sequence of events that was to lead to the fall of the Bastille on 14 July 1789 pointed towards two possible outcomes. One was a chaotic debt default that would result in civil war and a total overthrow of the government. The other was a determined and successful debt default that would not result in either. As it transpired, neither of these two events actually happened. Instead of a bankruptcy and a revolution, or a bankruptcy and no revolution,

---

[12] Arthur Young, *Travels in France*, ed. Constance Maxwell (Cambridge, 1929), 17 October 1787, 84–5.

what happened in 1789 was a revolution and no bankruptcy. Instead of a debt default, the royal debt became the nation's debt. Why did this happen?

Answering this question certainly calls for finding out more about French finances in the eighteenth century and for comparing the magnitudes and ratios of taxing and spending to borrowing and lending not only in France but also in Britain, Prussia, Russia and the Holy Roman Empire of the German Nation. This, perhaps, could show that French finances were in a more brittle state than those elsewhere. It could also, as Young indicated, show that policy makers in France faced several different dilemmas produced, on the one side, by earlier royal debt defaults and, on the other, by the tension between the internal and external ramifications of a debt default. At the time when Young recorded these speculations in 1787, France was an absolute monarchy and, since its king was also its sovereign, its government could simply default on its debts. This was what had happened in 1771–72 at the time of the Maupeou coup, when, in the context of a fierce political battle, Louis XV's controller-general of finances, Joseph Marie Terray, had unilaterally cancelled interest payments on a significant portion of the royal debt. The significance of the move was widely recognised. 'In a word', wrote the Anglo-Irish political commentator Edmund Burke in the British periodical the *Annual Register*, of 1772,

> if we seriously consider the mode of supporting great standing armies, which becomes daily more prevalent, it will appear evidently that nothing less than a convulsion, that will shake the globe to its centre, can ever restore the European nations to that liberty by which they were once so much distinguished. The western world was the seat of freedom, until another, more western, was discovered; and that other will probably be its asylum when it is hunted down in every other part. Happy it is, that the worst of times may have one refuge still left for humanity.[13]

Burke, like Arthur Young, was to say a great deal more about the French Revolution. But his reaction in 1772 to the Maupeou coup anticipated the logic of Young's account of political conversation in Paris in 1787. First, there was a problem caused by the French royal deficit. Then, there was

---

[13] *The Annual Register, or a View of the History, Politics and Literature for the Year 1772* (London, 1773), 79.

a range of possible outcomes. One, according to Young, was 'a bankruptcy, a civil war and a total overthrow of government'. A second, however, was certainly still a bankruptcy, but this time with no civil war and no overthrow of government. It would instead, as Burke put it, entail the extinction of 'that liberty' by which 'the European nations were once so much distinguished' unless, as he put it, it gave rise to 'nothing less than a convulsion that will shake the globe to its centre'.

This kind of speculation has largely disappeared from the historiography of the French Revolution. It was still alive, however, in the summer of 1788, nearly a year after Arthur Young recorded his account of a political conversation in Paris in 1787. According to a letter of 25 August 1788 to one of his Genevan compatriots by the Swiss political commentator Jacques-Pierre Mallet du Pan, one of a group of political journalists associated with the Parisian periodical the *Mercure de France*, the French monarchy had always solved its financial problems by means of political coups. 'History informs us', Mallet wrote, 'that, beginning with Sully, the ministers of that monarchy have always managed to pull it out of distress only by means of operations equivalent to bankruptcies'.

> Reflection easily offers an explanation of this conduct. It derives from the nature of the government and a national character that is incapable of order, thrift, and patience, as well as the almost insurmountable difficulty of righting wrongs in a great empire without producing great convulsions. You, sir, have been able to see the progress of the disorder and, in the light of what I have said, will be able to put your finger on the palpable reasons obstructing these remedies. The king needed authority, but the kingdom is in anarchy; he needed concerted action, but discord (*trouble*) exists everywhere; he needed great consideration and tact, but, steel in hand, national confidence has been cut off at its roots. Sovereign power has been compromised, just when it needed all its energy. It was believed that fine prologues to ridiculously paternalistic edicts were the way to govern the state and opinion (*l'état et les esprits*), and that the resources to be sought were the very ones that are bound to produce an upheaval. This is the first time, I think, that a sovereign, with no money, can be seen trying to carry out a revolution that will overturn the civil and judicial order of a kingdom of 30,000 square leagues.

'In any case', Mallet warned, 'expect this crisis to be very long, unless it is aggravated (*brusqué*) by operations of even greater violence than those yet tried'.[14]

We do not know how many people thought like Mallet du Pan, Arthur Young or Edmund Burke. But it is possible to show that eighteenth-century discussions of the properties and powers of public debt were more central to the conceptual switch from a revolt to a revolution as the name given to a transformative event and, more specifically, to the French Revolution than is now usually assumed. This discrepancy between the frequency and variety of eighteenth-century discussions of public debt and the relative paucity of its presence in modern historiography was, it could be said, a product of the French Revolution itself. Britain's capacity to finance the two decades of global war that preceded the allied military and naval victory in 1815 helped to entrench the modern funding system into European economic and political life more firmly and fully than had earlier seemed possible. After Waterloo and its relatively long peaceful aftermath, evaluations of public debt came to be given a more durably neutral administrative and technical quality than was usual in the eighteenth century. The sheer facts of success helped to screen out much of the range and diversity of earlier speculation about the future because, after 1815, much of its content had been consigned to historical and political irrelevance.

Before 1815, however, the future was considerably less clear-cut, and the range of possibilities associated with public debt was, accordingly, considerably wider, making the subject of the funding system the source of a larger body of political speculation than is now usually assumed. As with the four broad eighteenth-century concepts of enlightenment already described, there were several different eighteenth-century approaches to the subject of public debt. These arose initially because public debts could be associated either with war and the costs of external defence or with the domestic economy and the sources of internal prosperity. These two sides of public debt, one external and the other internal, could then be described as either fundamentally compatible or

---

[14] Mallet du Pan to Aubert de Tournes, banker of Geneva, 25 August 1788, in 'Deux lettres inédites de Mallet du Pan', in *Mémoires et documents de la société d'histoire et d'archéologie de Genève*, vol. 22 (Geneva, 1886), 9–11.

fundamentally incompatible. This difference was connected to two different concepts of credit, as either public or private, and, behind this difference, to two different concepts of money and the state. Private credit was part of ordinary economic life. Public credit, however, not only involved lending funds to a state, but also involved receiving an interest-bearing bond or a note as the price of the loan. There seemed, therefore, to be an element of monetary creation involved in public credit that did not occur with private credit. This difference gave rise to two broad concepts of money and two different evaluations of its properties, powers and relationship to a state.

The difference between money produced by states and money produced by transactions was the basis of two enduringly different versions of political economy. On one side were those who subscribed to the view that money began as a sign established to facilitate trade and transactions because its main function was to measure and compare. Creating more money, as seemed to be the case with public credit, looked to be self-defeating because it would cause prices to rise at home and create trade and payments imbalances abroad. On the other side, however, were those who subscribed to the view that money began as a value embedded in some particularly prized form of property, like livestock, gold or jewellery. Here, public credit could be given a more positive evaluation because the money (sometimes called a fiat currency) created by issuing debt could be used to offset an unequal distribution of the prized property. In France, but also all over Europe, these different evaluations of public and private credit and, in tandem, money as a sign versus money as a value were carried through by the middle of the eighteenth century into two different assessments of the relationship between finance, taxes and public and private prosperity. From one perspective, typified in France by François Arouet, better known as Voltaire, and his famous early eighteenth-century panegyric of the modern age the *Henriade*, the effects of public debt were largely positive. Debt-based monetary creation, as exemplified by modern Britain, had the power to drive agriculture, industry and trade to higher levels of prosperity, while a central bank made it possible not only to channel private funds into public finance but also to track state income and expenditure with enough precision to turn annual budgets and ministerial accountability into major features of modern politics.

From another perspective, however, typified in France by Voltaire's contemporary and rival Charles Louis de Secondat, baron de Montesquieu, the effects of public debt were largely negative. Debt-based monetary creation cut across the division between the commercial and non-commercial sectors of society that, according to Montesquieu, was the hallmark of monarchy and the basis of the system of trade that he called 'trade based on luxury' as against the 'trade based on economy'. Only the former, he claimed, was compatible with monarchy, while the latter was compatible with both republican and despotic types of government. Conflating the one with the other, as also exemplified by modern Britain, threatened to undermine the unusual combination of a single ruler and a number of subordinate, dependent and intermediate powers that, according to Montesquieu, gave monarchy its nature. For Voltaire, public debt was an antidote to social ossification and an obstacle to the transformation of classes into castes. For Montesquieu, public debt was a threat to liberty and one of the prime causes of the propensity of modern governments, whether royal or republican, to drift towards despotism. On his terms, the political risks of adding a debt to a state outweighed its putative economic benefits. Private credit, underpinned by the division of society into commercial and non-commercial sectors and transmitted to the public treasury by taxes on transactions, could provide governments with all the resources that they might need.

Physiocracy cut across these antithetical evaluations of public debt. It endorsed Montesquieu's hostility towards public debt, but also accepted Voltaire's recognition of the positive relationship between public debt and a fiscal state. To its supporters, Physiocracy called for a fiscal state even though what its advocates called a legal despotism actually had no public debt. For the marquis de Mirabeau, the most prominent of the apostles of Physiocracy's founder, François Quesnay, something about the existence of property made it possible not only to have a fiscal state without a public debt but also to have a fiscal system that was more deeply and durably entrenched than anything tied to public debt. To its supporters, Physiocracy was designed to put a ruined world right.[15] In the system advocated by the French economists (as they were also known),

---

[15] See Catherine Larrère, 'Malebranche revisité: l'économie naturelle des Physiocrates', *XVIIIe Siècle*, 26 (1994), 117–38; Sonenscher, *Before the Deluge*, 190–222. For a more traditional view, see Charly Coleman and Charles Walton,

land was something like the particularly prized form of property that, in one type of account of the origins of money, was associated with gold or precious stones. But, unlike those who argued that public debt could be an antidote to private property, the supporters of Physiocracy argued that the antidote was built into property itself. In this early version of libertarianism, property contained a built-in correcting mechanism that could do what the supporters of public debt claimed that only a public debt could do. It would embed taxation so deeply and durably into economic life that questions of distribution and justice could be left largely to the market rather than the state.

The key concept underlying this alternative to public debt as a redistributive mechanism was the concept of the net product, a concept that was coupled with the idea of a single tax on that net product. As a concept the net product was a kind of residual in economic life, meaning that it was the wealth left over after all the many advances – on buildings, materials, equipment, livestock, transport, consumption, wages and rent – had been covered within a specified period of time. Unlike those who took money to begin with something of value, the advocates of Physiocracy took money to begin with a sign. Any transaction could create money and, fully monetised, the net product could accordingly be measured, at least retrospectively, and in the light of its size could be used to set a ceiling on taxation. Setting the ceiling too low would eat into advances to production. Setting it too high would supply a windfall to the owners of landed property. Getting it right, however, would build a system of incentives into the whole economy. Taxing the landowners would give them an incentive to push up rents. Tenants, in turn, would then have an incentive to raise productivity. Higher productivity would in its turn feed its way through to agricultural prices, urban consumption and, ultimately, the price competitiveness of manufactured goods. Paradoxically, Montesquieu's concept of a society divided into commercial and non-commercial sectors turned, under the aegis of Physiocracy, into Voltaire's endorsement of public debt without, however, actually having a public debt.

Physiocracy was the most ambitious of the many responses to the prediction made in 1752 by the usually calm Scottish philosopher David Hume

'Abstract and Embodied: The Political Economy of the French Revolution', *French History*, 38 (2024), 41–57.

that 'either the nation must destroy public credit, or public credit will destroy the nation'.[16] The large body of speculation and discussion captured by Hume's prediction had a more significant bearing on the politics of the French Revolution than hindsight has sometimes seen. Here, four broad clusters of thought can be singled out. Some highlighted the compatibility between public debt and political stability. Others emphasised its social divisiveness and potential for conflict because of the discordant relationship promoted by public debt between taxpayers, who were often landowners, and annuitants, meaning the recipients of interest payments or *capitalistes* as they were called in France. Yet others, in the third place, stressed the ratchet-like quality of debt finance and the difficulty of maintaining a long-term commitment to generate tax revenue to meet interest payments without succumbing to the temptation to opt for a quick-fix by gambling on a diplomatic, military or imperial adventure. As Montesquieu pointed out, many of the frequent wars of succession that took place in Europe in the eighteenth century, from the War of the Spanish Succession at the beginning of the century to the War of the Bavarian Succession near the century's end, were an effect of this state of affairs and the zero-sum game produced by trying to offset the dead weight of debt by grasping at the evanescent opportunity of a vacant throne. Finally, at its most extreme, this type of speculation could encompass a combination of an aggressive war of conquest and a voluntary debt default, based in the first instance on ratcheting up public debt until the level of taxation needed to meet interest payments was equal to total national income so that, in the second instance, by defaulting on the debt all the income allocated to interest payment was available for state expenditure, thus turning the government into the effective owner of all the property in its territory and the *de facto* controller of the lives and goods of all the members of the state. The stakes of this type of amalgamation of domestic and international politics could be

---

[16] David Hume, 'Of Public Credit' [1752], in David Hume, *Essays*, ed. Eugene F. Miller (Indianapolis, 1985), 360–1. On the essay, see Istvan Hont, 'The Rhapsody of Public Debt: David Hume and Voluntary State Bankruptcy', in Nicholas Phillipson and Quentin Skinner (eds.), *Political Discourse in Early Modern Britain* (Cambridge, 1993), 321–48, reprinted in his *Jealousy of Trade. International Competition and the Nation-State in Historical Perspective* (Cambridge, MA, 2005), 325–353. See too Max Skjönsberg and Felix Waldmann (eds.), *Hume's Essays. A Critical Guide* (Cambridge, 2025).

very high because, as many commentators registered, a voluntary debt default could either be a prelude to total mobilisation, total victory and a new fusion of government, state and society or, equally conclusively, to the end and dissolution of both a state and a society. Either outcome supplied an imaginative link between older concepts of revolt and newer concepts of revolution.

Physiocracy was the most conceptually ambitious of these links because of the stress that it placed upon a single tax centred on the net product as the key to the type of revolution from above advocated by the marquis de Mirabeau. Others, however, relied less on taxation and more on institutional design and the balance of political power. An initial version of this type of project highlighted the stabilising effects of public debt. Here, fear, rather than hope, was its motivating force. This assessment of public debt arose because of the cluster of different interests and the escalating risks of conflict that public debt brought in its wake. These risks, it was claimed, gave public debt a power to become the basis of a strongly goal-oriented programme of reform. The centre-piece of this programme was a body of legal and political institutions able to generate compromise and stability out of the tension between borrowing and lending versus taxing and spending that was responsible for the discordant economic and social interests involved in public debt. Compromise, it was argued, usually called for virtue, or the power to override immediate interests and personal inclinations, and virtue was exercised most readily when the balance of institutions and the range of choices favoured small gestures of one kind or another. According to this argument, small gestures favoured mixed or balanced government, which in turn favoured stability, and stability in its turn favoured careful management of public debt. This characterisation of the relationship between public debt and the pressure to reform was produced in Britain shortly after the middle of the eighteenth century but was still remembered in France in 1789 when it came to form the basis of a concept of revolution associated with the thought of a French political moralist named the abbé Gabriel Bonnot de Mably, described by one of his admirers in 1790 as 'that prophet of liberty'.[17]

---

[17] Aubin-Louis Millin, *Antiquités nationales, ou recueil de monuments pour servir à l'histoire générale et particulière de l'empire français*, 5 vols. (Paris, 1790), vol. 1, 20. On

The concept of revolution that gave Mably his prophetic aura was, however, first set out in a widely read collection of letters written a generation earlier and published in 1774 by the widow of an English political commentator named Philip Dormer Stanhope, Earl of Chesterfield. 'The French nation reasons freely, which they never did before, upon matters of religion and government and begin to be s*pregiudicati*' (or free of prejudice), Chesterfield informed his son on Christmas Day 1753, five years after the end of the War of the Austrian Succession, but at the beginning of a long cycle of conflict between the French royal government and the magistrates of the thirteen French Parlements that ran throughout the final years of the reign of Louis XV from 1754 to 1774, and began again in the second half of the reign of Louis XVI, starting in 1783. 'The officers do so too', Chesterfield continued,

> in short all the symptoms which I have ever met with in history, previous to great changes and revolutions in government, now exist and daily increase in France. I am glad of it; the rest of Europe will be the quieter and have time to recover. England, I am sure, wants rest, for it wants men and money. The republic of the United Provinces wants both still more. The other powers cannot well dance when neither France nor the maritime powers can, as they used to do, pay the piper. The first squabble in Europe that I foresee will be about the Crown of Poland, should the present King die, and therefore I wish his Majesty a long life and a merry Christmas.[18]

The ingredients of Chesterfield's prediction are worth noting. One was war, and the problem of funding the costs of war either by means of debt or taxation. The second was the ambiguous status of the resulting mixture of debt and taxation. Too much of both could mean financial exhaustion, producing an incentive for peace. An imbalance between them, however, could mean extra resources for political adventure and, as Chesterfield indicated, these could be as numerous and varied as the range of opportunities and threats provided by a divided and competitive world. One

Millin, see Cecilia Hurley, *Monuments for the People: Aubin-Louis Millin's* Antiquités nationales (Turnhout, 2013).

[18] Philip Dormer Stanhope, *Letters to his Son*, ed. Eugenia Stanhope. 2 vols. (London, 1774), 2:. 332. The letter is quoted by Harold Laski in his *Democracy in Crisis* (London, 1933), p. 13, originally a lecture series given in the United States in 1931 to address, as its title indicates, a comparable set of subjects.

amplification of Chesterfield's prediction was published early in 1789 and associated his titular name with his family name, Stanhope. This later prediction was in fact the work of one of Chesterfield's contemporaries, Gabriel Bonnot de Mably, and it was probably written nearer to the time of Chesterfield's prediction in 1753 than to the date of its own publication in 1789 (four years after Mably's death). It was entitled *Des droits et des devoirs du citoyen* (On the Rights and Duties of the Citizen) and contained a much more detailed account of the kind of 'great changes and revolutions in government' that Chesterfield associated with the magistrates of the French Parlements.[19] As Mably presented his speculations (in the form of an imaginary conversation between a Frenchman, a Swede and an Englishman named 'Stanhope'), Chesterfield had actually shown that the modern French monarchy had a real capacity for reform.

In developing this claim, Mably went to some lengths to show that modern politics offered more hope for real change than had been available in ancient politics. This was because modern political societies housed centralised governments and royal authority as well as popular participation and political decentralisation. As Mably had already emphasised, particularly in his observations on the history of the Roman republic, the *Observations sur les Romains* of 1751, the Romans simply did not have the conceptual and, above all, the institutional resources needed to identify the underlying causes of the divisions and conflicts driving the ancient Roman republic towards its end. Among the many causes of its ruin, all that the Romans could perceive was inequality, and the corruption of manners that it brought in its wake. As Mably described their predicament, the Romans were unable to do more than echo Cato the Censor's lament about the corrosive effects of luxury, imagining that the impotent example of the virtue of a few honourable men might be enough to stem the tide of political decay. But, Mably emphasised, all that this moralistic declamation served to do was to create conditions for ambitious demagogues like the Gracchi to exploit popular misery. Countering demagogues called for extraordinary means.

---

[19] Gabriel Bonnot de Mably, *Des droits et des devoirs du citoyen* [1789], ed. Jean-Louis Lecercle (Paris, 1972). According to a note among the papers of one of Mably's executors, a man named Gabriel Brizard, the book was published at the time of the second assembly of notables, late in 1788: Bibliothèque de l'Arsénal (Paris), Mss. 6076, fol. 13.

By the time of Caesar's rise to power, Mably wrote, the only way to preserve the republic would have been to jettison the rule of law and do whatever was necessary to enable the republic to survive. Brutus, he observed, had been right to assassinate Caesar as a tyrant, but wrong to spare his allies and clients. His legalistic argument that, as Roman citizens, Caesar's allies were entitled to the benefits of the rule of law because, although they were planning to commit acts of tyranny, they had not actually done so was, Mably argued, incompatible with the survival of the republic. In some desperate circumstances, he wrote, politics calls for the punishment of intentions and even for retribution for the mere power to do harm. But, he warned, even if this more prudent policy had been followed, the republic would probably still have fallen. There was no liberty left for the Romans to aspire to, unless a single very unusual citizen, after making himself master of them all, changed the form of the state from top to bottom and, by giving up all of Rome's conquests, went on to compel the Romans to readopt the manners and poverty of their ancestors. Even if such a reform was practicable, Mably commented, it was highly unlikely that any Roman citizen would have enough virtue to usurp sovereign power and use it this way.[20] It is not hard, in the light of this passage, to see why Mably's thought had such resonance during the French Revolution.

The modern world, Mably argued, offered better prospects. Despite its corruption, the possibility of implementing a comprehensive programme of moral and social reform was, paradoxically, more readily available to the moderns than the ancients. Here, civil conflict could turn into what, in *Des droits et des devoirs du citoyen*, Mably called a 'managed revolution' (*une révolution ménagée*).[21] In part, this was an effect of the rise of modern monarchy. 'When', Mably noted in his parallel *Observations on the Greeks*,

> a free people is once corrupted, they grow familiar with their vices; they love
> them, they cherish them, and it is very rare to find that a private citizen has

---

[20] Gabriel Bonnot de Mably, *Observations sur les Romains* [1751], reprinted in his *Oeuvres*, 12 vols. (Paris, 1794–5), 4: 314–24, 356–8, and, in the 13 vol. (London, 1789–90) ed., vol. 4: 275–76, 302, 314–16, 317.

[21] Mably, *Des droits et des devoirs du citoyen*, ed. Lecercle, 161. On the concept of a *révolution ménagée*, see Keith Michael Baker, *Inventing the French Revolution* (Cambridge, 1990), 97, 211.

courage enough to struggle against the prejudices, passions, and customs which reign imperiously in the breast of the undocile multitude, or has credit enough to persuade his degenerate countrymen to make an effort upon themselves in order to recover the point of happiness from whence they are fallen.

Monarchies, however, had a real capacity for reform. 'The history of monarchies', Mably continued,

> is, on the contrary, full of those kinds of revolutions that are so scarce in republics. As the citizen in a monarchy is not his own legislator and as he is obliged to obey and to receive whatever impression his sovereign is pleased to impose, a great prince always has it in his power to form a new people. The subject awakes from his lethargy, quits his vices, and without hardly perceiving it, assumes a new character, and the portion of virtue that one chooses to give him.[22]

Even without a 'great prince', however, reform was still possible, at least in a French context. This was not simply a product of respect for the virtues of the ancients but was also an effect of the surviving residue of the passions created during France's feudal past. Absolute government and court society had not entirely eradicated the values of clerical piety, noble honour and bourgeois probity underpinning the old system of estates, and, as Mably went into considerable detail to show, their surviving embers could still be used by a resolute magistracy to build up enough popular support to force the royal government to revive the French Estates-General, so that it, rather than a king, would then have the initiative for reform. 'If', the English reformer named 'Stanhope' in Mably's *Des droits et des devoirs du citoyen* asked his French interlocutor, 'there was to be a reign when everything goes wrong, where each individual trembles for his domestic fortune, where the nation is even more wretched than usual at home, and dishonoured abroad, I ask you, are your souls really so besotted and depraved as to be insensible to this situation?'[23] Desperate

---

[22] Gabriel Bonnot de Mably, *Observations sur les Grecs* [1749], revised as *Observations sur l'histoire de la Grèce*, [1764], and, for this passage, see the translation published as *Observations on the Manners, Government, and Policy of the Greeks* (Oxford, 1784), 151–2.

[23] Mably, *Des droits et des devoirs du citoyen*, ed. Lecercle, 183.

circumstances would give rise to heroic measures and a successful campaign to revive the old French Estates-General would produce a 'tempered revolution' and the reinstatement of the old French system of estate-based constitutional government. As it has been described, Mably's book was something like a script for the beginning of the French Revolution.[24]

A more lurid prediction of revolution – one reprinted quite frequently when the actual French Revolution had run much of its course – was published a decade or so after Chesterfield's prediction. It too focussed on the part played by the French Parlements in igniting a process of political and social transformation but it appeared in an article entitled 'The True Causes of the Decline of the French Nation' that was published in an English periodical named *The Universal Museum and Complete Magazine* in October 1764. 'The parliaments of France', the article began, 'are obliged to conceal the strong spirit of liberty with which they are inflamed under the mask of loyalty and of attachment to the monarchy. They remonstrate with force and elevation against every measure that tends to the prejudice of the provinces they protect.'

> They can go no further. But they await the moment to strike the blow that shall lay the fabric of despotism in ruins! When this blow is struck, the effects of it will be equal to those of magic. The cottage will be put on a level with the palace, the peasant with the prince. Ranks shall be confounded. Titles, distinctions and birth shall tumble into an undistinguished heap of confusion. A new moral universe shall strike the view of an admiring universe, and France, like old Rome in her first flights to empire, shall appear with the sceptre of universal dominion burgeoning in her hands. Out of universal confusion, order shall arise. The great, of nature's creating, will assume their places; and the great, by title and accident, will drop despised into the common mass of the people.[25]

---

[24] Keith Michael Baker, 'A Script for a French Revolution: The Political Consciousness of the Abbé Mably', in *Inventing the French Revolution* (Cambridge, 1990), 86–106.

[25] [Anon.], 'True Causes of the Decline of the French Nation', *The Universal Museum and Complete Magazine*, October 1764, p. 368.

Although the part played by the Parlements in the collapse of absolute government was actually more complicated than this prediction suggests, its vividly meritocratic vision of a 'new moral universe' and its awed anticipation of a French 'sceptre of universal dominion' heralding a new age of Roman greatness bore enough similarity to subsequent events for the article to be cited approvingly by 'the prophet of Paddington Street' Richard Brothers in 1795 and by the French republican journal *Le Conservateur* when the article was published in French translation in 1798.[26] It may not have described the real French Revolution, but, by the end of the eighteenth century, it could still look like a startlingly prescient announcement of what the French Revolution had become.

On the basis of this type of prediction, the Terror came first. In imaginative terms, it was expected more fully and graphically than what actually happened. The mechanisms involved in turning France back into 'old Rome' with 'the sceptre of universal dominion burgeoning in her hands' were described very graphically in a series of predictions of revolution published after the end of the Seven Years War (1756–63) that were all later brought together in a pamphlet published in 1810 by an American commentator on political affairs named Robert Walsh. Where the Chesterfield-Mably concept of a 'managed revolution' presented a prospect of political stability and constitutional propriety as its target or goal, and where the 1764 prediction of revolution offered a vision of

---

[26] Richard Brothers, *Wonderful Prophecies. Being a Dissertation on the Existence, Nature and Extent of the Prophetic Powers in the Human Mind*, 3rd ed. (London, 1795), 51–2; *Le Conservateur* (22 January 1798/3 Pluviôse VI), 1151. Memories of the prediction were still alive in 1819, when it appeared in Richard Carlile, *The Republican*, 1(. 7) (1819), 103–04. It also appeared in the *Cabinet of Curiosities* (London, 1795), 63–5, 79–82; *The Illuminator* (London, 1797), 18–19; *The Universal Theological Magazine and Impartial Review* (August 1805), 72; David Simpson, *A Plea for Religion and the Sacred Writings Addressed to the Disciples of Thomas Paine* (Philadelphia, 1809), 262; *The Supernatural Magazine* (1809), 117; *Miraculous Prophecies and Predictions of Eminent Men from the Earliest Records Relation to the Revolutions of Empires and Kingdoms, Particularly England and France* (London, 1821), 1–5; and William Jones, *The History of England during the Reign of George III*, 3 vols. (London, 1825), 2: 3. It can also be found in an Irish publication entitled *The Press*, no. 63 (1798): see Eckhardt Rüdebusch, *Irland im Zeitalter der Revolution: Politik und Publizistik der United Irishmen, 1791–98* (Berne, 1989), 114, note 287.

'old Rome' as a model of political independence, social justice and equal opportunity, Walsh's compilation set out a concept of revolution as a springboard to universal empire. Many years before 1789, Walsh wrote in his introduction, 'it was predicted "that the continent would be speedily enslaved should a nation, with the resources of France, break through the forms and trammels of the civil constitutions of the period; shake off fiscal solicitudes by a general bankruptcy; turn her attention exclusively to military affairs and organize a regular plan of universal empire"'.[27] That prediction, whose words Walsh quoted, was made in 1772 by a precocious twenty-year-old French writer on military affairs named the comte de Guibert in his *Essai général sur la tactique* (A General Essay on Tactics). Walsh then went on to quote another prediction of revolution which, he claimed, also amounted to an unusually accurate description of the French revolution. This one was to be found in the Scottish Jacobite Sir James Steuart's *Inquiry into the Principles of Political Oeconomy*, a book first published in 1767. In it, Steuart had outlined a speculative scenario to show how the modern system of war finance had the potential to revive what he called 'the most perfect plan of political oeconomy ... anywhere to be met with, either in ancient or modern times', namely the political economy of the republic that Lycurgus had founded in Sparta.[28] It was 'perfect' because everything in Sparta was done for the service of the state, leaving no room at all for any private interest.

At first sight, Steuart had written, the prospect of bringing back the ancient Spartan political economy to the modern world looked to be extremely far-fetched because it seemed to call for the wholesale renunciation of landed possessions and every other kind of private property. But if, Steuart continued, 'that supposition should appear too absurd', there was still no reason to rule it out. All that was needed to re-establish the 'most perfect plan of political oeconomy' was for a prince 'to contract debts to the value of the whole property of the nation; let the land-tax be imposed at twenty shillings in the pound, and then let him become bankrupt to the

---

[27]   [Robert Walsh], *A Letter on the Genius and Dispositions of the French Government, including a View of the Taxation of the French Empire*, 3rd ed. (Philadelphia, 1810), 10–11.

[28]   Sir James Steuart, *An Inquiry into the Principles of Political Oeconomy [1767]*, ed. Andrew Skinner (Edinburgh, 1966), bk. ii, ch. xiv, 218.

creditors'. A voluntary debt default would place all property, income and service at the disposal of the state. 'I ask', Steuart concluded, 'what confederacy among the modern European Princes, would carry on a successful war against such a people? What article would be wanting to their ease, that is, to their ample subsistence? And what country could defend itself against the attack of such an enemy?'[29] Steuart's prediction, taken over and amplified from Hume's essay 'Of public credit' of 1752, came to look like an unusually prescient anticipation of the course and content of the French Revolution. From the vantage point of the first decade of the nineteenth century, there was enough similarity between what Steuart called a 'relaxation to the mind, like a farce between the acts of a serious opera' and the real sequence of events in France for Robert Walsh to cite it as evidence of the devastating political and military power of the resources supplied by the modern funding system and of how, deliberately or inadvertently, the French had managed to tap that power comprehensively.[30] The French Revolution was Steuart's 'farce' made real. 'Nothing, indeed', Walsh commented, 'but a total revolution in the internal constitutions of the other states could have prepared them to meet France on equal terms'.[31]

All these speculations could be subsumed under the more general prediction of revolution made in 1762 by Jean-Jacques Rousseau. 'We are', he announced in his *Emile* in 1762, 'approaching a state of crisis and the age of revolutions', because, he added in a note, it was 'impossible for the great monarchies of Europe to last much longer'.[32] It was a claim that he repeated in the *Considerations on the Government of Poland*, written some ten years after the publication of *Emile*. 'I see', he wrote in the second paragraph of the whole book, 'all the states of Europe rushing to their ruin. Monarchies, republics, all those nations with all their magnificent institutions, all those fine and wisely balanced governments have fallen

---

[29] Steuart, *Inquiry*, bk. ii, ch. xiv, pp. 226–7 (cf. Walsh, *Letter*, 11).

[30] The passage describing the projection as a 'farce' appears at the beginning of the next chapter: see Steuart, *Inquiry*, bk. ii, ch. xv, 227.

[31] Walsh, *Letter*, 18.

[32] Jean-Jacques Rousseau, *Emile, or on Education* [1762], in Jean-Jacques Rousseau, *Collected Writings*, 14 vols., ed. Allan Bloom, Christopher Kelly, Roger D. Masters, Philip Stewart, et al. (Hanover, New Hampshire and London, 1987–2007), vol. 13, book III, 343. Abbreviated subsequently as Rousseau, *CW*, followed by the volume, book and page numbers.

into decrepitude and threaten soon to die.'[33] On Rousseau's bleak terms, and under prevailing political and social conditions, no institutional bulwark, constitutional nicety, social interest or patriotic spirit could offer any identifiable shelter or protection from the imminence of Armageddon. Nor was the prediction unique. 'Societies become corrupt as they grow old', Mably's literary executors informed the future president of the United States Thomas Jefferson in 1791, 'and torrents of blood have to be spilled to regenerate them'.[34] Revolutions, on these premises, were better avoided than anticipated.

[33] Jean-Jacques Rousseau, *Considerations on the Government of Poland and on Its Planned Reformation [1782]*, ed. Christopher Kelly and Judith Bush, in Rousseau, *CW*, 11: 170. I have also used the translation given in Jean Jacques Rousseau, *The Social Contract and Other Political Writings*, ed. Victor Gourevitch (Cambridge, 1997), at, here, p. 178.

[34] The abbés Chalut and Arnoux to Thomas Jefferson, 20 May 1791, in Thomas Jefferson, *Papers*, ed. Julian P. Boyd, 25 vols. (Princeton, 1982), 20: 428.

CHAPTER THREE

Causes and Causation

Many of the more lurid predictions of the course of the French Revolution, such as the forecast of 'torrents of blood' made by Mably's executors to Thomas Jefferson in 1791, or the warning about 'fire and blood' famously issued by Edmund Burke in his *Reflections on the Revolution in France* of 1790, or the scenario set out much earlier by the comte de Guibert in 1772, now look quite prescient. Other predictions of revolution, however, simply failed to materialise. Two, in particular, slowly faded from the sequence of events that began to unfold in France between 1787 and 1789. One set of predictions was centred on opposition to the royal government by the French Parlements, while the other focussed on the idea of a patriot king. Despite their disappearance, however, both are still relevant to the sequence of events that gave rise to the French Revolution partly because they were canvassed very widely at its beginning, but mainly because they also throw real light on the tangle of different and often competing assessments or evaluations of social, economic, moral and political conditions in late-eighteenth-century France. To some, like Voltaire, France was significantly backward, or not modern enough. To others, however, France was far too modern and possibly at a tipping point. One looked forward to the future, while the other looked backwards to the past. Both, however, converged on finding fault with the present.

It is tempting to turn this difference into a binary opposition, but the contents of both types of assessment were too varied to form a clear-cut antithesis. While one type of assessment could be associated with Rousseau or Sieyès and another could be associated with Mably or Robespierre, the differences between them fail to exhaust the range of evaluations that could arise, for example, from a subject like equality and the question of whether equality was best seen as a historical starting point or a historical goal and, by extension, whether modern versions of equality were better understood to be legal and formal or substantive and real. In a superficial sense, these differences were connected to a kind of timescale running from backwardness to modernity. In a fuller sense, however, they were also connected to a range of more sharply divergent evaluations of the relationship between the past and the present and the direction of moral and political travel bound up with the passage of time. These divergences are particularly relevant to thinking about the origins of the French Revolution because many of the nineteenth- and twentieth-century arguments about its causes and consequences were based on the assumption that the direction of travel went only one way, starting with backwardness and the criticism of the French Old Regime generated by the Enlightenment and ending, according to the moral and political predilections of the historian in question, either in modernity or catastrophe.

Bringing ideas into the picture makes the story more complicated. They reveal a broader range of evaluations of the relationship between the old and the new, or the past and the present, and this in turn makes it possible to inject a new level of explanatory flexibility and analytical precision into the story. Including ideas turns the question of the direction of moral and political travel into a more open-ended examination of whether the travel in question was travel *to* or travel *from* and whether the resulting uncertainty calls in turn for a broader investigation of eighteenth-century assessments of the relationship between morality, history and politics. Instead of the rigidities built into interpreting the course and content of the French Revolution in terms of an already assumed opposition between the Old Regime and modernity – and in fitting such subjects as the public sphere, public opinion, modernisation, reform, resistance or revolution into this sort of binary framework – taking ideas as events reveals a broader array of historical and political possibilities. These, certainly, included counterposing modernity to what was to become the French Old Regime, but adding a fuller array of ideas to the subjects of what was old or new, ancient or modern, gothic or classic helps to reveal that the content and connotations of these apparently binary terms were not fixed. Different evaluations of both the past and the present could be connected to different and potentially discordant visions of the future. Using ideas as evidence makes it possible, in short, to ask two questions rather than one: both about what was expected but did not happen and about what was unexpected but really did happen.

The procedure applies particularly to the two predictions of revolution that, although widely canvassed before 1789, simply failed to materialise. The first was the prediction made by Philip Dormer Stanhope, Earl of Chesterfield, and echoed by the abbé Gabriel Bonnot de Mably of a push by the French Parlements to restore a mixed or balanced system of government in order to avert the threat of a debt default by the French royal government. In this Chesterfield-Mably-inspired scenario, the possibility of losing income from interest payments on investments in royal debt would cause the magistrates of the French Parlements to demand a revival of the old French Estates-General. In this revival of the past, the representatives of the clergy, nobility and the third estate would meet separately but regularly as an assembly of the Estates-General of the whole kingdom under the aegis of a monarch whose powers were limited both by the requirement to subject royal legislation to ratification by the three estates and by the conciliar structure of decision-making within the monarchy itself. In this system, decisions would be made by estates and councils, not by individual rulers and ministers. Absolute government would give way to constitutional government and royal power would be limited by a mixed or balanced systems of political representation and political decision-making. Something like this system of government was, finally, established in France, but only after the French monarchy was restored in 1815 and only after it was already clear that the government of what came to be called the Restoration was as controversial and contentious as any of the six earlier governments that ruled France between 1789 and 1815.

The other prediction that was rehearsed quite frequently in the years and months that preceded the fall of the Bastille was not as strongly centred on externally generated legal and institutional pressure to promote reform as on a centrally generated idea of reform from above by a public-spirited ruler. In this version of reform the emphasis fell less on the interests of the magistrates of the thirteen Parlements and more on the moral and political connotations of the concept of a patriot king. As Mably emphasised in his *De la législation, ou principes des lois* (On Legislation, or Principles of Law) of 1776, the two types of agency were certainly not incompatible. 'The prince', he wrote, 'will see that, in divesting himself of his power, he will augment it and that his subjects, guided by love, trust, esteem, respect and veneration will fall down at his feet'.

> As all the energy of his soul develops, he will come to enjoy the most extensive power that a man can possess, the glory of having made a free nation, the pleasure of affirming the fortune of his house and the thought that the virtuous generations to come will be his own work. Can it be believed that a new Charlemagne could not triumph over the corruption of his court and break through the obstacles used to oppose him? Look at what Peter I has done in Russia. The prince who I predict will, doubtless, make all these reflections.[1]

A year after Bastille had fallen, the passage, written by a 'great and worthy professor of liberty', was still cited as an example for Louis XVI to follow as part of the preparations for the Festival of the Federation on 14 July 1790, the first anniversary of the original event.

The concept of a patriot king that Mably rehearsed was in fact a prominent feature of the royal propaganda campaign launched by the incumbent controller-general of French finances, Charles-Alexandre de Calonne, as a prelude to the Assembly of the kingdom's most notable subjects that was summoned by Louis XVI to meet on 22 February 1787 to address the problem of the deficit. Its immediate brief was to discuss and, Calonne hoped, to endorse the package of fiscal and institutional reforms that he had outlined in his memorandum to Louis XVI on 20 August 1786. The first step, however, was to persuade the Notables to accept the package and this, at the outset, meant invoking the idea of a patriot king. 'Enough others', Calonne informed a now-forgotten poet named Pons-Denis Ecouchard Lebrun shortly before the assembly began, 'have sung the praises of the bloody exploits of the conquerors of the earth'. Lebrun's task, however, was to be different. As Calonne informed him, his 'heroic lyre' was to praise 'the useful virtues of a benevolent king' and to mobilise what the minister called 'the astonishing effects' that

---

[1] Gabriel Bonnot de Mably, *De la législation, ou principes des lois* [1776] (Amsterdam, 1777), book 3, ch. 2, 223. For a later citation of the passage, see Jean Dusaulx, *De l'insurrection parisienne et de la prise de la Bastille* (Paris, 1790), 255–6.

patriotism could produce. 'Divine patriotism', he suggested, had, there-fore, to be 'the muse of my Pindar' (Ecouchard Lebrun's admirers, it should be explained, had renamed him 'Pindar' Lebrun, after the ancient Greek founder of lyric poetry). Patriotism, Calonne continued, would certainly flee 'those unfortunate countries that slavery oppresses', and might still languish in countries in which 'a more temperate authority governs, but governs alone', but, he emphasised, it could not exist at all 'unless a nation also exists'. The poet's assignment was, therefore, to show how the forthcoming assembly – 'formed', the minister noted, 'by a more enlightened choice' than those once made in elections to the old French Estates-General – promised the kingdom a future that would match the image of her present king. Where Louis XIV's 'fatal ambition' and 'thirst for glory' had, during the reign of Louis XV, necessarily produced 'des-potism as its offspring' (the allusion was to the Maupeou coup), France now had a ruler of a different quality.

Louis XVI's destiny, Calonne explained, was to 'give the nation back its existence', enabling it, 'more than ever', to identify itself with its reigning king. If this was achieved, he continued, the 'most discordant constitution' would be 'restored to the most desirable unity' and the 'odious empire of arbitrariness' would be annihilated. Taxation would be lightened by a better distribution of the fiscal burden and, once it was, complaints about its unfairness would begin to die down together with the demise of 'the exceptions' that had produced them. Agriculture would be revived by the growing value of its products. Commerce would increase by way of the liberty 'that is its element', while 'those strange barriers separating different parts of the same empire' and 'those cruel rights' that subjected 'the commodity most necessary to life' to 'an excessive dearness' and condemned the con-sumers of bread and other cereal products 'to the most barbarous of vexations' would all disappear. In less florid language, and as Calonne actually went on to propose to the assembly of Notables, this meant that internal customs barriers, duties on subsistence goods and regulations surrounding the marketing of cereals would be abolished, leaving all domestic trade, including the grain trade, to become free trade. This, Calonne ended, was how 'nature's bard (*chantre*)', by becoming 'the bard of the fatherland (*patrie*)', might celebrate 'the most memorable epoch of the monarchy' (Lebrun, it should also be explained, was famous for an unfinished poem entitled 'Nature, or Rural and Philosophical Happiness' that he had begun in 1760).[2]

Lebrun duly obliged. His *Discours en vers, à l'occasion de l'assemblée des notables* (Discourse in Verse, on the Occasion of the Assembly of Notables) faithfully followed the minister's script. Contrary to malign rumour, the modern Pindar began, the forthcoming assembly was not a symptom of some hidden political disorder because France, as shown by the recent victorious war against Britain over American independence, was still a 'colossus'. But, Lebrun continued, France was also a 'confused collection of discordant principles and ancient abuse'. Error piled on error over thirteen centuries of assorted kings had left the nation without the laws required to secure its well-being and called now for 'wisdom and genius' to produce 'harmony as their offspring'. A state, Lebrun observed, could still languish 'in the midst of its glory'. The 'weaknesses of a king', and the 'errors of a minister', joined to 'the sinister legacy' of the succeeding reign (the allusions echoed Calonne's advice about how best to describe Louis XIV and Louis XV) could erode the foundations of the finest throne if 'cruel subsidy's erratic system' were to dry up the sources of public wealth. Now, however, hope was at hand. The 'days of horror and alarm', when 'desperate eyes' could see nothing in the state but 'misery coupled to luxury', and when 'the sons of Plutus dared to drink the tears of the fatherland from gilded cups', while 'pale, feeble wretches fought their frightened flocks for the grass on the ground', would, Lebrun announced, soon belong to the past. Like a 'wise cultivator' improving his fields, 'a wise king' had begun the work of reform. Wealth, he knew, was not to be found 'in the mines of Golconda', but in those 'smiling fields made fertile by labour'. Spain testified all too well to the sterility of 'gold-driven indigence'. Gold ran out but the land itself was 'inexhaustible'. Properly encouraged, France would soon shine again with renewed splendour. Abundance, the arts, and trade would flourish, credit would be healed of its ancient wounds, gold would flow safely along broad highways, allowing the humble 'cabin' to escape, finally, from its crushing burden. It was hard not to see, Lebrun concluded, that the blood line

---

[2] Calonne to Lebrun [late 1786, or early 1787], in Pons-Denis Ecouchard Lebrun, *Œuvres*, 4 vols. (Paris, 1811), 4: 273–79.

running from France's virtuous King Henri IV to her present ruler was a sign that Louis XVI would, in fact, be his reincarnation.[3]

The Calonne-Lebrun reform programme was matched, however, by another programme. Where the first was designed to promote prosperity, the second was designed to revive morality. This second programme was the work of Maximilien Robespierre, later to become famous (or notorious) as one of the authors of the Terror. Although there is no evidence that this was actually the case, Robespierre's programme, written in the spring of 1789, reads as if it was a direct reply to the one promoted by Calonne and Lebrun. 'Another sovereign', Robespierre began, taking aim at the call by Calonne and Lebrun for Louis XVI to follow their plan of economic and institutional reform, 'might limit his ambition to reviving and restoring those ancient and sacred maxims which protect the ownership of our goods. He might believe that he had accomplished everything by succeeding in re-opening all the sources of national wealth and by reassuring the alarms of trade and a languishing agriculture.'

> But the glory of procuring all the treasures of abundance for us, of embellishing your reign with all the finery and pleasures of luxury, success of that kind, which to the vulgar politician seems to be the most admirable masterpiece of human wisdom, is not the most interesting part of the august mission appointed to you both by heaven and your own soul. To guide men to happiness by means of virtue, and to virtue by means of a system of legislation based upon the immutable principles of immutable morality, principles that are designed to restore human nature to all its rights and to all its original dignity; to rebind the immortal chain linking man to God and to his fellows by destroying all the causes of oppression and tyranny, and the fear, suspicion, pride, servility, egoism, hatred, cupidity and all those vices they sow in their wake, and which take man far from that end to which the eternal legislator assigned society, this, Sire, is the glorious vocation to which he has called you.[4]

---

[3] Pons-Denis Ecouchard Lebrun, 'Discours en vers, à l'occasion de l'assemblée des notables', in his *Œuvres*, 2: 237–41.

[4] Maximilien Robespierre, 'Mémoire pour le Sieur Louis-Marie-Hyacinthe Dupond' [1789], in Victor Barbier and Charles Vellay (eds.), *Oeuvres complètes de Maximilien Robespierre*, 10 vols. (Paris, 1910–59), 1: 573- 682 (at, particularly, 661–5, 669–70,

Louis XVI, Robespierre continued, was in position 'to carry out a revolution attempted by Henri IV and Charlemagne, but which was not yet possible in the times in which they lived'. Times, however, had changed, and the moment to act was now at hand. But, Robespierre warned, 'if we are to let it slip, it may perhaps be decreed that the only glimmer of light left to us will be one that reveals no more than days of trouble, desolation and calamity! Ah Sire, hasten to seize it; take pity on an illustrious nation which loves you well, and ensure that there is at least one happy people on this earth.'[5]

Robespierre's appeal to Louis XVI relied on more than the idea of a patriot king. Its moral and political orientation was also indebted to a book entitled *The Adventures of Telemachus, Son of Ulysses* that was published towards the end of the seventeenth century by François de Salignac de la Mothe-Fénelon, archbishop of Cambrai, and then republished more fully in 1715, the year in which both Fénelon and Louis XIV died. Fénelon's book (apart from the Bible, it was the eighteenth century's best seller) was a plan for peace as well as prosperity. Its focus, accordingly, was less on the virtue of patriotism than on the merits of humanity. Robespierre's appeal echoed Fénelon's orientation. Its final peroration, with its call to the king to ensure that there was 'at least one happy people on this earth', can be taken as a guide to Robespierre's politics from the beginning to the end. As Fénelon had emphasised, love of self had to give way to love of family; love of family to love of country; and, finally, love of country to love of humanity. Virtue in this context was, ultimately, human, not civic and, according to Fénelon, relied on a concept of Christ that placed less emphasis on Christ's nature as a divine redeemer and more on his image as the human embodiment of divine love.[6] As with the ancient

672–3). The text is reproduced in the more recent edition of Maximilien Robespierre, *Oeuvres*, 12 vols. (Paris, 2007-22), XI: 50-126.

[5] Robespierre, 'Mémoire pour Dupond', in Robespierre, *Oeuvres complètes*, vol. 1, 672–3 (and, in the 2007 edition, vol. XI, p. 120).

[6] For two initial but somewhat limited examinations of Fénelon's Christology, see Jacques Lebrun, 'Mystique et christologie à la fin du xviie siècle', in Maria-Cristina Pitassi (ed.), *Le Christ entre orthodoxie et lumières* (Geneva, 1994), 31–47 and Karen Pagani, 'If Voltaire Ceased to be Voltaire: The Influence of Quietism on Voltaire's Later Works', in Christoph Schmitt-Maaß, Stefanie Stockhorst and Doohwan Ahn (eds.), *Fénelon and the Enlightenment: Traditions, Adaptations, and*

Greek Stoics or Cynics, its principles were cosmopolitan, not patriotic, however much the very scale of humanity as an object of allegiance added an extra level of virtue to patriotic commitment.

The idea of a patriot king had a Franco-British origin. In France, its most striking symbol was the country's first Bourbon king, Henri IV, commemorated both for his stance towards the sectarian divisions and social misery generated by the kingdom's sixteenth-century religious wars and for his later incarnation in Voltaire's frequently reprinted epic poem the *Henriade*, published at the beginning of the reign of Louis XV to herald a new age of peace and prosperity after the long wars of the final years of the reign of Louis XIV. In Britain, the figure of the patriot king was associated with the eponymous pamphlet *The Idea of a Patriot King*, written in 1738 and published in 1749 by Voltaire's acquaintance Henry Saint-John, Viscount Bolingbroke. The two versions of the idea produced by Voltaire and Bolingbroke anticipated the later tension between promoting prosperity and recovering morality that separated the two reform programmes of Calonne and Robespierre. Where the *Henriade* highlighted the importance of industry, trade and public debt as the basis of a British-style system of balanced government and royal authority, *The Idea of a Patriot King* highlighted the importance of balanced government and royal authority as the means to keep industry, trade and public debt in check. The difference between these two programmes meant that it was not clear throughout the eighteenth century whether a patriot king was a cause or an effect, a highly respected agent of authority or a widely admired product of prosperity and, in the light of this uncertainty, whether it was more important, at least in the first instance, to promote prosperity or recover morality. In Britain, in the thought of David Hume, Adam Smith and Edmund Burke, the dilemma was narrowed down to a combination of liberty and authority. In France, the dilemma was carried through into the financial and political crisis that began to develop after 1787.

Variations (Amsterdam, 2014), 38–41. See also Bernard Cottret, *Le Christ des lumières* (Paris, 1990), 173–86 and Bernard Cottret Rousseau, and Monique Cottret, 'Simul Justus, simul peccator. Jean-Jacques Rousseau était-il protestant?', *Bulletin de la Société de l'Histoire du Protestantisme Français*, 151 (2005), 107–26.

The several different connotations of the idea of balanced government as either a product of or antidote to the world of industry, trade and public debt and the equally different range of assessments of the internal and external dimensions of the idea of a patriot king were matched by a further set of considerations centred on the subject of monarchy itself. This third subject had its starting point in a famous passage in the Old Testament in which God issued a warning to the people of Israel about their request to be given a king. The passage, set down in the first Book of Samuel, Chapter Eight, was cited very frequently in many parts of early modern Europe, particularly at the time of the revolt of the Netherlands in the sixteenth and early seventeenth centuries and during the various seventeenth-century British revolutions. In it, God ordered Samuel to tell the people of Israel:

> This will be the manner of the king that shall reign over you. Your sons he will take and make them his charioteers and his horsemen and runners before his chariots. He will make of them captains over thousands, captains over hundreds, captains over fifties, and captains over tens. He will take of them to till his grounds and reap his harvests; to make his weapons of war and instruments of his chariots. Your daughters he will take to be ointment-makers, cooks and bakers. The best of your fields, vineyards and olive-yards, he will take and give to his servants. And he will take the tenth of your seed and your vineyards and give to his officers and his servants. The choicest and best of your menservants and of your maidservants, of your cattle and of your asses, he will take and put to his own work. Your very flocks he will tithe; and his servants you shall be. And you will cry out in that day because of your king which shall have chosen you and the Lord will not hear you in that day.[7]

---

[7] For the passage, slightly modernised here, see *The Holy Bible*, ed. Alexander Geddes, 2 vols. (London, 1797), 2: 58–59. On its significance, see Eric Nelson, *The Hebrew Republic: Jewish Sources and the Transformation of European Thought* (Cambridge, Mass., 2010), 26–35. See too Adolphe Lods, 'Les sources des récits du premier livre de Samuel sur l'institution de la royauté israélite', in Faculté de Théologie de Montauban (ed.), *Etudes de théologie et d'histoire* (Paris, 1901), 259–84, and the editor's introduction to Carlo Sigonio, *The Hebrew Republic*, ed. Guido Bartolucci (Jerusalem, 2010); Thomas Maissen and Fania Oz-Salzberger (eds.), *The Liberal-Republican Quandary in Israel, Europe and the United States: Early Modern Thought Meets Current Affairs* (Boston, 2012); and Ofri Ilany, *In Search of the Hebrew People: Bible and Nation in the German Enlightenment* (Bloomington, 2018).

'Read the treatise on taxation (*traité de l'impôt*) by Samuel to the Jewish people on their demand to have a king in place of their judges', wrote a future member of the Jacobin club named François Boissel in his highly successful *Catéchisme du genre humain* (Catechism of the Human Race) when it was published in 1789.[8] In the nineteenth century, Boissel was taken to be a precursor of communism. In fact, he was simply one of a long line of thinkers who continued to make use of the passage from Samuel until well into the nineteenth century. By the time that Boissel came to publish his *Catechism*, the passage had acquired an almost emblematic status because it supplied the template of the short and frequently reprinted *History of the Troglodytes* published in 1721 as one of the *Persian Letters* by the French magistrate Montesquieu. In his adaptation of God's admonition to Samuel, Montesquieu continued to rehearse the Hebrew story but presented it more deliberately and explicitly as a choice between virtue without monarchy and monarchy without virtue. Presented this way, the alternatives were clear-cut. Montesquieu chose the second, but more than one eighteenth-century French commentator was prepared to choose the first and, in the light of how the Scriptural story was recycled by Montesquieu, was willing to claim, particularly during the period of the French Revolution, that reading between the lines, Montesquieu was, in fact, a covert republican. Where liberty was concerned, as the subject was put in pamphlet entitled *Le jugement dernier des rois* ('The Last Judgment of Kings') that was published in 1793 by Sylvain Maréchal, who recycled its content from a fable he had published in 1789, 'savages' were the 'elders' of the *sans-culottes* because they had never had kings. 'Born free, they lived and died as they were born.'[9]

The success of Montesquieu's version of the scriptural story was one reason for the resonance that God's admonition to Samuel came to have in eighteenth-century France. It was matched, later in the century, by the many other variations on the scriptural story published by Montesquieu's rival Voltaire, particularly in his iconoclastically burlesque tragedy

---

[8] François Boissel, *Catéchisme du genre humain* (no place of publication, 1789), 80. On Boissel, see Pierre-Antoine Courouble, 'Francôis Boissel, le Jacobin oublié', *Annales historiques de la révolution française*, 362 (2010), 151–74.

[9] Sylvain Maréchal, *The Last Judgment of Kings/Le jugement dernier des rois* [1793], ed. Yann Robert (Lewisburg, 2024), 119.

Saul, and, in parallel, by the more brutal verdict of Voltaire's friend the baron d'Holbach in his *Théologie portative* (Portable Theology) of 1768. As Holbach's entry on the judge put it, 'Samuel: an angry Jewish prophet who did not spend much time studying the law of nations in Grotius and Pufendorf. He made mincemeat of the kings of other countries, but made or unmade the kings of his own.'[10] The more fundamental reason for the story's resonance, however, was the subject of absolute government (meaning a king who was also a sovereign) and the combination of its disputed political and theological origins and its potentially catastrophic political consequences. 'Samuel', wrote Jean-Jacques Rousseau in his *Social Contract,* 'represented this in the strongest manner to the Hebrews, and Machiavel has proved it by incontestable evidence. Indeed this celebrated politician, while he pretends to be giving lessons to kings, gives the noblest lesson to the people and *The Prince* of Machiavel is the book of republicans.'[11] In more straightforwardly historical terms, the system of absolute government usually associated with France's Bourbon kings and, in particular, the long reign of Louis XIV from 1643 to 1715 was standardly taken to be Roman in origin. Rome had been an empire and the system of imperial authority established by the Roman Caesars and codified gradually in Roman law had been transmitted to France under Roman rule. From this perspective, France's kings were heirs to the legal and institutional arrangements underpinning the Roman Empire. In a deeper sense, however, absolute government had a more uncertain status and a less unequivocal legitimacy because of the different theological and political interpretations that could be made of God's warning to Samuel. These interpretations, put summarily, centred

---

[10] On Voltaire's play, see John Bagnell Bury, *A History of Freedom of Thought* (London, 1913), 154–55, and the 'Introduction' to Voltaire, *Saul,* ed. Henri Lagrave and Marie-Helene Cotoni, in Voltaire, *Oeuvres Completes,* vol. 56A (Oxford, 2001), 327–457. See too Paul-Henri Thiry baron d'Holbach, *Théologie portative* (London, 1768), 214–15.

[11] Jean-Jacques Rousseau, *On the Social Contract* [1762], in Rousseau, *CW,* 4: 177. On the Hebrew republic in Rousseau, see Barbara Abrams, Mira Morgenstern and Karen Sullivan, *Reframing Rousseau's* Levite d'Ephraim: *The Hebrew Bible, Hospitality and Modern Identity* (Liverpool, 2021), 5–30, and Michael Sonenscher, 'From the Hebrew Commonwealth to Party Politics: Rousseau's Legacy and the Nation-State in Nineteenth-Century Political Thought', *Modern Intellectual History* 21 (2024), 1–34.

on two rival accounts of the condition of humanity before and after the Fall and, more specifically, on two different answers to the question of whether it was correct to describe the earlier or the later condition of humanity as a state of nature or a state of grace.

The first answer owed a great deal to a widely publicised Catholic heresy known as Jansenism (after its originator, a seventeenth-century Belgian theologian named Cornelius Jansen). For Jansen and the Jansenists, the original condition of humanity was a state of nature because in that condition Adam (and perhaps Eve) had integrity. The Fall, therefore, was at once a loss of integrity, an exile from God and a reorientation of human nature from virtue to vice. Henceforth, to meet the purposes of the creation, humanity was required to rely entirely on the various types of grace, such as general grace, redeeming grace, supervening grace or efficacious grace, that were made available to Adam's descendants by God and by God incarnate in Christ. Divine grace was, therefore, part of human history. It added a layer of divine provision from a now inaccessible God to the more schematic telos of Scripture and, in keeping with this combination of divine provision and divine inaccessibility, meant that Jansenist political theology placed a high value on the virtues of clarity, continuity and consistency in both human affairs and scriptural interpretation. In this context, God's warning to Samuel about the perils of establishing a king had a real and lasting significance. It highlighted the dangers of innovation in politics and human affairs and supplied a powerful set of reasons and precedents for resisting royal authority if that authority was used to promote any kind of regal, legal, financial or fiscal innovation.

The second answer was a mirror image of the first. In it, the switch from humanity's original condition to its fallen position was a switch from a state of grace to a state of nature. This was the position maintained by more orthodox Catholics throughout the eighteenth century. As it implied, grace was part of the human condition before the Fall while the succeeding state of nature was, at least initially, a state of misery and deprivation but, in the light of what had been lost, also a state of discovery and, potentially, recovery. The difference between the two accounts meant that God's warning to Samuel could be interpreted in two incompatible ways, as either an endorsement of the original condition and an objection to innovation, or as an acknowledgement of human fallibility and a recognition of the need for recovery. In the first account, sovereignty and government were radically separate because God, as sovereign, made laws that were enforced by the judges of the Hebrew commonwealth. In the second, government and sovereignty were closely intertwined, generating a recurrent need for vigilance to prevent the abuse of power. The price to be paid for having a king was, accordingly, either an elusive memory of lost virtue or an abiding injunction to keep virtue alive. 'But where say some', wrote Tom Paine in 1776 in his *Common Sense*, 'is the king of America?. I'll tell you friend, he reigns above, and doth not make havoc of mankind like the Royal Brute of Great Britain.'[12]

References to the many different connotations of the passage from Scripture were made by almost every significant seventeenth- or eighteenth-century political thinker. Although the two types of political theology appeared to converge, they boiled down to either embracing or uprooting modernity. This meant that the idea of a patriot king was given a number of different, and not readily reconcilable, objectives. From one perspective (supplied by Chesterfield and Mably), the prime responsibility of a patriot king was to revive the old system of estates to balance and reconcile divergent interests. From a second perspective (supplied by Voltaire, Bolingbroke and Calonne), the prime task was to promote prosperity and reduce inequality. From a third (supplied by Fénelon), the prime concern was to combine justice at home with peace abroad. This initial trio of objectives was far from exhausting the range of interpretations that the passage could carry. To some, including Jacques Bénigné Bossuet, God's message to Samuel had highlighted the rights and powers of kings and the part played by Providence in human history. To others, including John Locke, the same message had highlighted the original status of the right to punish in the state of nature and the purely military quality of monarchy in its original form. Kings on Locke's interpretation were once purely military leaders until the children of Israel called upon God to grant them a king with the power to judge.[13] To

---

12 Thomas Paine, *Common Sense* [1776], in his *Selected Works*, ed. Howard Fast (New York, 1943–45), 30. Cited in Gabriel Calori, 'La vision théologique de l'histoire à travers le langage politique de Thomas Paine: Présence et rôle du mythe biblique', *Etudes Anglaises* 66 (1976), 257–70, which is probably the best short study of Paine's thought.

13 See, for example, John Locke, *Two Treatises of Government*, ed. Peter Laslett [1960] (Cambridge, 2023), §109, 340–41: 'And thus in *Israel* itself, the chief business of

yet others writing in Locke's wake, including Montesquieu, Rousseau and, as to be shown in the next chapter, one of Rousseau's most attentive followers, the abbé Emmanuel-Joseph Sieyès, God's warning to Samuel highlighted the difference between primitive simplicity and modern complexity and, by extension, reinforced the importance of separating sovereignty from government by designing a set of institutions able to establish and maintain a categorical difference between a single royal sovereign and an elected head of state.[14] The first gave rise to what Sieyès called a *ré-privé*, but the second gave rise to what he called a *ré-publique*.

Despite these radical differences in envisaged outcomes, all the initial diagnoses of the underlying problems began with almost identical descriptions of the current state of France. According to all, France was a large populous country, with a huge impoverished rural society and a tiny, opulent, privileged elite. But where from one point of view inequality was a product of the long afterlife of the relics of France's gothic and feudal past, from another viewpoint it was a product of a more firmly modern set of developments in warfare, trade and industry. The two claims were not necessarily incompatible because it was still possible to claim that the thousands of venal offices and the arsenal of court patronage centred on Louis XIV's palace at Versailles which, together, gave the royal government much of its internal architecture, had also given the vestiges of feudalism a fiscal life-support system made up of the honours, exemptions and resources that office and patronage made available to a favoured few. This apparent convergence, however, did not entail a new synthesis. Instead, eliminating venality and turning off the tap of patronage could either mean making prosperity more generally available or,

their judges and first kings seems to have been to be *Captains in War* and leaders of their armies' (italics in original).

[14] For initial examples, see Harold Laski (ed.), *A Defence of Liberty against Tyrants: A Translation of the Vindiciae Contra Tyrannos by Junius Brutus* (London, 1924), 72–4, 87–91, 162, 174, 190–91, 208, 220, 228 and William E. H. Lecky, *Rationalism in Europe* [1865], ed. Archibald Robinson, 2 Parts (London, 1946), Part II, 70–2. As is well known, Rousseau initially envisaged giving the title of *Instituts politiques* to what became his *Du contrat social*, echoing the *Institutes* of the Roman jurists Justinian and Caius. On this subject, see Claudia Moatti, *Res publica: histoire romaine de la chose publique* (Paris, 2018) and *Sur la politique: cinq grandes leçons romanes* (Paris, 2025).

alternatively, turning merit, talent and individual ability into the only acceptable criteria for public distinction.

Again, it should also be emphasised, the two outcomes were not fundamentally incompatible even if wealth and virtue were not quite the same. The ambiguity did not prevent the different diagnoses underlying the two types of assessment of the present state of France from converging quite readily on the same set of images. Alongside the rococo splendour of Versailles and Paris, away from the more recent commercial prosperity of Marseille and Bordeaux, and beyond the vast landed estates and copious income streams available to the overlapping circles made up of the kingdom's great nobles, clerical grandees and high royal officials lay cascades of urban and rural poverty that broadened massively and deepened savagely when harvests fluctuated, livestock died or trade and industry dried up, filling the roads with migrants, crowding the hospitals with the old and the very young and marking out the places of asylum where the two streams converged as stark and forbidding gateways to death.[15] Imagery like this ran from one end of the eighteenth century to the other. 'You who till without a plough, who reap where you have not sown', thundered the abbé Hyacinthe de Gasquet in 1766, 'who earn when both sleeping and waking and spend nights and days doing nothing but feeding on the work, the sweat and the substance of others' would still – finally – be called to account, even if in the next life rather than this.[16] The details of accusations like this may have varied, but the gravity of the conditions to which they referred remained constant. 'Proud idleness lives off the past, but if your hand is on the plough, can you afford to look behind?' asked the abbé Joseph Pétiot in 1784 in a passage that helps to explain why he was singled out in 1791 by the Girondin leader Jacques-Pierre Brissot as someone who,

---

[15] For an example, see Colin Jones and Michael Sonenscher, 'The Social Function of the Eighteenth-Century French Hospital: The Case of the Hôtel Dieu of Nîmes', *French Historical Studies*, 13 (1983), 172–214.

[16] Hyacinthe de Gasquet, *L'usure démasqué* (Avignon, 1766), 453. The passage is translated in Bernard Groethuysen, *The Bourgeois: Catholicism versus Capitalism in 18th Century France* [1927] (London, 1968), 223, and was singled out for comment by J. H. Plumb in a review of Groethuysen's book in the *New York Review of Books* of 24 October 1968. On Christian evaluations of inequality, see Andre Delaporte, *L'idée d'égalité en France au xviiie siècle* (Paris, 1987), particularly the striking passage from Bossuet cited at p. 103.

as Brissot put it, could have been 'of value to the people if he did not defend them with enigmas and knew how to explain his thought because, since he writes and speaks, it is to be assumed that he can think'.[17] The real divergences began only with the analyses of their underlying causes. From one perspective, the many dimensions of inequality that France displayed showed how far the kingdom lagged behind modernity's ascending curve. From another perspective, however, exactly the same set of qualities showed just how far ahead of the curve France had come, but with the further implication that one more step might lead to ruin.

It is hard to know how to measure the extent to which diagnostic divergences like these made it more or less difficult to promote either a revival of mixed or balanced government or to establish a programme of reform under the aegis of a patriot king between 1787 and 1789. By 1790, however, their joint disappearance from the political agenda was all too clear. The point is worth emphasising because, with the conspicuous exception of Physiocracy, almost every programme of institutional reform in France before 1789 highlighted the value of a mixed system. A strong early case in its favour, based on the widely read *Essay on the Constitution of England* published in 1776 by the Swiss political commentator Jean-Louis Delolme, was made in the summer and autumn of 1789 by a lawyer from Grenoble named Jean-Joseph Mounier who for a time became a prominent member of the National Assembly. The difficulty, however, of creating a British-style House of Lords out of the 50,000-strong French nobility quickly ruled out the possibility of making the new French system a facsimile of its British counterpart. The British-style constitutional project championed by Mounier and the Monarchiens (as they came to be called) never really got off the ground, despite muted support from another of Delolme's followers, Louis XVI's finance minister Jacques Necker, and, after the fall of the Bastille, a recurrent hope that Necker and the hero of the American Revolution General Lafayette would join forces to create a French

---

[17] Jacques-Pierre Brissot, *Mémoires* (compiled by his son), 4 vols. (Paris, 1832), 4: 23, referring to Joseph Pétiot, *Autres rêveries sur le magnétisme animal à un académicien de province* (Brussels, 1784), 42. On Petiot and, too, the source of Brissot's characterisation in an entry to his periodical, *Le Patriote français*, 16 March 1791, see Robert C. Darnton, *Mesmerism and the End of the Enlightenment in France* (Cambridge, MA, 1968), 103–4.

equivalent of the patriotic civil and military authority that the Americans had found in *The Federalist Papers* and George Washington. Real as these hopes might have been, differences in circumstance ruled out a French equivalent of Madison and Washington.[18]

The result, as the Anglo-Irish political commentator Edmund Burke pointed out in 1790 in his *Reflections on the Revolution in France*, was that very few of the constitutional ingredients of the new French regime had a recognised political pedigree. The only precedent for the highly unusual single legislative chamber established by the French Constituent Assembly in 1790 was the unicameral legislature of the American state of Pennsylvania and, even there, the single legislature was matched by a constitutionally specified Council of Censors.[19] France, however, was neither Pennsylvania nor Massachusetts, nor even Britain, with its relatively tiny hereditary peerage. 'You might if you pleased', Burke wrote, 'have profited of our example and have given to your recovered freedom a correspondent dignity'.

> Those opposed and conflicting interests which you considered as so great a blemish in your old and in our present constitution interpose a salutary check to all precipitate resolutions. They render deliberation a matter, not of choice, but of necessity; they make all change a subject of *compromise,* which naturally begets moderation; they produce *temperaments* preventing the sore evil of harsh, crude, unqualified reformations, and rendering all the headlong exertions of arbitrary power, in the few or in the many, for ever impracticable. Through that diversity of members and interests, general liberty had as many securities as there were separate views in the several orders, whilst, by pressing down the whole by the weight of a real monarchy, the separate parts would have been prevented from warping and starting from their allotted places.[20]

---

[18]   On this aspect of French politics, not only after 1789 but also after 1815, see a four-part series of articles on Lafayette published in 1822 by the self-styled Baron d'Eckstein in *Annales de la littérature et des arts*, notably vol. 9 (1822), 8–10.

[19]   Angus Harwood Brown, 'The Pennsylvania Council of Censors and the Debate on the Constitutional Guardian in the Early United States', *American Journal of Legal History*, 64 (2024), 1–26.

[20]   Edmund Burke, *Reflections on the Revolution in France* [1790], ed. John Greville Agar Pocock (Indianapolis, 1987), 31.

Burke's verdict on the new regime may have been negative, but even its supporters recognised that its institutional arrangements were something new.

Burke's charge of constitutional failure has been accepted more readily than there have been available explanations of the failure itself. One possible reason for the failure that has already been indicated is that the calls to revive a mixed or balanced system of government or, in parallel, to rely on a patriot king to promote a range of legal, fiscal or institutional reforms were based on such radically different diagnoses of the present state of France that they simply cancelled one another out. France could not be far too modern and not modern enough at one and the same time. The more fundamental moral and historical evaluations underlying both sets of claims fed readily into the legacy of conflict between ministers and magistrates inherited by the royal government from the reign of Louis XV and into the high-level political infighting generated by the shifting allegiances of the king, the queen and other members of the royal family to the rival ministerial factions associated respectively with the duc d'Aiguillon and the duc de Choiseul that were also inherited from the reign of Louis XV.[21] They fed their way too into the various alliances and possibilities of alliance that were available to France before and after the War of American Independence and, too, into the possible aftershocks and reverberation of a French debt default on the kingdom's allies or clients in Switzerland, the Netherlands or the Italian Peninsula. Although, echoing Burke, it was once usual to associate the French Revolution with a failure to reform, it is equally possible to associate it with a plethora of incompatible projects for reform. Where it was once possible to take the phrase *après-nous le déluge* (after us, the deluge) attributed to Louis XV's mistress Mme de Pompadour to be evidence of a more generic and heedless indifference to the gravity of circumstances, it is equally possible to interpret the phrase as simply one of many other anticipations of Armageddon. In itself, it could have meant either.

---

[21] On these subjects, see John Hardman, *French Politics 1774–1789. From the Accession of Louis XVI to the Fall of the Bastille* (London, 1995); Julian Swann, *Politics and the Parlements of Paris under Louis XV* (Cambridge, 1995) and Munro Price, *The Fall of the French Monarchy* (London, 2002).

The resulting absence of the expected solution calls for a final, more general comment about causation. One way of trying to address it is to follow events as they unfolded in France from the late summer of 1786 to the spring of 1789 and beyond. This type of historical narrative seems to have the advantage of integrating the question of causation into a specifiable sequence of choices and decisions made by determinate sets of individual or collective agents, like the king, his ministers, the queen, the princes of the royal blood, the assembly of Notables, the French royal Parlements, the representatives of the French third estate, the officers and troops of French royal army or, later, the members of the French National and Legislative assemblies, the constitutional Convention of the first French republic and the various provincial and Parisian Jacobin clubs. The same procedure could also be applied, but with more of a question mark about whether they were quite the same sort of identifiably cohesive and continuous agent, to the people of Paris, or of France as a whole. Cumulatively, they all did the things that made up the French Revolution.

The difficulty with this procedure is that the same type of historical narrative can be applied to any sequence of events, some ordinary, others extraordinary, but with nothing in the sequence itself that makes it possible to distinguish the one from the other. Under stable conditions, a well-organised narrative can explain quite a lot. Under unstable conditions, it simply cannot.[22] The coronation of Louis XVI in 1774 was, with some ceremonial modification, an ordinary event, occasioned by the death of his grandfather Louis XV, and was caused by the application of the rules governing the succession to the French throne. The execution of Louis XVI in 1793 was an extraordinary event even if, according to some, it could be justified by the very status that Louis XVI had acquired at his coronation. '*One cannot reign innocently*', the twenty-five year old Jacobin leader Louis-Antoine Saint-Just told the French republican Convention on 13 November 1792 to clinch the case for the regicide.[23]

---

[22] The point is one of the features of the work of John Dunn, notably his *Modern Revolutions: An Introduction to the Analysis of a Political Phenomenon* [1972] (Cambridge, 1989), and one reason for its abiding salience. For illustration of the problem, see John Hardman, *The French Revolution: A Political History* (New Haven, 2025).

[23] The original statement was '*On ne peut point régner innocemment*': Louis-Antoine Saint-Just, speech to the Convention on how to try Louis XVI, 13 November 1792,

But even the most intricately detailed of historical narratives would be quite hard-pressed to interpret Saint-Just literally and take Louis XVI's coronation to be the cause of his execution. By definition, extraordinary events escape ordinary classification, which is why it is so difficult to avoid tautology (or circularity) in explaining why they occur.

Trying, as many historians have done, to get behind the sequence of events by looking elsewhere – to changing economic circumstances, rising bourgeois aspirations, developing institutional weaknesses, mounting international pressures, faltering political legitimacy, growing enlightenment criticism, lingering religious antagonisms, increasing class conflict or an emerging public sphere – still leaves a gap in the causation. All these things may well have happened, but it is not clear how, whether jointly or severally, they were connected to the events themselves, nor why any or all of them eventuated in something whose content was as specific as the content of the French Revolution. The difficulties begin because some events occurred only because other events ruled out more ordinary or predictable courses of action, ensuring that the effects of hesitation, improvisation or inspiration would look more strongly causally determined than, in fact, they were. In this sense, dealing with the subject of causation is like watching a negative turn positive when printing an old black and white photograph.[24] Shadows become highlights and brightness turns into darkness, making what once was there look so different that it seems to have disappeared from view. Something similar, it could be said, happened with the French Revolution, with extraordinary events ruling out more ordinary events, leaving other events and other possible causes to come to the fore. Opportunities could fade into obscurity while contingencies could crystallise into certainties. The resulting mixture of continuity and discontinuity is what has made it so difficult to decide where causes end and their effects begin thus starting the slide into circularity (as, most obviously, would be the case by taking faltering political legitimacy to be a cause). The question of causation seems, consequently, to entail a double bind. Narratives have

in Louis-Antoine Saint-Just, *Oeuvres complètes*, ed. Miguel Abensour (Paris, Gallimard, 2004), p. 480 (italicized in the original).

[24] For comparable use of the metaphor, see Hans Blumenberg, *Concepts en histoire* [1998] (Paris, 2017), 5–6. For a more alarming examination of causation, see Bertrand Russell, 'On the Notion of Cause', in *His Mysticism and Logic* [1918] (London, 1953), 171–96.

the advantage of dealing with real events, either ordinary or extraordinary, but the disadvantage of not being able to discriminate between them. Bringing more general causes into the picture makes it difficult to get back to the events themselves at least without smuggling in some kind of circularity. There seems to be no easy way to deal with the question of causation without falling into either undifferentiated uniformity or unverifiable generalisation.

One way out, as should now be clear, is to try to find out as much as can be found about what was expected, but did not happen, as about what was unexpected, but really did. This, it needs to be emphasised again, does not mean speculating about counterfactuals or about what might have happened if, for example, the royal army had moved more rapidly on Paris in July 1789 or if, in June 1791, Louis XVI had not been captured at Varennes.[25] By definition, that type of nonevent leaves no historical evidence. But the other type of nonevent, the type that was expected, but did not happen, has in fact left a great deal of historical evidence in the many books, pamphlets, newspapers, speeches, letters, notes or private papers that survive from the time. There, it is not hard to find a huge array of contemporary descriptions, assessments or evaluations of France's past, present and many possible futures. Dealing with the question of causation in the light of this mixture of retrospective and prospective points of view has several distinct advantages. First, it makes it easier to explain how possible extraneous causes – like changing economic circumstances, rising bourgeois aspirations, developing institutional weaknesses, mounting international pressures, faltering political legitimacy, growing enlightenment criticism, lingering religious antagonisms, increasing class conflict or an emerging public sphere – were incorporated into current assessments of political possibilities or constraints to become part of the motivation for, or justification of, the unfolding sequence of events. Second, it makes it easier to identify a rather smaller, if still heterogeneous, number of issues that, at different times, really were causally

---

[25] On counterfactuals, see Quentin Deluermoz and Pierre Singaravélou, *Pour une histoire des possibles* (Paris, 2016); and Catherine Gallagher, *Telling It Like It Wasn't: The Counterfactual Imagination in History and Fiction* (Chicago, 2018) as well as her earlier, 'What Would Napoleon Do? Historical, Fictional, and Counterfactual Characters', *New Literary History*, 42 (2011), 315–36.

important in making the French Revolution the type of revolution that it became. Third, and as will be shown in more detail in the following pages, it also makes it easier to see how relatively late in the day it was before anyone began to think that the events taking place in France really were extraordinary, not only because they deviated unexpectedly from earlier parallels but also because they diverged just as strikingly from what might have been expected of the future. Fourth, this gradually dawning, but also intrinsically unstable, awareness of the differences between the expected and unexpected makes it easier to deal with the generic problem of unintended consequences that were as much a feature of the French Revolution as of any other extraordinary event. As the volatile pattern of events unfolded, it suggested other examples and different parallels and these in turn gave rise to further assessments or opened up new, but previously unforeseen possibilities or constraints.

All four advantages add up to quite a good set of reasons for trying to approach the events of the French Revolution from its protagonists' points of view. A narrative able to accommodate both ordinary and extraordinary events calls for this type of future-oriented perspective because it is the only one that can provide as much historical and analytical purchase on failures that have now been forgotten as on successes that were never foreseen. The idea of a patriot king was, arguably, one of the former. The idea of a representative system was, equally arguably, one of the latter. Explaining the French Revolution calls for this mixture of the possible and the actual and the underlying combination of things that were expected but did not happen and things that were forgotten but could then look brand new. The point was registered more fully and clearly than posterity has recognised by several of those most immediately and directly exposed to the events of the French Revolution. One of them, the German philosopher Johann Gottlieb Fichte, set out to show that history was, in fact, made up of just this combination of the ordinary and routine along with the extraordinary and unprecedented. Fichte gave this combination of causation and creation the name of facticity. As will be shown towards the end of this book, it became one of the more durable legacies of the French Revolution.

CHAPTER FOUR

Cutting the Cable: Rousseau, Sieyès and the Idea of a Representative System

The mixture of the possible and the actual is particularly applicable to the thought of Emmanuel-Joseph Sieyès because much of his political and intellectual life was made up of a sequence of largely unsuccessful attempts to bridge the gap between the two. Sieyès's intellectual abilities have come to be widely recognised and his thought has been associated with a surprisingly wide variety of earlier political thinkers, from Thomas Hobbes, Baruch Spinoza and James Harrington in the seventeenth century to Montesquieu, Rousseau and Adam Smith in the second half of the eighteenth century. 'Among the crowd of men of wit and talent who adorned the Constituent Assembly', wrote one of his recurrent political opponents, Antoine-Joseph Barnave, 'only two seemed to me able to aspire to the title of a creative mind: the abbé Sieyès and Dupont (de Nemours)'.[1] But, notwithstanding this unforced compliment and the generally impressive intellectual pedigree associated with his thought, only a very unusual combination of circumstances formed the context that, in 1789, gave Sieyès's ideas a sudden and almost entirely unexpected prominence. Many of them, however, were soon rejected or implemented in so limited or partial a way that much of their original content and purpose came to be misrecognised particularly, and most significantly, in relation to Sieyès's close intellectual engagement with the thought of Jean-Jacques Rousseau.

According to some interpretations, centred on the subject of sociability, Sieyès differed from Rousseau because Rousseau's thought had more in common with Thomas Hobbes's minimalist version of sociability, while Sieyès's did not. According to others, centred on the subject of

---

[1] Antoine-Joseph Barnave, *Œuvres*, 4 vols. (Paris, 1843), 2: 65.

representation, Sieyès differed from Rousseau, this time because Sieyès had more in common with Hobbes's strong version of representative sovereignty, while Rousseau did not. According to yet others, centred on the subject of democracy, Sieyès differed from both Hobbes and Rousseau on the political foundations of democratic sovereignty because Sieyès was conspicuously silent on the subject of a social contract, as well as, but in a more literal than a conceptual sense, the subject of the general will.[2] One of the aims of this chapter is to show that in all these subjects Sieyès actually had more in common with Rousseau than posterity has come to see and that this can be supported by strong textual evidence. In this context, Hobbes was simply part of the intellectual background, one that changed radically after the publication in 1748 of Montesquieu's *The Spirit of Laws*. Positioning Sieyès's thought in this post-Montesquieuian context helps to throw new light on the common conceptual ground that Sieyès shared with Rousseau. Both endorsed Montesquieu's assertion in *The Spirit of Laws* that 'liberty, not being the fruit of every climate, is not accessible to all peoples' because both understood the argument about economic productivity and fiscal accountability on which Montesquieu's assertion was based. On the premises of that argument, checks and balances were built into the institutional framework of the whole system because the tension between the state's need for tax revenue and its members' need for justice kept honour alive as the underlying principle of monarchy and, later, made the politics of social comparison – or social envy – the underlying principle of representative government. Rousseau and Sieyès largely reinforced Montesquieu's point by giving it a stronger electoral twist.[3] Circumstances in 1788 and 1789 also, however, supplied

---

[2] On Sieyès, Hobbes and sociability, see Richard Tuck, *The Sleeping Sovereign* (Cambridge, 2008), 121–80, and his more recent *Active and Passive Citizens: A Defense of Majoritarian Democracy* (Princeton, 2024), 15–43. On Sieyès, Hobbes and representation, see Pasquale Pasquino, *Sieyès et l'invention de la constitution en France* (Paris, 1998); and, for two different approaches to Sieyès and democracy, see Myriam-Isabelle Ducrocq, *La République de Harrington dans la France des Lumières et de la Révolution* (Oxford, 2022) and Lucia Rubinelli, *Constituent Power: A History* (Cambridge, 2023), 33–74.

[3] For fuller development, see Michael Sonenscher, *Jean-Jacques Rousseau: The Division of Labour, the Politics of the Imagination and the Concept of Federal Government* (Leiden, 2020), 80–1.

the conditions in which the intellectual convergence became a political convergence. Sieyès certainly did not create these circumstances, but positioning his thought in the double context formed both by Rousseau's intellectual legacy and by the high politics of the Old Regime helps to explain the sudden prominence that his ideas acquired.

Sieyès, arguably, was the most durably significant political presence in the French Revolution. His pamphlet *Qu'est-ce qu'est le tiers état?* (*What Is the Third Estate?*), published early in 1789, is usually taken to be its manifesto text. His relationship with the upper echelons in the French army in 1799 was central to the military coup that brought Napoleon Bonaparte to power in November of that year. For a time, between 1799 and 1801, Sieyès was one of the republic's three consuls, sitting alongside Bonaparte and Roger Ducos as one of the triumvirate at the head of the new French regime. After 1801, however, when the republic became an empire, he was elbowed aside by Bonaparte and pushed subsequently into gilded obscurity when, in 1804, the empire was turned into a hereditary empire. In keeping with his own idea of how to neutralise political opponents, he was made a count of the French Empire and subsequently went into exile from France to live in Brussels when the Bourbon monarchy was restored in 1815. He returned to France at the age of eighty-two in 1830 (he was born in 1748) and lived on, silently and invisibly, for a further six years. Asked whether he wished to resume his membership of the French Institute that he had played a part in establishing in 1797, he declined. At his age, he was reported to have said, his dwindling mental capacity meant that he would either talk too much or say too little. It was a sardonically self-aware verdict on his whole political life, echoing in a number of different registers the remark made in May 1790 by the comte de Mirabeau that it was 'a national calamity' for Sieyès to remain silent on the question of whether the king or the National Assembly should have the right to declare war and peace.[4]

Sieyès was almost entirely unknown before 1789. He soon came to be seen, however, as the theoretical architect of the French Revolution. The origin and orientation of his political thought have remained something of a mystery ever since his three famous pamphlets – the *Essay on Privileges,*

---

[4] John Harold Clapham, *The Abbé Sieyès: An Essay in the Politics of the French Revolution* (London, 1912), 119.

What Is the Third Estate? and the *Views of the Executive Means Available to the Representatives of France in 1789* – were published in a space of six months between the winter of 1788 and the spring of 1789, as the French Revolution really began. Some years later when, in 1795, a translation of the seventeenth-century English republican James Harrington's *Oceana* was published in Paris, one of Sieyès's closest political allies, Pierre-Louis Roederer, noted in a review of the translation that the legislative system that Harrington had commended, with one part of the legislature deliberating and the other part deciding, was rather like the one recently proposed to the French Convention by an unnamed individual who Roederer called 'the most profound of our legislators' and who, transparently, was Sieyès. It was a pity, Roederer continued, that the translation had not been published three months earlier because, he wrote, 'it might then have been possible to accept truths from a dead foreigner that were too difficult to accept from a living citizen'.[5]

Roederer was not the last to compare Sieyès to Harrington although, in contradistinction to later commentators, he made the comparison to highlight the similarity rather than to attribute the influence.[6] In this respect, his assessment was more accurate. Apart from the division of the legislature into two parts and, as Roederer emphasised, the French failure to adopt Sieyès's version of this idea (because, unlike the arrangements advocated by Sieyès, each of the two legislative chambers established in 1795 under the constitution of the French Directory was to make separate decisions, giving them a mixed, rather than a single, decision-making procedure), Sieyès attached considerably more significance to the relationship between the division of labour and political representation than

---

[5] The review, by Pierre-Louis Roederer, was published in the *Journal de Paris* on 1 September 1795 and reprinted in Pierre-Louis Roederer, *Oeuvres*, 7 vols., ed. A-M. Roederer (Paris, 1853–57), 4: 525–26 (at 526 for the passages quoted).

[6] See, for example, Jean J. Thonissen, 'Du Rôle de l'utopie dans l'histoire de la philosophie politique: James Harrington', *Bulletin de l'Académie royale de Belgique*, 2nd series, 15 (1863), 3–27 (at 21, note 2). Clapham, *The Abbé Sieyès*, 31–32, 109, 174, 264–65. More recently, see Myriam-Isabelle Ducrocq, *La République de Harrington dans la France des Lumières* (Oxford, 2022); Dirk Weimann and Gaby Mahlberg (eds.), *Perspectives on English Revolutionary Republicanism* (Aldershot, 2014); Rachel Hammersley, *The English Republican Tradition and Eighteenth-Century France: Between the Ancients and the Moderns* (Manchester, 2010).

Harrington had done. Although, in a loose sense, his political thought repeated the Harringtonian claim that the balance of political power followed the balance of property, Sieyès associated modern political power with different types of property and different types of political institution from those identified by Harrington. Despite these similarities, Sieyès's greatest intellectual debt was not to Harrington but to the political thought of Jean-Jacques Rousseau.

Sieyès did not, in fact, need to have any direct knowledge of Harrington's thought for the similarity that Roederer noticed to have occurred. It occurred because Sieyès, in the first place, was very familiar with Rousseau's thought and, in the second place, because Rousseau had highlighted Harrington's significance in the context of a surprisingly positive comment on the thought of one of his many imagined enemies and persecutors, the Scottish philosopher David Hume. The comment in question helps to explain the convergence between Harrington and Sieyès that Roederer and posterity subsequently noticed. It appeared in Rousseau's *Confessions* and began with a statement that he had known of Hume partly because he had read the volume of his *History of England* that covered the Stuart monarchy and had been published in French translation. 'For lack of having read his other works', Rousseau continued, 'I was persuaded, based on what I had been told about him, that M. Hume associated a very republican soul with the English paradoxes in favour of luxury. Based on this opinion, I looked at his whole apology for Charles I as a prodigy of impartiality and I had as great an idea of his virtue as of his genius.'[7] Rousseau did not expand on this assessment of Hume's 'very republican soul' but it is likely that it was based on the essay entitled 'Idea of a Perfect Commonwealth' that Hume published in 1752.[8] That essay, which was published in French translation in 1754, was both an endorsement and a criticism of Harrington's *Oceana*, the text that, as Hume wrote, was 'the only valuable model of a commonwealth that has yet been offered

---

[7] Jean-Jacques Rousseau, *Confessions* [1783], in Jean-Jacques Rousseau, *Collected Writings*, 14 vols., ed. Christopher Kelly, Roger D. Masters, Philip Stewart and Peter G. Stillman. (Hanover, New Hampshire, 1987–2007), 5: XII, 527.

[8] On the Rousseau-Hume relationship, see notably Ryu Susato, 'How Rousseau Read Hume's *Political Discourses*: Hints of Unexpected Agreement in the Views of Money and Luxury', *European Journal of the History of Economic Thought*, 26 (2019), 23–50.

to the public' and, as such, was superior to both Plato's *Republic* and Thomas More's *Utopia*.[9]

There is, therefore, good reason to think that it was Rousseau, with his comment on Hume, who was responsible for establishing a connection between Sieyès and Harrington. To find out about Harrington, all that Sieyès needed to do was to notice Rousseau's description of Hume's 'very republican soul' and read the French translation of his 'Idea of a Perfect Commonwealth'. Although it is not usually emphasised, Sieyès (like Immanuel Kant) was a very careful reader of Rousseau. Evidence of this engagement is not hard to find. The first piece of evidence is a comment made by Rousseau about the Polish people that Sieyès took over and applied to the French Third Estate. If, Rousseau wrote in his posthumously published *Considerations on the Government of Poland*, the Polish nation was to have 'a certain force' and 'a certain stability', it followed that the Polish people, who 'until now counted for nothing', should 'finally count for something'.[10] The passage echoed the earlier assessment of the status of the French Third Estate that Rousseau made in his *Social Contract* in 1762. When, Rousseau wrote there, political decision-making was made by the three estates of the clergy, nobility and commoners, 'the assembly of these representatives is called in some countries the third estate of the nation, so that the particular interests of two orders are placed in the first and second ranks and the public interest only in the third'.[11] Both passages were transferred, almost verbatim, to the biting comparison between the present status of the third estate (nothing) and what it aspired to become (something) that Sieyès published in 1789 at the very beginning of *What Is the Third Estate?*

---

[9]   David Hume, 'Idea of a Perfect Commonwealth' [1752], in Hume, *Political Essays*, ed. Knud Haakonssen (Cambridge, 1994), 222. See also Max Skjönsberg and Felix Waldmann (eds.), *Hume's Essays: A Critical Guide* (Cambridge, 2025).

[10]   Jean-Jacques Rousseau, *Considerations on the Government of Poland*, in Rousseau, CW, 11: ch. 6, 184, and ch. 13, 226. The overlap is also signalled by Thérence Carvalho and Bernard Herencia in their *Les Lumières au Chevet de la Pologne* (Geneva: 2024), 37, note 61. See also Gabrielle Radica, 'Républicanisme et contractualisme dans les *Considérations sur le gouvernement de Pologne* de Rousseau', *Ethique, Politique, Religions*, 26 (2025), 41–56 (at p. 50).

[11]   Rousseau, *CS*, Bk. III, ch. 15, in Roussseau, *CW*, 4: 192.

Here, for corroboration, is Rousseau on Poland in French: 'La république de Pologne, a-t-on souvent dit et répété', he wrote, 'est composée de trois ordres: l'ordre équestre, le sénat et le roi. J'aimerais mieux dire que la nation polonaise est composée de trois ordres: les nobles, qui sont tout, les bourgeois, qui ne sont rien, et les paysans qui sont moins que rien.' Together, he continued, the latter two orders made up the people to form one side of a social hierarchy that rose upwards towards the king. 'Commençons', Rousseau wrote, 'par le premier, jusqu'ici compté pour rien, mais qu'il importe enfin de compter pour quelque chose'.[12] Here, also in French, is Sieyès on the third estate. 'Le plan de cet écrit', he wrote, 'est assez simple. Nous avons trois questions à nous faire.'

'1   / Qu'est-ce que le tiers état? – TOUT.
2   / Qu'a-t-il été jusqu'à présent dans l'ordre politique? -RIEN.
3   / Que demande-t-il? – A ETRE QUELQUE CHOSE.'[13]

It was simply a quicker and more concise version of Rousseau's formulation.

The second piece of evidence is the high level of verbal and conceptual similarity between the descriptions of the subject of government made by Rousseau and Sieyès. 'A hereditary crown prevents trouble', Rousseau wrote, also in his *Considerations on the Government of Poland*, 'but brings on servitude; election maintains freedom, but shakes the state with each new reign'.[14] To avoid either possibility, he proposed that Poland's kings should be chosen by lot from among the thirty-three heads of the Polish administrative units known as Palatinates. Three candidates would be selected in this way and one would then be elected as king by the Polish Diet. With this form, Rousseau wrote: 'we combine all the advantages of election with those of hereditary succession'.[15] He had originally used the phrase in 1767 in a letter to Physiocracy's standard-bearer, the marquis de

---

[12]   The French passages are taken from Jean-Jacques Rousseau, *Ecrits politiques*, ed. J. D. Selche (Paris, 1972), 216 & 285.

[13]   Emmanuel-Joseph Sieyès, *Qu'est-ce que le tiers état?* [1789], in Roberto Zapperi (ed.), *Ecrits politiques* (Paris, 1985), 117.

[14]   Rousseau, *Considerations*, ch. 14, in Rousseau, CW, 11: 230.

[15]   Rousseau, *Considerations*, ch. 14, in Rousseau, CW, 11: 233. In this, and in the preceding citation, I have modified the translation.

Mirabeau. Rousseau's letter was published in 1768 as part of a pamphlet by Mirabeau entitled *Précis de l'ordre légal* ('An outline of the legal order') and then reprinted, with Rousseau's permission, in the second, 1775, edition of another book by Mirabeau entitled *Lettres sur la législation, ou l'ordre légal dépravé, rétabli et perpétué* ('Letters on legislation, or the legal order depraved, restored and perpetuated').

The phrase resurfaced in 1791, this time in the public debate that took place between Sieyès and the Anglo-American political radical Tom Paine after Louis XVI's flight from Paris when it seemed possible that the royal government would be replaced by a republican form of government. In this debate, Sieyès argued that something analogous to a monarchy was preferable to what he called polyarchy, or a government with a collective head of state, because, he wrote, it was possible to establish a form of election that, as he put it, was 'very applicable to the first public function'.[16] Although he did not specify how this electoral system would work, his claim that it would 'unite all the advantages attributed to *hereditary* without any of its inconveniences and all the advantages of *election*, without its inconveniences' is sufficiently redolent of Rousseau to indicate that it was simply a French version of the political system that Rousseau had commended to the Poles. Sieyès repeated both the phrase and its purpose in 1795 in drafting a proposal for what he called 'the peaceful and permanent nomination of the Great Elector', which, he wrote, 'would combine all the advantages of the election of a head without having to fear its inconveniences and all the advantages of inheritance without any of its innumerable dangers'.[17]

In emphasising the desirability of having a single head of state, but not an absolute monarch, Sieyès referred repeatedly to a passage from Pliny's *Panegyric to Trajan* that Rousseau had quoted in his *Discourse on the Origin of Inequality* to explain the desirability's significance. The passage ran: 'Let

---

[16] For the text, see Emmanuel-Joseph Sieyès, *Political Writings*, ed. Michael Sonenscher (Indianapolis, 2003), 170. Sieyès placed quotation marks around the words in a later manuscript entitled 'Bases de l'ordre social', written at the time of the constitutional discussions of 1795 and now printed in Pasquino, *Sieyès*, 181–91 (at 191).

[17] Christine Fauré, Jacques Guilhaumou, and Jacques Valier (eds.), *Des manuscrits de Sieyès*, 2 vols. (Paris, 1999 & 2007), 1: 514. Henceforth, Sieyès, *Manuscrits* followed by the volume and page numbers.

us have a prince to save us from the peril of having a master.'[18] There was, in short, a substantial overlap between Rousseau and Sieyès on the subject of constitutional design. This, however, was not the only area in which their thought converged. It extended to a common, but highly critical, engagement with the thought of the French philosopher Etienne Bonnot de Condillac. 'It is extremely necessary', Sieyès noted as he began to read his way through Condillac's *Traité des sensations* ('Treatise on Sensations'), 'to follow Condillac to have an accurate idea of what we know and how we know it'. Several pages later, however, he had changed his mind. 'There are', he now noted, 'simply too many mistakes in Condillac's writing for it to be worth continuing. One has to stop and correct him at every step. It is simply false to say that a single sense can be the nucleus of all the faculties of the soul.'[19] As with Rousseau, the processing power of the human mind and the mixture of memory, imagination, sensation and emotion on which the mind relied gave it a capacity for creativity that could not be captured by the combination of memory and analysis that was the most prominent feature of Condillac's thought. Human life was language based as well as physically based and, as with Rousseau, was lived in what Sieyès called a lingual world. Sieyès was clearly fascinated by this aspect of human life and its capacity to generate many of the abruptly incisive formulations and striking neologisms that are one of the features of his thought.

The overlap between Rousseau and Sieyès went even further. It extended to Sieyès's speculations, in an undated note that he headed 'slaves', about the implications of breeding a species of humanoid to do the hard physical work that was likely to cause misery and blight human lives. These speculations have been given several quite lurid interpretations.[20] Here too, however, the initial idea came from Rousseau. 'The pity we have for the misfortunes of others', Rousseau wrote in *Emile*, the book that was his most wide-ranging examination of morality and politics, 'is not measured by the quantity of that misfortune,

---

[18] Sieyès, *Manuscrits*, 1: 427.   [19] Sieyès, *Manuscrits*, 1: 77 & 93.

[20] See William J Sewell, *A Rhetoric of Bourgeois Revolution: The Abbé Sieyès and* What *Is the Third Estate?* (Durham, 1994), 145–65 and Angus Harwood Brown, 'Republican Nostalgia, the Division of Labour and the Origins of Inequality in the Thought of the Abbé Sieyès', *Intellectual History Review*, 34 (2024), 433–56.

but by the feelings that we attribute to those who suffer it'. This, he explained, was 'one of the causes which hardens us more to the ills of animals than to those of men, although the common sensibility ought to make us identify with them equally'. The inability of humans to imagine that animals could feel pain was why people were prepared to expose sheep or horses to severe physical hardship in their service to humanity. It was also, Rousseau added, why 'the rich console themselves for the harm they do to the poor by supposing them stupid enough not to feel it'.[21]

Sieyès's speculations followed the logic of Rousseau's comparison. Human slaves certainly suffered. But humanoids could play the same part in human life that animals really did because, as was the case with animals, their suffering would not be humanly recognisable. As Sieyès put it in his note, they would be 'another species that has fewer needs and is less apt to excite human compassion'. The point of the note was, in short, not a point about eugenics or class division, but a Rousseau-inspired point about slavery and human suffering. It was comparable in orientation to Rousseau's parallel point, in the *Social Contract*, about the modern division of labour as the price that humanity had been required to pay for the abolition of ancient slavery. The loss of the time and the freedom to participate in civic life that slavery had once made available to the Greeks and Romans, Rousseau argued, now had to be offset by different forms of political participation and a different type of government. Rousseau called it an elected aristocracy; Sieyès called it a representative system. In substance, however, the two systems were the same, with what Sieyès called 'electism', or an electoral system, replacing ancient slavery. Much the same point about emancipating humanity from hard physical labour is now sometimes made about washing machines or robots.

The overlap between Rousseau and Sieyès was, however, most visible in the context of three related subjects. The one that is now best known is the complicated subject of constituent power. In the early twentieth century it gave Sieyès the reputation of something like a precursor of the political thought of Carl Schmitt. When set alongside the other two subjects, however, it becomes clear that Sieyès's version of the concept of constituent power had as much to do with public debt as with political

---

[21] Jean-Jacques Rousseau, *Emile* [1762], ed. Allan Bloom, Book IV, Third Maxim (New York, 1979), 225.

decision-making. The first of these subjects was the electoral system that, in his *Considerations on the Government of Poland*, Rousseau called a system of gradated promotion. Sieyès simply took it over as the basis of the new political system that he envisaged for France. In this system, eligibility for election to office called for an earlier period of service in an office lower down the electoral scale. Promotion to office thus meant starting at the very bottom of the gradated scale and working slowly to be elected, step by step, all the way to the top. The second subject was formed by the set of distinctions differentiating what Sieyès called the constituent, constituting and constituted powers. Although the terminology did not originate with either Rousseau or Sieyès (it was probably picked up by Sieyès from a French translation of an examination of the British constitution by the Scottish painter and political critic Allan Ramsay), the concepts to which it referred were the basis of the strong distinction between ancient and modern political societies that was common to the political thought of both Rousseau and Sieyès. Although the word republic – from the Latin *res publica* (public thing) – has a generic quality, both Rousseau and Sieyès emphasised that the arrangements, institutions and activities of a modern republic were fundamentally different from those of an ancient republic. The key difference was a product of the division of labour and, in place of slavery, of the economic and social interdependence that the division of labour produced. Alongside the division of labour, there was also the new set of interests generated by public debt and the new type of constituent power that it produced alongside the ownership of land or moveable forms of property. The third subject in which the similarity between Rousseau and Sieyès was most marked was the abolition of the old French provinces and the old division of the kingdom into fiscal and administrative units known as *pays d'états* and *pays d'élections* (meaning, roughly, regions with elected estates and regions with nominated administrators) and their replacement by the eighty-three departments that still remain the principal administrative and electoral divisions of the French republic. Together they added up to what Sieyès called a representative system.

It is still usual to assume that this emphasis on political representation meant that Sieyès and Rousseau were far apart. This, however, is a mistake. It was produced both historically and historiographically by conflating the distinction between democratic sovereignty and representative government that was common to their political thought. That common ground can be identified initially from Rousseau's treatment of what he called the democratic constitution. 'The democratic constitution', he wrote in the eighth of his *Letters from the Mountain* of 1764,

> has been hitherto very poorly examined. All those who have treated this subject were either ignorant of it, too little interested in it, or interested in misrepresenting it. None of them has sufficiently distinguished the sovereign from the government, the legislative power from the executive. There is no other mode of government in which these two powers are so separate, and in which they have been so much confounded, by the affectation of writers.

Some, Rousseau continued, 'imagine that a democracy is a government in which the whole people is magistrate and judge', while others 'do not see liberty except in the right to elect one's leaders and (being subject only to princes) believe that the one who commands is always the sovereign'. None of this, Rousseau implied, was correct because liberty was more than the right to elect one's leaders, while sovereignty was not only, or not always, a capacity to command. If, Rousseau wrote, the correct distinctions (between sovereignty and government and between the legislative and executive) had been fully understood, then, he wrote, 'the democratic constitution is certainly the masterpiece of the political art; but the more admirable the mechanism of it, the less it belongs to common eyes to penetrate into it'.[22]

Rousseau's conception of this 'masterpiece of the political art' had a number of different components. The first was the figure of the legislator. The second was the division of political society into a number of different, hierarchically arranged, units and subunits. The third was the connection, based on individual votes, between the constitutional proposals supplied by the first and the multiplicity of different decision-making units involved in the second. The result was a state made up of several different municipal, regional, provincial or national branches of government and a government containing several different ministries, councils, committees or agencies, while society itself would house the

---

[22] Rousseau, *CW*, 9: 257.

many different occupations, activities or levels of qualification that enabled a nation to exist. Irrespective of their various individual purposes or composition, however, each unit would have the same type of democratic constitution as all the rest. This meant that decision-making within each unit would be the work of a general will, but that decision-making by any particular part of the larger whole would be the work of a particular will. As Rousseau emphasised at the beginning of Book 3, Chapter 5 of the *Social Contract*, both the sovereign and the government were 'two quite distinct moral persons' with 'consequently two general wills, one relative to all the citizens, the other solely for the members of the administration'.[23] Sovereignty was certainly singular, but government and administration could be made up of many different levels, with, on the one hand, general wills within each unit but, on the other, with many particular wills within the whole administrative hierarchy.

The complicated quality of the resulting hierarchical arrangement makes it possible to clarify Rousseau's otherwise opaque assertion that in a democratic constitution nothing was more separate than the sovereign and the government and, by extension, the legislative and executive powers. The same hierarchical arrangement also helps to explain what Rousseau meant by claiming that sovereignty was something more than the power to command because, as should be obvious, that power was as much a power of government as of sovereignty. Sovereignty, or the general will, was instead what made that power legitimate because it added something extra to the idea of majority rule. Here too Rousseau was explicit, notably in the context of explaining how sovereignty turned possession into property. It could perform this legitimating function because the general will was based on the more fundamental principle sanctioned by the initial, unanimous, social contract that stipulated that a majority decision would be a legitimate decision. Majorities and minorities would arise at every level of the political and administrative system, but the resulting array of more or less local differences would be given their legitimacy by the general will. At the same time, and equally importantly, the sovereign and its legislative power would be pushed into the background by the multiplication of governmental and executive powers.

---

[23] Rousseau, *CW*, 4:174. Here also, see Sonenscher, *Jean-Jacques Rousseau*, 24, 71, 75, 113, 155–56, 159, 167.

Government, with Rousseau, displaced sovereignty. Sovereignty, in keeping with Rousseau's claim at the beginning of the *Social Contract*, was the power to legitimate, or the power to make something lawful, rather than the power to command. Sovereignty limited government but also reinforced government because it added legitimacy to the many decisions based on the principle of majority rule made among the assorted units and subunits of the whole system. On the inside, these decisions could be described as legislation, or the work of a general will, but from the outside they would, instead, be no more than administrative decisions, straightforward decrees, or the work of particular wills. The general will in this context was normative, while government added power to the legitimacy supplied by the general will. The array of overlapping distinctions also helps to clarify why, in Rousseau's rendition, the general will applied ultimately to individuals, while majority rule applied to collectivities. In the final analysis, however, the two would coincide because a will that was truly general would have to encompass the will of every individual, including those whose votes had gone to the other side. Here, what mattered to Rousseau was that a democratic constitution would have several different levels of scale and scope and, consequently, several different levels of decision-making and government. Majorities and minorities would vary from level to level and this too was compatible with the idea of a general will. Despite its complexity, the whole system would begin and end with individual freedom.

There are strong reasons, therefore, to highlight a very considerable level of conceptual continuity from Rousseau to Sieyès. Sieyès, it could be said, took over Rousseau's approach to the relationship between majorities and minorities at different levels of the political and administrative hierarchy and, in the first edition of *What Is the Third Estate?*, applied the concept of *science sociale* or social science to the problem of majority rule.[24] Rousseau's treatment of the relationship between democratic sovereignty and representative

---

[24] See Michael Sonenscher, 'The Moment of Social Science: The *Décade Philosophique* and Late Eighteenth-Century French Thought', *Modern Intellectual History*, 6 (2009), 121–46; 'Ideology, Social Science and General Facts in Late Eighteenth-Century French Political Thought', *History of European Ideas*, 35 (2009), 24–37; and, more recently, 'Physiocracy, Globalization and Capitalism', in Auguste Bertholet and Béla Kapossy (eds.), *La Physiocratie et la Suisse* (Geneva, 2023), 159–64.

government meant, as Sieyès put it memorably, that the old distinctions between monarchy, aristocracy and democracy could fall by the wayside because the new distinctions would centre on the differences between what he called a *ré-privé*, a *ré-total* and a *ré-publique*, meaning a republic, with its clear distinction between sovereignty and government, as against either absolute government (a *ré-privé*) on the one side or democratic government (a *ré-total*) on the other. In a republic the distinction between sovereignty and government was clear, but in the other two alternatives the distinction collapsed.[25] A republic was two-sided, but under the other systems of rule the two sides of the sovereignty–government distinction fused into one. With Sieyès, as with Rousseau, sovereignty legitimated, but governments ruled. This was why the two sides, one dealing with morality and the other with power, had to be kept separate. Under electoral conditions and majority rule, a government that was illegitimate could be replaced by one that was legitimate, leaving the subject of sovereignty undisturbed. As with Rousseau too, there was something that appeared to be paradoxical in Sieyès's insistence on the sovereignty of the nation but the primacy of the government. To many of his contemporaries, the combination appeared either to assert too much about the entitlements of the nation or to confer too much power to the government. In the context of the events that began to unfold between 1786 and 1789, the combination was designed, as Sieyès set out to show in the first of the three pamphlets that he wrote, but the third of the three that he published in 1789, to present a sequence of steps that, cumulatively and peacefully, would transfer sovereignty from the king to the nation and replace the many legal, financial, fiscal components of the royal government by a new political and administrative hierarchy made up of largely elected officials.

This pamphlet, entitled *Vues sur les moyens d'exécution dont les représentants de France pourront disposer en 1789* ('Views of the executive means available to the representatives of France in 1789'), helps to

---

[25] On this terminology, see Sieyès, *Political Writings*, xxi, and Sieyès, *Manuscrits*, 1: 511. For further discussion, centred on the concepts of the nation and the people as authorising agents, see Sonenscher, 'From the Hebrew Commonwealth to Party Politics' (above, ch. 3, fn. 11) and, because I did not then know of it, Ahmed Slimani, *La modernité du concept de nation au xviiie siècle: apports des thèses parlementaires et des idées politiques du temps* (Aix-Marseille, 2004), 37–58. See too Robert R. Palmer, "The National Idea in France before the Revolution", *Journal of the History of Ideas*, 1 (1940), 95–111.

explain the resonance that Sieyès's political thought came to have in 1789. As its title indicates, it set out a clear strategy for replacing hereditary government by elected government. In this respect, it also set out a clear alternative both to the idea of a patriot king, with its emphasis on reform from above, and to the standoff between the Parlements and the royal government, with its emphasis on reviving the Estates-General to establish a modified version of mixed government. It also offered an alternative to the many other proposals for reform that had circulated in France in earlier parts of the eighteenth century. One, also to be found in the publications of the abbé Gabriel Bonnot de Mably, envisaged scaling up the mixed system advocated by Chesterfield (and many others) and transforming the French monarchy into a large federal republic comparable to the system of government that, according to Mably, had existed under Charlemagne's empire. A second, to be found in the works of Voltaire's admirer Claude-Adrien Helvétius, also highlighted the desirability of a more federal system of government, with the old French provinces forming the basis of a new, elected, system of regional administration. A third, usually identified with the circle associated with Louis XVI's first minister of finance, Anne-Robert-Jacques Turgot, a circle that included the marquis de Condorcet, Pierre-Samuel Dupont de Nemours, the abbé André Morellet and the Italian American Filippo Mazzei, envisaged a system similar to the one that Calonne presented to the assembly of notables in 1787. Its cornerstone was to be a network of provincial assemblies to replace the old system of provincial estates that was designed to change the old division of the kingdom with its three different estates and three separate sets of representatives or delegates into a single system of political administration and representation with landownership at its core.

The strategy that Sieyès set out in his 'Views of the executive means' was similar to, but diverged from, all these alternatives to absolute government. It was, in the first place, inclusive and made no distinction between the ownership of different types of property as a basis of citizenship. Although it did not do so explicitly, it also made it clear that citizenship could include women as well as men and that any distinction between active and passive citizenship, a distinction that, again, Sieyès took over from Rousseau, would be fluid and open rather than rigid and fixed. It also, in the second place, set out a clearly demarcated sequence of steps, modelled on Turgot's *Mémoire sur les municipalités* (Memorandum on Municipalities), that were designed to turn absolute monarchy into representative government.[26] There would, in the first place, be a constituent assembly, elected with a brief to draft a new constitution for France. Once drafted, the constitution would be presented to the French nation for ratification and, to meet this brief, the nation would, in its turn, be divided into a hierarchy of elected municipalities or *communes*, districts or *arrondissements*, and departments. There would, therefore, be a dual process of election and ratification as the new divisions and new electorates were put into place. Primary assemblies would elect municipal officers who, in turn, would elect the officials and administrators of the districts and *arrondissements* and they, in their turn, would do the same to the administrators and officials of the departments. There was, in short, a clear sequence of steps and, when it had run its course, there would still be a king, but the nation would now be sovereign and its government would have a constitution.

Four developments gave the representatives of the third estate an opportunity to take the political initiative and adopt the strategy contained in Sieyès's three pamphlets in the spring and summer of 1789. The first was the political rebellion that began in the United Provinces of the Netherlands as part of the fallout from the American War of Independence. During that war, the Netherlands had been allied to France against Britain, but, to Dutch patriots, a succession of naval disasters in the course of the war appeared to indicate a lack of real commitment by the Dutch Stadtholder William V to the American cause and the French alliance and a lingering willingness to collude with Britain's Hanoverian rulers. The ensuing patriot campaign against the House of Orange after 1781 meant, from a French perspective, supporting the Dutch opposition to William V in order to bring the United Provinces more fully into the anti-British coalition. It also had the financial advantage of adding the resources of patriot capital in Amsterdam to the Franco-American war effort. By the autumn of 1787, however, the situation became more complicated. William V was expelled from the Hague in 1786 but, with the help of the Prussian army, was restored to his position a year later. The coincidence of the Prussian invasion of the

---

[26] Sieyès, *Manuscrits*, 2: 444, n. 27, 447, n.30.

Netherlands in 1787 with the ongoing dispute over the deficit in France created an awkward political dilemma. In the context of the Prussian invasion of the Netherlands, a replay of the events surrounding the Maupeou coup of 1771–72 would simply ruin France's patriot allies and set the seal on the restoration of the House of Orange under Prussian and British aegis. This was one reason why there was no royal debt default in the autumn of 1787.

The second development was internal rather than external in origin and it occurred a year later. It arose from a dispute that began in the French army but spilled over to encompass the broader subjects of the nature and composition of the French nobility and the competing claims of merit and inheritance as sources of entitlement to honours.[27] Its immediate cause was a royal ordinance of 17 March 1788 stipulating that to be eligible for promotion every army officer above the rank of sub-lieutenant was required to prove that he came from a family having four degrees of nobility (meaning that the individual in question had to present proof of nobility going back at least four generations). In itself, the stipulation was not a novelty. It had been made at the time of the foundation of the French Royal Military School in 1751 and had been repeated in the provisions of the famous Ségur ordinance of 22 May 1781 (named after Philippe-Henri, marquis de Ségur, the incumbent war minister). The controversial aspect of the ordinance of March 1788 was to be found in its fourteenth article. It specified that the king retained the right to make promotions directly to some military offices in order, as the wording of the article put it, 'to secure outlets for that portion of his nobility that is called on more particularly to command his regiments'.[28]

The article in question was part of a broader reforming strategy designed to establish a clearer distinction between what might be called the dignified and efficient parts of the French army by filtering out unsuitable candidates from positions of military command to leave what according to its advocates would be a more homogenously effective officer corps. Beyond its more immediate military purpose, the strategy was

---

[27] See, most fully, Rafe Blaufarb, *The French Army 1750–1820: Careers, Talent, Merit* (Manchester, 2002).

[28] For the provisions of the article and one of many hostile reactions, see [Anon.], *L'armée française au conseil de la guerre* (n. p. n. d., but early 1789 from the content), 1.

also connected to the monarchy's financial problems because, as was the case in every eighteenth-century state, French military expenditure accounted for by far the largest proportion (well over two-thirds) of government spending. In this sense, military reform matched the royal government's broader objective of dealing with the deficit both by reducing the costs of the army and, in the longer term, by cutting the size and changing the distribution of the tax burden. The article was designed to establish a twin-track system of military promotion, with both tracks nominally being subject to the requirement to prove four degrees of nobility, but with one set of largely supernumerary offices used to siphon off unqualified candidates with no identifiable military ability, leaving the other set of offices reserved for those with both a real military pedigree and an established record of command. The scheme entailed creating a number of largely dignified offices, with titles like sub-lieutenant, second-captain, deputy-major, adjutant-colonel or aide-major-general, to complement the efficient part of the military establishment. Promotion to these offices could be fast-tracked, making it easier to weed out the wrong type of noble without actually having to purge the army, thus leaving the right type of putatively more competent army officer more securely in place.

This, at any rate, was the aim, but it backfired spectacularly. Instead of being seen as an attempt to entrench ability, experience and established military pedigree into the chain of army command, it came to be seen as an attempt to reward insiders, court favourites and exactly those recently ennobled nobles that it was designed to weed out, with the inflated supply of dignified offices, and the concurrent relative fall in the number of efficient offices leading to a further scramble for positions of influence and power within the new military hierarchy. Instead of favouring ancient military lineage, as it was intended to do, army reform came to look like patronage for well-heeled clients. The result was an outburst of criticism from both inside and outside the army that soon turned into a more wide-ranging argument over the effects of privilege and court patronage on the nature and composition of the nobility itself. Examples of unearned privilege and the abuse of patronage were not hard to find, whether in some of the more lurid episodes of the reign of Louis XV or in the more recent aura of scandal that had come to surround the new queen, Marie Antoinette, particularly in the wake of the Diamond Necklace Affair of

1784 and 1785, when an apparently innocent gift from an obsequious cardinal was quickly enveloped in charges of sleaze, greed and political intrigue. It is important to remember, however, that all these subjects could have been grist to the mill of a patriot king. A model was available in 1789 in the form of Prussia's king Frederick II. As one of his panegyrists, the Scottish historian John Gillies, wrote in that year: 'the example of Frederick will serve to convince modern incredulity of the wonderful revolution that may be produced by the exertions of one man in the republic which he guides, or the kingdom which he governs'.[29] But the botched attempt at reforming the French army in the spring and summer of 1788 made the risks of repeating Maupeou's coup against the Parlements in that autumn as high as defaulting on the debt had been in 1787 at the time of the Prussian invasion of Holland. Events, in short, conspired to rule out the possibility of Louis XVI becoming a patriot king.

The third of this sequence of unexpected developments was a result of a change in the nature of government borrowing that took place in France in the third quarter of the eighteenth century between roughly the end of the War of the Austrian Succession in 1748 and the end of the American War in 1783. That change amounted to relying more on banking houses and the international capital markets than on domestic financial institutions and tax officials like the royal farmers general to fund the costs of war. The change placed a new emphasis on the comparative costs of public finance in an international context and gave a new salience to long-standing, mainly British, arguments about the properties of public debt. Constitutional government, it was claimed, was good for public debt because it helped to set limits on government expenditure on the one hand but enabled governments on the other hand to raise taxes to cover the interest payments required to service debt. The argument carried particular weight in the context of comparative power politics. It highlighted the risk premium associated both with absolute government and the largely domestic financial instruments on which absolute monarchies were forced to rely because of their more limited exposure to international capital markets. Both constraints meant that French government debt was more costly to service than its British counterpart and, in

---

[29] John Gillies, *A View of the Reign of Frederick II of Prussia with a Parallel between that Prince and Philip II of Macedon* (London, 1789), 503.

a French context, this gave a sharper edge to the argument in favour of British public finance. The argument had a particular salience after the end of the American War of Independence. Sooner or later, it was claimed, there would be a further round of hostilities between France and Britain and, as Prussia's ruler, Frederick the Great, was reported to have said, victory would no longer go to the state with the biggest armies, but to the one with the deepest pockets. In a world of international capital markets, power politics called for both fiscal reform and constitutional change. The point was recognised by both Calonne and Necker but was also compatible with Sieyès's concept of a representative system.

That system was a consistent feature of the three pamphlets that Sieyès wrote between 1787 and 1789. But the last of the four unexpected developments that took place during what amounted to a one-year period gave rise to a change of tactics, if not of strategy. This was a memorandum to the king published late in 1788 under the name of the comte d'Artois, the youngest of the king's two brothers, that endorsed the idea of a political schism and a possible recourse to force if Louis XVI chose to opt for an Estates-General that would deliberate and decide as a single body. Its rejection of any modification to the old system of separate estates echoed earlier ministerial assertions of absolute royal sovereignty and matched a proclamation by the Parlement of Paris in September 1788 supporting the same political intransigence.[30] It is not clear whether the long-term objective of both pronouncements was simply to maintain the form of the old Estates-General of 1614 or to create enough deadlock to clear a way for the establishment of a Chamber of Peers as, in accordance with the ideas of their political mentor the duc de Choiseul, both the comte d'Artois and the queen were rumoured to favour. Sieyès, however, turned the intransigence into an opportunity. The threat of a schism, he emphasised in *What Is the Third Estate?*, was actually an open invitation to

---

[30] On this *Mémoire présenté au roi par Mgr le comte d'Artois* (Paris, 1788), see Bernard Manin, '*Un voile sur la liberté': La Révolution française du libéralisme à la Terreur* (Paris, 2025), 147. On ministerial assertions of royal sovereignty, notably by the Keeper of the King's Seals. Chrétien-François de Lamoignon, see Peter de Bolla and Christopher Prendergast, *The Two Julys* (Cambridge, 2024), 213, and, on the Parlement of Paris, Bailey Stone, *The Parlement of Paris 1774–1789* (Chapel Hill, 1981) and *The French Parlements and the Crisis of the Old Régime* (Chapel Hill, 1986).

the representatives of the Third Estate to seize the political initiative and unilaterally implement the strategy set out in his *Views of the Executive Means*.[31] The Third Estate, he now asserted, was a complete nation. Its representatives were entitled, therefore, to draft a constitution for its government because they could, in effect, become a national and constituent assembly.

Cumulatively, these four unexpected developments blocked the range of recognised courses of action followed on earlier occasions by the French royal government. These, as Mallet du Pan noted in 1788, usually culminated in a *coup d'état* (there were reasons, it could be said, why the French had a word for it). The difficulties and dilemmas for decision-making and choice created by this sequence of events goes some way towards explaining the high-level political intrigue and recurrent faction-fighting within both the royal government and the royal household that continued all the way up to the fall of the Bastille. If, as diplomats reported and insiders lamented, there was a king's party and a queen's party and clusters of assorted bishops, nobles, ministers and administrators aligned with each side, the swirling divisions and alignments that they created were a measure of the many all-too-readily identifiable disasters that could be associated with established courses of action. In this context, the strategy that was set out in the three pamphlets that Sieyès published in 1788 and 1789 amounted to a real and organised alternative. If, as William Wordsworth put it famously, it was bliss to be alive in 1789, this was partly because Sieyès, with Rousseau behind him, seemed to have shown how it was possible to use the stabilising potential of constituent power to avert Armageddon.

---

[31] See too Sieyès, *Political Writings*, xxii–xxiii.

CHAPTER FIVE

Public Debt as the Cement of Society

At the height of the fierce political infighting among Jacobins, royalists, Girondins and an assortment of French but also British, Italian and German political conspirators that took hold in France before Napoleon Bonaparte seized power in 1799, Sieyès was accused by his supporters of not showing enough firmness towards the Jacobins. 'There is a sect that is even more redoubtable than the Jacobins', he was reported to have replied, 'it is the sect of those who are impatient'.[1] It is a revealing comment not only because it captures something long-lasting in Sieyès's view of how events in France had unfolded over the past decade but also because it highlighted the mixture of blindness and insight that was one of the abiding characteristics of his political vision. Sieyès had a plan, based in large measure on Rousseau's political thought and, more specifically, on Rousseau's advice to his Polish interlocutors about how to prevent Poland from falling off the political map. It was a clear, coherent and sequentially integrated plan that was designed, step by step, to turn the islands of privilege running from street porters, labourers and wig-makers to dukes, counts and bishops into a unitary nation with a representative government. The problem, however, was that it would take time.

So too, however, would other schedules with other imperatives. Time mattered in 1789 in several different and potentially incompatible ways. The first and most straightforward of these schedules was formed by the

---

[1] '*Il est un secte*', répondit-il, '*plus redoutable encore que les Jacobins, c'est celle des impatiens*'. Jacques Mallet du Pan, *Mercure Britannique, ou Notices historiques et critiques sur les affaires du tems.* 5 vols. (London, 1798–1800), 4 (1799), 73 (the italics are in the original).

many obligations that stretched forwards into the future. Administrators, officials and defence establishments needed funds; taxes and rent had to be paid; goods and services to be produced; transactions completed and payments made. Meeting these obligations and matching their schedules was the key to maintaining economic and social stability. But time also mattered in a second way, now looking back to the past. Here, it supplied a more cloudy set of rights and expectations that, it was claimed, allowed laws and customs transmitted from earlier times to authorise actions in the present. Of these, the most salient in the early summer of 1789 was what was called the *droit de commune*. An English equivalent of the term is hard to find because the *droit de commune* was different from a common right. It meant, more literally, the right to be a *commune* or community that was able to act morally, legally and, possibly, even physically because it had the legal, material and human resources that gave it a capacity to be a person. Usually, this concept of collective personality relied on royal authorisation and was associated with Roman law. Without royal authorisation, the legitimacy and status of this type of corporate personality was not a particularly prominent part of the life of the eighteenth-century French monarchy. It had a shadowy presence in the life of the urban trades and in the lawsuits brought intermittently by large numbers of journeymen against employers or guilds because legal actions brought by scores of different individuals presupposed collectivities and common resources in all but name. It had a more assured status in relationships between entities like villages, towns, suburbs or tenants on the one side and feudal, seigneurial or monastic institutions on the other.[2] But both the scale and extent of the rights or of the size and composition of the communities associated with the concept of a *droit de commune* were fluid and, in the eighteenth century, were a subject of careful legal scholarship. If, according to the heterodox eighteenth-century commentator the

---

[2] On the urban trades, see Michael Sonenscher, 'Journeymen, the Courts and the French Trades, 1781–1791', *Past and Present*, 114 (1987), 77–109 and, on rural society, see Hilton Root, *Peasants and King in Burgundy: Agrarian Foundations of French Absolutism* (Berkeley, 1987). The fact that the concept of a *droit de commune* does not appear in Michael P. Breen, *Law, City, and King: Legal Culture, Municipal Politics and State Formation in Early Modern Dijon* (Rochester, 2007) or Marie Seong-Hak Kim, *Custom, Law, and Monarchy: A Legal History of Early Modern France* (Oxford, 2021) suggests that it was a sixteenth-century innovation or, possibly, later.

marquis d'Argenson, it amounted to 'a veritable democracy residing in the middle of monarchy', the monarchy's own historians relegated it to an earlier time in French history, while the abbé Gabriel Bonnot de Mably, in his widely read *Observations sur l'histoire de France*, made a point of associating the right with the emergence of royal government towards the end of the middle ages. He did so, however, by claiming that it began as a scheme superimposed by the French king Louis the Fat (whose reign ran from 1108 to1137) on a right that was naturally available to everyone. Knowing that he did not have the power or resources to deal with the predatory behaviour of armed feudal lords, the cunning king had 'as a favour and a privilege' sold off what was actually a natural right to allow the members of a commune to assemble, deliberate, govern themselves and provide for their security. The result, however, was doubly beneficial, with more power below and less responsibility above.[3] On this basis, the *droit de commune* could be invoked, as Mably went on to show, to endorse the combination of royal authority and communal government that he identified with the huge republic headed earlier by Charlemagne. From the vantage point of a later, very didactic, account of Mably's political vision written in prison in 1794 by a French jurist named Jacques-Guillaume Thouret for the benefit of his own son, the French term *grande nation* was simply a translation of the Latin term *civitas maxima* used most famously by the German philosopher Gottfried Wilhelm Leibniz to describe this type of large republic.[4]

In keeping with both d'Argenson's and Mably's descriptions, the *droit de commune* was one of the rights invoked in March 1789 by the Parisian municipal administration to support its claim that Paris was entitled to

---

[3] On the *droit de commune*, see René-Louis de Voyer de Paulmy, marquis d'Argenson, *Considerations sur le gouvernement ancien et présent de la France*, 2nd ed. (Amsterdam, 1784), 28. See also the fine modern edition, ed. Andrew Jainchill (Oxford, 2019), 35, 85–6. For official scholarship on the concept, see Louis-Guillaume de Vilevault and Louis George Feudrix de Bréquigny, *Ordonnances des rois de France de la troisième race, recueillies par ordre chronologique*, 22 vols. (Paris, 1723–1849), XI (1769), i–vi., and, in Mably, see his *Observations sur l'histoire de France* [1765], ed. Francois Guizot, 2 vols. (Paris, 1823), vol. 1, 451–7.

[4] Jacques-Guillaume Thouret, *Abrégé des révolutions de l'ancien gouvernement français, ouvrage élémentaire extrait de l'abbé Dubos et de l'abbé Mably* (Paris, 1800), 131–2. On Thouret and his posthumous editor Francois de Neufchateau, see James Livesey, *Making Democracy in the French Revolution* (Cambridge, MA, 2001), 192–3.

elect a single set of representatives at the forthcoming meeting of the Estates-General with no distinction between the clergy, nobility and the third estate. More importantly, it was also invoked four months later to forestall a repetition of the Maupeou coup of 1771 and protect Paris from the royal army. It has often been claimed that lawyers played a disproportionately prominent part in the events of the French Revolution. One reason for this prominence, it could be said, was their familiarity with French customary law. On 10 July 1789, as the threat of armed intervention grew, a motion was passed by the electoral assembly of the city of Paris asserting that 'the establishment of *communes* in this town and in all the towns of the kingdom is the primary authentic principle of every civil and political association' and that 'considering that the town of Paris, having enjoyed the right to be a commune under the first two royal dynasties, should never have been deprived of a right that cannot be proscribed'. Paris, the motion continued, declared accordingly that it could reclaim all the rights associated with the *droit de commune*, including 'the guard and defence of the city and the rights and properties of the *commune*'.[5] In practice, this meant reviving the old *garde bourgeoise* of Paris and many other major French towns.

From this perspective, the dismissal of Jacques Necker on 11 July 1789 was not only the occasion that precipitated an insurrection but also one that brought the past back to life in the form of an organised militia. In this context, among the more widely remembered advocates of the Parisian electors' call in early July 1789 to reinstate the *droit de commune*

---

[5] Charles-Louis Chassin, *Les élections et les cahiers de Paris en 1789*, 4 vols. (Paris, 1888–89), 1: 353–8, and, on the later proclamation, see Charles Comte and Horace Raisson, *Histoire complète de la garde nationale* (Paris, 1831), 28–32. Both the phrase and the concept were still present in Augustin Thierry, *Lettres sur l'histoire de France* [1820], 5th ed. (Brussels, 1840), 159, 210, 233, 248, 250, 254, but disappeared during the nineteenth century. One measure of its disappearance, notwithstanding the Paris commune of 1871, is its absence from Dan Edelstein and Jennifer Pitts (eds.), *Cambridge History of Rights* (Cambridge, 2025) and, earlier, Louis Fougère (ed.),. *Les communes et le pouvoir: histoire politique des communes françaises de 1789 à nos jours* (Paris, 2002). The concept is equally absent from Roger Dupuy and Serge Bianchi (eds.), *La garde nationale entre nation et peuple en armes: mythes et réalités, 1789–1871* (Rennes, 2006) and Roger Dupuy, *La garde nationale, 1789–1872* (Paris, 2010). See also, however, Mathilde Larrère, *L'urne et le fusil: La garde nationale parisienne de 1830 à 1848* (Paris, 2016), 14, n. 1.

were the lawyers Camille Desmoulins, Nicolas Bonneville and Jean-Henri Bancal des Issarts, all of whom went on to play significant parts in revolutionary politics and whose legal training was consonant with the requisite knowledge of this aspect of French customary law. By the end of the month, the Bastille had fallen, the *garde bourgeoise* was becoming the National Guard and the standoff between the royal government and the representatives of the Third Estate had delivered a National and Constituent Assembly. The past, in this sense, delivered a more powerful but less calibrated plan of revolution than Sieyès had imagined.

The outcome was substantially different from the structured sequence of steps set out in Sieyès's pamphlets. The tension between the two divergent imperatives produced by inherited expectation on the one side and future commitment on the other meant that time pressed down on Sieyès's plan in ways that were difficult to reconcile. Sieyès's plan called for building up a system of government from the bottom up. Maintaining financial and fiscal stability called instead for exercising authority from the top down. The tension between these two imperatives was reinforced by the same set of circumstances that in 1788 and 1789 gave rise to the opportunity to put Sieyès's plan into practice and start to turn absolute monarchy into representative government. Political instability abroad, first in the Netherlands and then in Brabant and the Flemish provinces of the Holy Roman Empire, ruled out using force to impose political stability at home. Inversely, political instability at home, arising first from the standoff between the ministry and the magistracy and then from the botched programme of army reform, played into the more alarming prospect of impotence abroad and instability at home. Rumours of the imminence of a *coup d'état* in the days before 14 July 1789 were magnified by the uncertainties of communication and the heightened expectations generated by the stalemate between the third estate and the members of other two orders that began when the Estates-General started to meet on 6 May 1789. As rumours of a coup began to circulate, so too did invocations of the *droit de commune* and assertions, in what came to be called the *grande peur* (Great Fear), of the rights of towns, villages and parishes to ring church bells, call out their inhabitants and take arms to defend lives and property from the anticipated threat of soldiers and brigands. Here too what was what expected did not happen, but what was unexpected really did. Although the rumours failed to materialise, the fall of the Bastille and the events of the following three weeks not only gave France a National Assembly and a national debt but a National Guard as well.

Time, in this context, mattered, but not in ways that matched Sieyès's plan. The tension between rights inherited from the past and duties stretching into the future was played out over the remainder of 1789 as a sequence of choices and decisions whose effects were to magnify the deficit far beyond the sum that, two years earlier, gave rise to Louis XVI's decision to summon an Assembly of Notables. The first event in this sequence was the famous night of 4 August 1789 when the National Assembly abolished seigneurial rights and venal offices. The second event was the National Assembly's decision to abolish the clerical tithe and, following Talleyrand's proposal on 14 October 1789, its decision to nationalise church property on 2 November 1789. The third event was the decision by the National Assembly to reject the system of gradated promotion that, echoing Rousseau and, more remotely, Hume and Harrington, Sieyès had proposed as the basis of local and national elections. Sieyès took no part in these events and publicly opposed the decision to abolish the tithe. Its abolition and the nationalisation of church property amounted, he argued, not only to giving the landowners a tax-free windfall (with the abolition of the tithe) but also magnified the problems of funding the deficit (by turning church expenditure into national expenditure).[6] Uniting the nation in this way was, he claimed, radically self-defeating. It would add to public spending while reducing public income, stripping future governments of the leverage that they would need to maintain security abroad and justice at home.

Despite the strong support that Sieyès's system of gradated promotion received from the dominant figure in the National Assembly, the comte de Mirabeau, as well as the parallel that its supporters drew between the system of gradated promotion and Rousseau's idea of an 'elective aristocracy', Sieyès's alternative to absolute government never got off the ground. To its critics, the long period of time required before a new national legislature could come into being, coupled with the large number of steps involved in rising from municipal to national office, meant

---

[6] Emmanuel-Joseph Sieyès, *Observations sommaires sur les biens ecclésiastiques* (Paris, 1789), p. 1.

that a political or administrative career was likely to be available only to those with substantial financial resources. According to its opponents, the outcome of the system of gradated promotion looked less like an 'elective aristocracy' than a self-sustaining oligarchy. The early opposition to Sieyès was driven not so much by the supporters of Robespierre and his Jacobin allies as by those known in 1791 as the more moderate Feuillants (named after the former Feuillantine convent at which their meetings took place). As Sieyès recalled with some venom nearly ten years later, Antoine-Joseph Barnave, one of the future Feuillant leaders, warned in a speech on 10 December 1789 that if the system of gradated promotion was put into effect, the revolution would have to last for ten more years because it would take that long for all the proposed legislation to be put into effect. Barnave's political ally, the former magistrate in the Paris Parlements Adrien Duport, was equally scathing in March 1790 about Sieyès's proposals for a new, more specialised, legal system ('they are the greatest proof', he told the National Assembly, 'that those who conceived of them have no acquaintance with, or even knowledge of, the subject').[7] For both Barnave and Duport, political legitimacy and legal authority required something else.

This fierce hostility towards Sieyès's political proposals was a product of a rather different concept of France's future. In historiographical terms, the politics of the group of individuals (headed by Barnave, Duport and the Lameth brothers) who, over the summer of 1791, came to be called the Feuillants have been somewhat overshadowed by those of their better known Girondin or Jacobin contemporaries, such as Brissot, Condorcet, Paine, Desmoulins, Marat, Robespierre and Saint-Just.[8] Before 1791,

---

[7] For discussion of the idea of gradated promotion, and Barnave's hostility towards it, see *Courier de Provence*, 72 (9–10 December 1789), 10–26, and Sonenscher, *Before the Deluge*, pp. 15, 76–77, 83, 237, 266, 279, 314–17, 319, 334. On Sieyès's recollection of Barnave's warning, see [Anon.], *Exposé historique des écrits de Sieyès* (no place of publication, an VIII/1799), 40, note 10. The claim is a slightly distorted recollection of Barnave's statement that he could not conceive of how, in light of Mirabeau's proposal to establish a system of gradated promotion, 'on peut proposer une loi qui ne pourra être exécuté que dans dix ans', *Archives Parlementaires*, ed. M. J. Mavidal, E. Laurent and E. Clavel, 82 vols. (Paris, 1872–1913), 10 (10 December 1789), 497. Henceforth referred to as *AP*.

[8] For an overview, see François Furet and Mona Ozouf (eds.), *Terminer la révolution. Mounier et Barnave dans la révolution française* (Grenoble, 1990).

however, Barnave and his allies promoted a body of policies and opinions that made them the most consistent advocates of almost all the measures taken by the French National Assembly to bring the Old Regime to an end. They played a major part in igniting the debate of the night of 4 August 1789 that abolished feudalism in France. They strongly opposed giving the king an absolute royal veto in later discussion of the new French constitution, but strongly supported the nationalisation of the property of the French church on 2 November 1789, as well as the suspension of the thirteen French Parlements a day later.[9] They promoted the National Assembly's decision on 21 December 1789 to issue government bonds, or *assignats*, to be sold to individuals to enable them to buy nationalised church property and a year later, on 29 September 1790, they endorsed the further decision to turn the *assignat* into a circulating paper currency.[10] They argued in favour of transferring the right to declare war and peace from the king to the legislature and, as a corollary, they supported the part to be played by the National Guard in the new system of national defence that was established alongside the still nominally royal army. Most strikingly, in a departure from the order of subjects listed for debate on 19 June 1790 and in a clearly coordinated set of speeches, they bounced the National Assembly into abolishing all noble titles on the following day.[11] The measure effectively confirmed the fact that, as the Assembly's Committee on Feudal Rights put it in February 1790 in an earlier official report on the situation to be created by their abolition,

---

[9] During the debate on the royal veto in September 1789, Barnave insisted that no decision should be taken on giving the king even a suspensive veto until Louis XVI had given his assent to the abolition of feudalism on 4 August 1789: see *Courier de Provence*, 41 (11–14 September 1789), 23.

[10] On the *assignat*, see, particularly, François Crouzet, *La grande inflation. La monnaie en France de Louis XVI à Napoléon* (Paris, 1993), and Ferenc Feher, *The Frozen Revolution: An Essay on Jacobinism* (Cambridge, 1987), 30–48.

[11] On the future Feuillants' role in preparing the events of the night of 4 August 1789, see Georges Michon, *Essai sur l'histoire du parti feuillant: Adrien Duport* (Paris, 1924), 59–61; and, on the abolition of noble titles, Blaufarb, *French Army*, 62–3; Timothy Tackett, *Becoming a Revolutionary: The Deputies of the French National Assembly and the Emergence of a Revolutionary Culture* (Princeton, 1996), 292–6; and William Doyle, 'The French Revolution and the Abolition of Nobility', in Hamish Scott and Brendan Simms (eds.), *Cultures of Power in Europe during the Long Eighteenth Century* (Cambridge, 2007), 289–303.

'the lords (*seigneurs*) have descended to the rank of simple creditors'.[12] Henceforth, there were simply citizens and property, along with all the attendant arrangements and transactions affecting both citizens and property. Alongside the abolition of inherited distinction, the new National Guard appeared to offer substantial savings on public expenditure by reducing the size of the standing army. It also presented the prospect of a new democratically generated elite as a solution to the questions of merit and distinction raised by the bitter conflict over army reform. Finally and concurrently, the new National Guard promised to provide a real institutional mechanism for local involvement in the public life of the reformed French monarchy.

Three subjects gave rise to this comprehensive programme of regime change. The first was the old subject of the deficit that was now the new subject of the national debt. The second was the subject of a constituent power, while the third was the subject of the status of the French church. The relationship between the three subjects encompassed all the various tensions – between inherited rights and future obligations, existing commitments and future entitlements, individual beliefs and common institutions – that Sieyès later summed up as a tension between patience and impatience. The deficit was real and, notwithstanding the considerable technical difficulties involved in aggregating the various locations and durations of its many components, it was nonetheless measurable. The subject of a constituent power was less measurable and, accordingly, was susceptible to a broader range of interpretations, all largely incompatible with one another. The status of the French church was connected to both, partly because it owned or had been bequeathed a large amount of landed property, and also because it received part of its income in the form of the clerical tithe. But the real link between the three subjects was formed by the concept of constituent power. This was because the concept of constituent power could be applied as much to the church as to the state. Applied to the state, the concept gave rise to a constitution.

---

[12] On the report see Philippe-Antoine Merlin de Douai, *Rapport fait à l'assemblée nationale au nom du comité de féodalité, le 8 février 1790* (Paris, 1790), p. 7, and, more generally, James Q. Whitman, 'The Seigneurs Descend to the Rank of Creditors: The Abolition of Respect', *Yale Journal of Law and Humanities*, 6 (1994), 249–83, together with his *From Masters of Slaves to Lords of Lands: The Transformation of Ownership in the Western World* (Cambridge, 2025), 1–33, 236–90.

Applied to the church, however, it gave rise to a clear separation of church and state or to a distinction between religion and what the seventeenth-century English political theorist John Locke called the religion of the magistrate. The phrase now looks as if it refers to a state religion, but it was actually used to mean something like its opposite. Where religion referred to those beliefs and behaviour that affected the next life as well as this, the concept of the religion of the magistrate referred to behaviour solely affecting this life alone. It broke the connection between religious belief and secular behaviour and, in keeping with its name, left religious belief to private judgement while transferring secular behaviour to the judgement of magistrates constituted by the constituent power.

The concept of constituent power is usually associated with Sieyès, but as with the concept of the religion of the magistrate, the phrase was actually British in origin and it is likely that Sieyès simply took it over from a French translation of a widely reviewed pamphlet entitled *An Essay on the Constitution of England* that was published anonymously in London in 1765, but appeared in a German translation in 1767 under the name of the Scottish portraitist and political commentator Allan Ramsay. A short set of extracts from the pamphlet were published in the 8–10 January 1765 issue of *The London Chronicle* and were noticed by the philosopher David Hume. As Hume informed his publisher William Strahan in a letter of 26 January 1765, the extracts from the 'treatise' (as he called it) indicated that Ramsay's pamphlet 'seems to be nothing but at an abridgement of my *History*', even though, he continued, 'I shall engage that the author has not named me from the beginning to the end of his performance'.[13] Hume had a point. Although he did not use the phrase 'constituent power' in his *History*, his use of the term 'constituent' – to refer, for example, to the barons or bishops as constituents of the English Parliament – was consonant with Ramsay's usage. According to Hume, the early seventeenth-century improvements in the arts, navigation and 'the general system of politics in Europe' meant, as he put it, that 'the several constituent parts of the gothic governments, which seem to have

---

[13] Hume to Strahan, Paris, 26 January 1765, in *The Letters of David Hume*, ed. J. Y. T. Greig [1932], 2 vols. (Oxford, 1969), 1: 492. For the notice publicising the pamphlet and the extracts from it, see *The London Chronicle*, 3–5 January 1765, 23; 8–10 January 1765, 36–7.

lain asleep for so many ages, began, everywhere, to operate and encroach on each other'. These developments, he explained, gave rise on the continent to 'unlimited authority' but, in England, to 'a passion for a limited constitution'.[14] The ideas, if not the terminology, were almost identical and, notwithstanding his complaint about priority, Hume and Ramsay remained friends. Adam Smith followed the same usage in 1776. The 'great, original and constituent orders of every civilized society', he wrote famously, were the owners of land, labour and capital.[15]

The broad principle underlying Ramsay's pamphlet was, as he put it himself, that '*the constitution of every country constantly changes with its* constituent *power*'.[16] As one of its first French reviewers was quick to note, this meant that the concept of a constituent power was, as his reviewer put it, a 'new twist' on the principle that the balance of political power followed the balance of property made famous in his *Oceana* by the seventeenth-century English republican James Harrington.[17] In England, Ramsay wrote, constituent power had once been in the hands of the landowners, but with the growth of Britain's public debt an entirely new constituent power had emerged. 'With the debt of the nation', he explained, 'so grew,

[14] David Hume, *A History of Great Britain*, 6 vols. (London, 1762), 5: 14.

[15] Adam Smith, *An Inquiry into the Nature and Causes of the Wealth of Nations [1776]* (Oxford, 1976), Bk I, ch. xi, vol. 1, 265–7.

[16] [Allan Ramsay], *An Essay on the Constitution of England* (London, 1765), 23 (the passage is italicised in the original). Ramsay's name is printed on the title page and the phrase 'constituent power' appears in brackets and in English in the German translation, *Versuch über die Konstitution von Engelland* (Frankfurt and Leipzig, 1767), 2nd section, 10. Ramsay, unusually, knew and read German: see Iain Gordon Brown, 'Allan Ramsay's Rise and Reputation', *The Walpole Society*, 50 (1984), 209–47 (at p. 212), and his ' The Pamphlets of Allan Ramsay the Younger', *The Book Collector*, 37 (1988), 54–85. See also Alaistair Smart, *The Life and Art of Allan Ramsay* (London, 1952), 140–2, and his later *Allan Ramsay: Painter, Essayist and Man of the Enlightenment* (New Haven, 1992), 212–14, 299–300, as well as Bernard D. Frischer and Ian Gordon Brown (eds.), *Allan Ramsay and the Search for Horace's Villa* (London, 2001), 1–25. For discussion, see David Williams, 'French Opinion Concerning the English Constitution in the Eighteenth Century', *Economica*, 30 (1930), 295–308 (at pp. 307–8); Christopher Hill, 'The Norman Yoke' in John Saville (ed.), *Democracy and the Labour Movement: Essays in Honour of Dona Torr* (London, 1954), 11–66 (at p. 43) and Herbert Butterfield, *George III, Lord North and the People* (London, 1949), 349–50.

[17] See *Gazette Littéraire de l'Europe*, 5 (March–May 1765), 242–53 (at p. 245).

in proportion to its credit, and by degrees produced a new set of constituents who, without being necessarily connected with the land, with the trade, with either of the Houses of Parliament, or with any corporation or regular body of men in the kingdom, became no less formidable than they were useful to the government'.[18]

Alongside this new set of constituents, there was also a new relationship between church and state, to which Ramsay gave the name of 'the religion of the magistrate'. He used the phrase in much the same sense as it had been used by John Locke in his *Letter Concerning Toleration* and his often misinterpreted *The Reasonableness of Christianity* of 1695. As Locke argued consistently, the mysteries of revealed religion were beyond reason's grasp, which was why no religious dogma could be sanctioned by the state.[19] This was also the view that Ramsay adopted. 'No religion', he wrote, 'which requires an assent to any particular opinion can ever become a religion for the magistrate'. Religion applied to the afterlife while the religion of the magistrate applied to this life. The first applied to what was internal or to thoughts, feelings and desires; the second to what was external or to actions and their consequences. The polytheism of the Romans, Ramsay claimed, had made the distinction possible in republican Rome, just as the new relationship between the church and the state established in Britain after the Hanoverian succession now promised to make the same non-dogmatic 'religion of the magistrate' the antidote to the use of religion as a tool of faction.[20]

This emphasis on public debt as a constituent power and on the religion of the magistrate as the secular basis of civil life was carried through into two French versions of Ramsay's pamphlet that were

---

[18]   [Ramsay], *Essay*, at pp. 10 (for the phrase 'the constituent power'), 70–1. On the early French interest in Ramsay's *Essay*, see Emilio Mazza, 'Mille choses de sa part. Hume, Ramsay and Beccaria', *Diciottesimo Secolo*, 4 (2019), 121–9 (see p. 123, n. 27).

[19]   As Locke put it, 'those that are averse to the religion of the magistrate', meaning all non-Anglicans, 'will think themselves so much more bound to maintain the peace of the commonwealth' if 'the partiality that is used towards them in matters of common right' was removed. John Locke, *A Letter Concerning Toleration*, [1689] (London, 1765), 61–3.

[20]   [Ramsay], *Essay*, pp. 37, 48, 75. For a concurrent discussion, see Colin Kidd, 'Civil Theology and Church Establishment in Revolutionary America', *Historical Journal*, 42 (1999), 1007–26.

published in 1789 by a man named Jean Chas, who by 1791 had become a prominent pro-Feuillant political journalist.[21] Together, they amounted to a fusion of the legacies of James Harrington and John Locke. The overlap between the two legacies stands in sharp contradistinction to more recent claims about the differences between the putative republicanism and civic humanism of the former and the liberalism and natural jurisprudence of the latter. It also chimes readily with both the distinction and the complementary relationship between the constituting and constituted powers of a nation made at the same time by Sieyès. The fusion gave what Sieyès's critics called the 'metaphysical' character of his terminology a more readily identifiable economic and social content by linking his political thought to the claim made by Harrington that the balance of political power followed the balance of property. Put summarily, public debt was the new constituent power. In this initial rendition, the concept of constituent power had an economic and social dimension that stretched beyond the confines of constitutional design or sovereign decision-making. Public debt was real and, it could be claimed, its reality set limits on the procedures and content of constituent power. Public debt also, however, had properties of its own and these, it was claimed, could be the basis of a new and more egalitarian social order.

The relationship between the two claims was underlined in a pamphlet entitled *Jean-Jacques Rousseau à l'Assemblée Nationale* that was published towards the end of 1789 by an individual named François-Philibert Aubert de Vitry. In the pamphlet, Aubert de Vitry took on the mantel of Rousseau's authority to attack the concept of constituent power as it had been used by Sieyès and, concurrently, by one of Sieyès's later critics, the future Girondin political leader Jacques-Pierre Brissot. In making their distinctions between constituent power and legislative power, Aubert argued, both Sieyès and Brissot had relied too heavily on the procedures for constitutional ratification that had been followed in the United States. Sieyès had in fact made the distinction the basis of his insistence on constitutional ratification by the primary assemblies of the *communes* in the system that he envisaged, while Brissot had relied on much the same

---

[21] [Jean Chas], *Réflexions sur la constitution de l'Angleterre* (London, 1789), and A l'assemblée des états-généraux, ou coup d'œil sur la constitution, sur le prêt et l'emprunt (London, 1789).

distinction in calling for the future constitution to be ratified by the nation as a whole. To Aubert de Vitry, both versions of the distinction between constituent and legislative power were based on mistaken assumptions about legal and political institutions that were likely to give rise to divisions, disputes and possibly civil war (a subject that he associated with the thought of the abbé Gabriel Bonnot de Mably whose endorsement of civil war he singled out for attack).

The only genuine constituent power, Aubert de Vitry asserted, was the power to create a society. Once a society was in existence, it was, by definition, equipped with a capacity to make laws. Some laws might be made by a single armed leader, others might establish specialised institutions, while still others could simply leave society alone. In all cases, however, they would still be laws. From this perspective, the distinction between the putative constituent and legislative powers was nugatory and, in France, the capacity to establish a new constitution was now located entirely in the National Assembly. According to Aubert de Vitry, the more urgent task was to begin the work of reducing economic and social inequality along the lines proposed by a long list of earlier writers whose publications he proceeded to summarise. The list included Fénelon, the marquis de Mirabeau, Mably and Rousseau, but was headed by the then keeper of Rousseau's flame, the writer Jacques-Henri Bernardin de Saint-Pierre, whose *Études de la nature* (Studies of Nature) relied on concepts of sociability and natural society that were substantially different from Rousseau's own. The high profile that Aubert gave to Bernardin de Saint-Pierre was matched by the equally high profile that he gave to a very explicit admirer of the English republican James Harrington, a Franco-Irish playwright and pamphleteer named James (or Jacques) Rutledge who, long before the French Revolution, had published a play entitled *Le Bureau d'esprit* (or 'The Office of Wit') – written in collaboration with another playwright and satirist named Louis Sebastien Mercier – that was designed to be a satire on salon society.[22] The play in question contained

---

[22] According to the catalogue of the Bibliothèque nationale de France, evidence of the authorial collaboration of Rutledge and Mercier is contained in the 1777, Liège, edition of Rutledge's play. On the target of the play see Maurice Hamon, *Madame Geoffrin. Femme d'influence, femme d'affaires au temps des Lumières* (Paris, 2010), 388-89.

a joke about salons, men of letters and breeches that formed the original context of how a *sans-culotte* could be described. In Aubert de Vitry's later rendition of Rutledge's thought, Harrington was set against Sieyès rather than aligned with him because Harrington's identification of the relationship between the balance of property and the balance of political power was used here to justify an ambitious programme of property redistribution under the aegis of an agrarian law.

Aubert de Vitry is now almost entirely unknown. The list of forty individual authorities that he invoked in his pamphlet can, however, be taken as a reasonable guide to the mainstream of French thought at the beginning of the French Revolution. It is a measure of the broad intellectual consensus that had come into being during the winter of 1789–90 over the relationship between the three subjects of the national debt, the status and property of the church, and the scale and scope of the constituent power. It was a consensus based largely, however, on its members' opposition to two sets of proposals. The first was the opposition headed by Barnave in December 1789 to Sieyès's and Mirabeau's Rousseau-inspired system of gradated promotion. The second was the opposition that emerged in the spring of 1790 to an attempt by the royal government to solve the related problems of the debt, the church and the constitution by turning to the coordinated influence of the royal ministry and the municipality of Paris. This project had an explicitly American parallel because it centred on the possibility of finding two French political figures comparable in stature to Benjamin Franklin and George Washington to supply the authority and guidance needed to enable the monarchy to establish a new basis for constitutional, financial and religious stability. The two obvious candidates were the mayor of Paris, Jacques-Sylvain Bailly, who, like Franklin, was a man of science with an international reputation, and secondly, the commander of the Parisian National Guard, the marquis de Lafayette, who, like Washington, had acquired his status in the course of the American War and had reinforced his stature when he had escorted the king and the queen from Versailles to Paris on 5 October 1789 when large numbers of the people of Paris had marched on the royal palace to demand better supplies of bread at more affordable prices. Together, Bailly and Lafayette were seen, notably by Jacques Necker, the most publicly influential minister remaining in the royal government after the fall of the Bastille, as the two best hopes for creating a new and reformed French monarchy.[23]

The ministry's projected solution to the related problems of the debt, the church and the constitution had already been canvassed in the autumn of 1789 when Necker called for the conversion of an existing discount bank, the Caisse d'Escompte, into what was to be called a National Bank. The new bank would manage public finances and, crucially, would raise capital secured on the future sale of church property from consortiums of private capitalists. Essentially, the newly nationalised church property would be mortgaged to the bank in exchange for as large an injection of capital as possible. Pressure to implement the plan emerged early in 1790, when, on 10 March of that year, a deputation from the municipality of Paris headed by Jean-Sylvain Bailly presented a memorandum to the National Assembly offering to buy up half the quantity of *assignats* (or 200 million of the total of 400 million livres) that, on 21 December 1789, the Assembly had decided to issue to enable future purchasers of former church property to invest in as a down-payment towards the final purchase of the property. As Bailly explained, there was a contradiction between the widely accepted need to raise revenue as quickly as possible and a likely slump in land prices caused by the sudden arrival of so large a supply of land onto the market. He proposed accordingly that the National Assembly should authorise the municipality of Paris to buy up all the former church property in its jurisdiction and acquire half the total issue of *assignats* to do so. It would pay for the *assignats* in fifteen instalments of ten million livres a year, funding the first payment by way of a loan, with the returns from subsequent sales paying for the rest. The same procedure, he suggested, could be applied in their turn to the remaining *assignats* by the larger municipalities of provincial France. To cover the cost of the initial purchase, both the Parisian and provincial municipalities would issue interest-bearing bills in relatively small denominations (of between 200 and 1,000 livres) to be used to give additional security to private transactions and, at the same time, to prevent a credit crunch from bringing economic life to a halt.

---

[23] See, on these hopes, the four-part series of articles on Lafayette published in 1822 by the self-styled Baron d'Eckstein in *Annales de la littérature et des arts*, notably vol. 9 (1822), 8–10.

The fifty million livres profit on the whole transaction that would go to the municipality of Paris would, Bailly emphasised, be used to fund the cost of public works, including the construction of 'a palace' to house the National Assembly.[24] As he explained in a further speech, on 16 March 1790, 'Paris made the revolution; Paris secured the revolution; but the whole burden of the revolution, and all its evils, fell on Paris'. For six months, he added, the people of Paris had relied on alms. They were now, he concluded, entitled to demand that 'Paris, whose fate is inseparable from that of the provinces; Paris which is the centre of the kingdom; Paris which is the abode of a great people, made up of all the peoples of France, should not be crushed by the effects of a revolution in which it has both played so great a part, and borne the whole burden'.[25]

On 18 March 1790, the National Assembly decided to back Bailly's proposal and authorised the sale of the full 400 million livres worth of *assignats* to the municipalities of both Paris and the rest of the kingdom.[26] Some two months later, however, it began to have second thoughts. It did so partly in response to a speech on 13 May 1790 by an individual named Jacques-François Menou who later became a member of the Feuillant club and, subsequently, the general who led the French army into the *faubourg* Saint-Antoine to crush the last popular Parisian insurrection in the spring of 1795. It did so mainly, however, because of the furious reaction in Paris that Menou's speech provoked. In his speech, Menou told the assembly that he had been offered a bribe during the negotiations between the Parisian municipality and the financiers whose credit was to be used to underwrite its initial payment for the nationalised church property. The speech discredited the scheme overnight. The future Feuillant leaders Duport and Lameth now joined Menou in opposing Bailly's proposal. For Duport, it amounted to giving 'a present of three million *livres* to the capitalists of Paris'. For Charles Lameth, 'it was a mistake to think that the security offered by capitalists was required to

---

[24] *AP*, 12 (10 March 1790), 112–15. The episode is mentioned briefly in Bernard Bodinier and Eric Teyssier, 'L'événement le plus important de la révolution ': *La vente des biens nationaux (1789–1867) en France et dans les territoires annexes* (Paris, 2000), 387–8.

[25] *AP*, 12 (16 March 1790), 195–6. On this episode, see Crouzet, *La grande inflation*, 111.

[26] *AP*, 12 (18 March 1790), 212.

give the *assignats* credit. If anything is likely to discredit the *assignats*, it is to involve capitalists in the acquisition and sale of these assets. Underwriting would have been shameful even under Calonne. The National Assembly cannot countenance an operation like this.'[27] The episode played into the already difficult relationship between Bailly, the Parisian municipality and the sixty districts (soon to become forty-eight sections) into which the capital was divided. The municipality's communal assembly had already criticised Bailly's proposal, arguing instead that the Parisian districts should deal directly with the National Assembly over the future fate of church property, and Menou's speech helped to reinforce its hostility.[28] On 20 May, a public *Lettre adressée par les représentants de la commune à leurs commettants* ('Letter from the representatives of the commune to their constituents') amplified on what Menou had said and called for the scheme to be dropped. Although Bailly replied in kind and snubbed a meeting with the representatives of the commune, the scheme was effectively dead.

Six months later, however, there was a new solution. Its author was a Swiss banker and political journalist named Etienne Clavière.[29] Instead of mortgaging nationalised church property to a network of banks, Clavière's solution amounted to mortgaging what previously belonged to the church to the whole nation. The outcome was the system of public finance based on what came to be called the *assignat.* The term meant, more literally, an assignation to buy land after first buying a bond, or assignation, that entitled its owner to buy land nationalised from the church when it came onto the market. The original idea for the creation of the *assignat* came from Clavière. It echoed the financial projections of

---

[27] The only detailed account of the episode is to be found in Sigismond Lacroix, *Actes de la commune de Paris pendant la révolution*, 1st series, 7 vols. (Paris, 1894–98), 5: 375–489 (the remarks by Lameth and Duport are quoted at 378, 381). See also *AP*, 15 (13 May 1790), 501–2.

[28] See, for the wider context, Gary Kates, *The* Cercle Social, *the Girondins, and the French Revolution* (Princeton, 1985), 33–66 (at 59, 64–65 for this episode), and Maurice Genty, *L'apprentissage de la citoyenneté. Paris 1789–1795* (Paris, 1987), 35–62 (at p. 50).

[29] On Clavière, see Mathieu Chaptal, *D'une révolution à l'autre: Etienne Clavière (1735–1793)* (Paris, 2023) and Lynn Hunt, *The Revolutionary Self: Social Change and the Emergence of the Modern Individual (1770–1800)* (New York, 2025), 8–9, 115–48, and Trevor Jackson, *Impunity and Capitalism: The Afterlives of European Financial Crises, 1690–1830* (Cambridge, 2022), 134–176.

a number of eighteenth-century theorists of public debt, ranging from John Law at the beginning of the century to Sir James Steuart, William Ogilvie and David Williams going into the time of the French Revolution. Clavière began to promote the association between the *assignat* and equality even before church property was actually nationalised by publishing a series of letters in the early autumn of 1789 in the comte de Mirabeau's periodical, the *Courier de Provence*. His first proposal centred on using public debt to enable anyone owning or renting land to avoid payment of the tithe to the Catholic church. The proposal involved using the funds supplied by a voluntary patriotic gift (*don patriotique*) established at the time of the fall of the Bastille to float a larger loan that would be authorised by the National Assembly to form a fund whose bonds could be bought by private individuals and then used to buy themselves out of paying the tithe. The *assignat* was a massively scaled-up version of the same idea. It was created on 19 December 1789, six weeks after the vote by the National Assembly of 2 November 1789 to confiscate ecclesiastical property. On 17 April 1790, the Assembly confirmed its decision to establish the bond and authorised the issue of 400 million livres worth of *assignats*. It also ruled that *assignats* could be used as a currency rather than owned only as an entitlement to buy nationalised land. Clavière, Mirabeau wrote in a secret note to the royal court in September 1790, was 'the author of the *assignat*' and on this basis could take over the ministry of finance and responsibility for liquidating the public debt. If the *assignat* was to fail, Mirabeau added brutally, Clavière would be no more than 'a victim without consequences'.[30]

The consequences, in fact, were high. Initially, the currency was given a relatively high denomination – of 200, 300 or 1,000 livres – and its owners were entitled to an interest payment of 3 per cent on the face value of the bond. Production of the paper currency was quite slow and, for much of 1790, holders of paper issued by a royal discount bank (the *Caisse d'Escompte*) established in 1776 were authorised to use its bills as *assignats*. On 9 May 1790, the National Assembly added the domains belonging to the crown to the property of the nation and, on 17 May 1790, made it clear that it intended to use the nationalised property for more redistributive and egalitarian purposes. Municipalities were now

---

[30] Guy Chaussinand-Nogaret, *Mirabeau: entre le roi et la révolution* (Paris, 1986), 92.

required to fix land prices at a multiple of twelve times their annual yield, and to offer units for sale for a down payment of 20 per cent, with the remainder paid off over a period of twelve years. On 9 July 1790, it repeated its decision but now introduced a variable rate of down payment of between 12 per cent and 30 per cent, with the remainder paid off over a period of a dozen years at an annual interest rate of 5 per cent on outstanding balances. Three months later, on 29 September 1790, the National Assembly voted to issue a further quantity of *assignats* worth 800 million livres and did so again on 19 June 1791 with the issue of several further tranches of *assignats* to an additional total of 600 million livres. These decisions effectively cemented the *assignat* into French finances and French society. They meant that the *assignat* was now first in the line of defence upholding the balance between income and expenditure in the new regime's financial system. It also, however, added a further price to both the costs and the risks. It added to the costs because investors in *assignats* were paid a rate of interest to offset the opportunity costs that might otherwise have discouraged potential land buyers from buying *assignats*. It added to the risks because the need to make interest payments in full and on time ratcheted up the pressure to maintain fiscal and monetary stability. If tax revenue began to dry up, or if the currency began to lose its purchasing power, the new French regime faced the prospect of adding the Charybdis of inflation to the Scylla of state bankruptcy.

In some respects, this solution was redolent of the ambitious, but catastrophic, debt-reduction scheme based on a Royal Bank and a trading company called the Mississippi Company that had been established in the early eighteenth century by a Scottish financier named John Law. In other respects, however, it was redolent of Allan Ramsay's *Essay on the Constitution of England* of 1765 with its identification of the owners of capital, not land, as the modern constituent power. The new solution won support from a wide political spectrum. Its author Clavière had the backing of the future Girondin leaders Jérôme Pétion and Jacques-Pierre Brissot. It also, however, had the support of the future Feuillant leaders Adrien Duport and Antoine Barnave. 'Some', Duport said in a speech to the National Assembly on 29 September 1790, 'have tried to frighten you by reminding you of Law's system and by reviving that hereditary terror that he succeeded in transmitting down to us'. But, he continued, the 'imaginary Mississippi' on which Law's system was based had been replaced by one that was real because it was based on the recently nationalised property of the French church. With land, not foreign trade, as the basis of this variation on Law's system, economic prosperity and political stability would go hand in hand.

The comparison between the two sources of financial stability enabled Duport to end his speech with a further comparison, this time between Britain and France, that was much to the advantage of the latter, but which also rehearsed much the same argument as Ramsay's *Essay on the Constitution of England* had done. 'You have been told', Duport ended, 'that it is necessary to bind every individual interest to the constitution and one example may serve to persuade you of the strength of this argument'. The example in question was England and the failure of the English Society for Constitutional Information to change the corrupt British electoral system. The reason, Duport claimed, was that the British public debt gave every individual an overriding interest in the status quo. The same convergence of interests, he argued, now applied to France but this time to bind individuals to a free constitution. 'Think, Gentlemen', Duport concluded, 'about the power of such a bond once it has come to hold together a free constitution, one that already favours reason and justice, as well as every interest. *Walpole* made the English contract debts to bind them to the House of Brunswick, while we have ours to bind the French to the work of their representatives, thus uniting justice to politics in an indissoluble manner.'[31] As Hume and Ramsay had shown, public debt was the modern constituent power. 'If the Mississippi could have been transported to France', one of Duport's allies told the Parisian Jacobin club, citing Duport's earlier analogy, 'Law's bills would have been excellent. But we, in fact, do have the Mississippi.'[32]

---

[31] Adrien Duport, *Des assignats* (Paris, 1790), pp. 14, 26. On the speech, see Michon, *Adrien Duport*, 129, and, on the decision in April 1790 to add a further 1,200 million livres to the initial issue of 400 million livres, see Tackett, *Becoming a Revolutionary*, 265–69. See also, but without the comparison, Rebecca Spang, *Stuff and Money in the Time of the French Revolution* (Cambridge, MA, 2015).

[32] Maurice Gouget-Deslandres, *Sérieux et dernier examen sur le rachat de la chose publique* (Paris, 1790), reprinted in Alphonse Aulard, *La société des Jacobins. Recueil de documents pour l'histoire du club des Jacobins de Paris*, 6 vols. (Paris, 1889–97), vol. 1, 204–25 (at 225 for the phrase cited).

It was a striking metaphor. It also underlined the comprehensive transformation of the plan that Sieyès had laid out in the three pamphlets that he published between the autumn of 1788 and the spring of 1789. That plan amounted to turning what Sieyès called the inverted triangle of absolute government right side up, with the apex at the top and the base at the bottom. This meant transferring sovereign power from the top to the bottom and, as Rousseau had shown in his characterisation of the democratic constitution in his *Letters from the Mountain*, it also meant highlighting sovereignty's power to legitimate rather than its power to command. This latter power would still remain but it would now be a power of government rather than the untrammelled power of the sovereign. Government itself would be given the pyramidal structure of municipalities, *districts* and departments that would rise upwards towards the national legislature and the national government but the power to command would largely be exercised piecemeal or locally and partially unless there was a national emergency. By late 1790, however, the pyramidal structure was still intact, but government had come to be poised precariously between the centralised character of public finance and the decentralised character of the system responsible for its management. The tight nexus formed by the three subjects of the debt, the concept of a constituent power and the status of the church now meant that decision-making was centralised but that administration was decentralised. Politics, accordingly, could be either overcentralised or not centralised enough. With time, solutions were possible. But, as Sieyès later acknowledged, events sometimes meant that solutions could run out of time.

CHAPTER SIX

Constituent Power and Political Power

Sieyès's political thought stood at the confluence of the intellectual legacies of Hume and Rousseau. There were, certainly, important intermediaries such as Ramsay in Britain and Turgot in France, but the original conceptual building blocks were the work of the earlier pair. From Hume, Sieyès took over the concept of constituent power and the neo-Harringtonian claim about the relationship between property and political power that Ramsay adopted from Hume's *History*. From Rousseau, Sieyès took over the concept of a social contract and its place within the structure of rights and obligations that Rousseau associated both with the concept of a general, or common, will and with the distinction between sovereignty and government as the basis of what, in his *Letters from the Mountain*, Rousseau had called the democratic constitution. From both, Sieyès also had available the possibility of a synthesis indicated by Rousseau's claim that Hume 'associated a very republican soul with the English paradoxes in favour of luxury'.[1] One measure of Sieyès's intellectual ambition is that he set out to establish a system in which the two legacies could be combined. The key to this combination of constituent power and a social contract was Sieyès's unusual claim that the division of labour was a representative system and that the forms of representation that it contained were compatible with all the more obvious forms of representation involved, for example, in electing a member of a legislature, selecting the leader of a political party or giving a lawyer a power of attorney. On Sieyès's terms, all these forms of representation were variations on the more general attributes of the division of labour that, initially, made it a system equipped in its own right with a range of

---

[1] See Ch. 4.

causal powers and properties that made it a conceptual and practical bridge between the intellectual legacies of Hume and Rousseau or, more specifically, between the concepts of constituent power and a social contract.

As Sieyès's conceived it, the division of labour encompassed both occupational specialisation and the separation of powers. These two aspects of the division of labour could, however, be interpreted in different ways. Occupational specialisation could arise among or within different activities, with the former involving more separation, but with the latter, as in Adam Smith's concept of a pin factory, involving more integration. The same indeterminacy applied to the separation of powers because they could be separated either vertically into substantively distinct activities like legislation, execution or adjudication, or separated horizontally into activities that took place at, for example, municipal, regional, provincial or national levels. It is not clear whether the two types of occupational and institutional differentiation were readily compatible without the many different units and subunits that Rousseau and Sieyès (and, later, Hegel) associated with what Rousseau called the democratic constitution. Without both types of differentiation, the division of labour understood as occupational or technical specialisation could exist without the separation of powers, just as the separation of powers could exist without the division of labour. Putting the two together could, on one side, entail more generalised representation but could, on another, entail more pronounced social fragmentation, a more rigidly stratified social hierarchy and a more highly centralised power.

Sieyès recurrently referred to the years around 1770 as the time when he began to formulate his system (he would then have been about twenty-two years old). 'Work (*travail*) favours liberty only in becoming representative', he wrote in an undated note.

What seems to have been most applauded in France in Smith's work [*The Wealth of Nations*] is its first chapter on *the division of labour.* Yet there is nothing in his ideas that was not common among all those of my fellow citizens who took an interest in economic matters. . . . As for myself, I had gone further than Smith as from 1770. I saw not only that the *division* of labour in the same trade, namely under *the same higher level of management,* was the surest way to reduce the costs and increase the quantity of products,

> I also envisaged the *distribution* of the great occupations or trades as the true
> principle of the social state. ... Multiply the *means*, or the power, to satisfy
> our *needs*; enjoy more, but work less (*jouir plus, travailler moins*), this is what
> defines the natural increase of liberty in the social state. Thus, the progress
> of liberty follows naturally from the establishment of *representative* work.[2]

He made the same point in 1789 in the *Views of the executive means*. 'The
more a society progresses in the arts of trade and production', he wrote
there, 'the more apparent it becomes that the work connected to public
functions should, like private employments, be carried out less expen-
sively and more efficiently by men who make it their exclusive occupation.
This truth is well known.'[3]

In the original version of the concept produced by Hume and Ramsay,
the emphasis in the concept of constituent power fell largely on causation. Changes in the nature and composition of different types of property gave rise to different sets of social arrangements, economic activities,
legal systems and political institutions. Sieyès, however, gave the concept
a further set of connotations by adding the subjects of collective choice
and collective action to the Hume–Ramsay version of constituent power.
As he set out to show in the final chapters of *What Is the Third Estate?*,
changes in the nature and composition of different types of property and
occupation gave rise not only to different sets of social arrangements and
their corollaries but also to entities with a more collective or composite
quality such as, most obviously, a state, but also municipalities, univer-
sities, hospitals or corporations and this in turn meant that political
societies were made up of components that were both singular and plural,
individual and collective, unitary and multiple. As Sieyès emphasised in
the final parts of his pamphlet, the many occupations and activities
performed by the members of the Third Estate not only made it
a complete nation but also made it one that housed two types of will
and two types of power, one singular and the other plural. On these terms,
the concept of the division of labour encompassed both occupational and
institutional differentiation. Ramsay's Humean version catered for the
first, while Rousseau's social contract highlighted the second. Sieyès's

[2]   A. N. 284 AP 2, dossier 13 (sheet-headed 'travail') and Roberto Zapperi (ed.),
      Emmanuel-Joseph Sieyès, Ecrits politiques (Paris, 1985), 62.
[3]   Sieyès, *Political Writings*, 48.

concept of constituent power combined the two. From this perspective, adding the concept of the division of labour to the concept of constituent power made it possible to combine agency with causation in both a collective and individual sense.

Sieyès's modifications covered all these possibilities. Substituting the concept of constituent power for the more politically charged concept of sovereign power matched the parallel substitution of 'the nation' for 'the state' that Sieyès made to indicate the ultimate source – or final location – of political power. In both cases, however, it was hard to escape from the ambiguities that come with ideas. In one sense, the substitutions could have been designed to bypass or overcome the conceptual vocabulary associated with royal authority, particularly the idea of a patriot king. In another and possibly complementary sense, however, they could also have been designed to bypass or overcome the notoriously fractious relationship between Rousseau, Diderot and their respective followers. Even a cursory comparison is enough to show that Sieyès had little in common with many of Rousseau's most prominent admirers such as the writer and student of nature Jacques Henri Bernardin de Saint-Pierre. His own intellectual orientation was closer to that of the much larger group of Diderot's friends and collaborators to his *Encyclopédie*, including Pierre-Paul Thiry, baron d'Holbach, Guillaume-Thomas Raynal, André Morellet, Jean-Baptiste-Antoine Suard, Nicolas de Caritat, marquis de Condorcet, François-Jean, comte de Chastellux and, most famously, Louis XVI's first controller-general of finance, Anne-Robert Turgot. This was the group that, in personal terms, was particularly close to Hume, Ramsay and Adam Smith in course of their various visits to France in the 1760s and, at the time of the publication of Ramsay's essay, was largely responsible for giving Ramsay's version of the concept of constituent power the fairly considerable level of attention that it received.

In Ramsay's usage, the concept of constituent power had a Harringtonian and Humean dimension that was soon overshadowed by the events of the French Revolution. Sieyès's adoption of the term made it more like Rousseau's concept of a legislator, or a figure outside society able to persuade, without having to convince, a society to adopt the institutions and arrangements compatible with a social contract. Here, Ramsay's original concept had an immediate salience because its treatment of different types of property relied heavily on the concept of the division of labour as the basis of constituent power. The problem, however, was that the division of labour was as ambiguous a concept as constituent power itself. In one guise, it could be described as agent of prosperity or an engine of productivity. In another, it could be seen as the basis of a social structure and the hierarchy of ranks. In a third, it could be understood to be the key to institutional differentiation and the separation of powers. In a fourth, however, it could be described as a source of social fragmentation or a solvent of political unity. If Sieyès's intention was to use the concept of constituent power to build a bridge between the followers of Rousseau and Diderot, it was a short-term success but a longer-term failure. What was designed to be a bridge turned into a void because the concept of the division of labour housed too many different interpretations for them all to be compatible with the concept of constituent power.

In 1788 and 1789, the concept of constituent power was common ground for the opponents of absolute government and its programme of royal reform. By 1790 and 1791, however, the use that Sieyès made of the additional concept of the division of labour to bridge the gap between the intellectual legacies of Rousseau and Diderot turned the concept of constituent power into a cause of conflict, particularly among the followers of Diderot. Rousseau's characterisation of the division of labour is still well known. So long, he wrote, as men 'applied themselves only to tasks a single individual could perform and to arts that did not require the collaboration of several hands', they could live 'free, healthy, good and happy' lives. But 'the moment that one man needed the help of another' and 'as soon as it was found to be necessary to be useful for one to have provisions for two, equality disappeared, property appeared, work became necessary' and 'slavery and misery were soon seen to sprout and grow together with the harvests'.[4] Here, the emphasis fell on inequality and, as a response, the concept of a social contract, a concept that Rousseau virtually patented. If, as Rousseau wrote at the beginning of *The Social Contract*, it was impossible to find an unequivocal explanation of how man was born free but everywhere in chains, it was still possible, as he went on to show in his eponymous book, to explain how that condition could be made

---

[4] Jean-Jacques Rousseau, 'Discourse on the Origin of Inequality', in Victor Gourevitch (ed.), *Rousseau: The Discourses and Other Early Political Writings* (Cambridge, 1997), 167.

legitimate.[5] There was a contractual solution to the social problem and, for Rousseau and, later, Adam Smith, the productivity of the division of labour could be harnessed to supply the state with fiscal and financial resources while taxes and the money supply could be managed to offset some of the effects of inequality.

There was, however, another characterisation of the division of labour that placed less stress on productivity, political economy and taxation and gave more significance to its relationship to civility, propriety and the system of ranks. This characterisation of the division of labour was made by Ramsay in a letter to Diderot written in 1766, soon after the publication of his own essay on the English constitution.[6] As Ramsay indicated in his letter, he entirely endorsed Diderot's hostility towards Rousseau and, in passing, made several allusions to their joint friendship with David Hume and their common endorsement of Hume's treatment of utility and civility. The substance of the letter, however, was about André Morellet's French translation of Cesare Beccaria's Rousseau-inspired treatise on crimes and punishments and, in making his assessment of its merits and limitations, Ramsay set out a radically different interpretation of the division of labour from the productivity-oriented concept highlighted by Rousseau. In contradistinction to both Beccaria and Rousseau, Ramsay's concept was based on what he called a 'purely experimental morality', meaning a morality based on observation and experience rather than authority and deduction. Without this type of experimental test, Ramsay wrote, applying the concept of a social contract to the subject of crimes and punishment was likely to eventuate either in something arbitrary or would end up instead as a banal endorsement of the status quo.

[5] See Yair Mintzker, '"A Word Newly Introduced into Language": The Appearance and Spread of "Social" in French Enlightened Thought, 1745–1765', *History of European Ideas*, 34 (2008), 500–13. Thanks to John Robertson for alerting me to this article.

[6] The letter was published as 'Lettre de M. de Ramsay, peintre du roi d'Angleterre, à M. Diderot' in Denis Diderot', in Jean-André Naigeon (ed.), *Oeuvres*, 15 vols. (Paris, 1798), vol. 9 (Paris, an VIII), 426–4, and republished by Franco Venturi in his edition of Beccaria's *Dei delitti et dei pene* (Turin, 1965), 536–45. On Ramsay in Morellet's correspondence with Beccaria, see Cesare Beccaria, *Opere*, ed. Luigi Firpo and others, 16 vols. (Rome, 1978–2008), vol. 4, pp. 350, 524. On Diderot's acquaintanceship with Ramsay's circle, see Gianluigi Goggi, "Diderot-Raynal, l'esclavage et les Lumières ecossaises", in Jean Mondot (ed.), *L'esclavage et la traite sous le regard des Lumières* (Bordeaux, 2004), 53–94.

To Ramsay, the concept of a contract was too generic to provide guidance in matters of crime and punishment. Some sort of tacit social contract, he told Diderot, could be found in the dealings of the Great Mogul with his subjects, or the American colonists with their slaves while, he added, the contract that was actually executed most fully and faithfully was between a ploughman and his ox. Crimes and punishments were matters of time, place, manners and customs, and these in turn were products of the differentiation of conditions and the scale and extent of the social and occupational hierarchy. 'I well know', Ramsay concluded,

> that the longer and more distinct that scale has become, and the more firmly each individual has been settled at every step of the ladder, the more a monarch differs from a despot or a tyrant. But I defy the author of *Des délits et des peines* (Of Crimes and Punishments) and all the philosophers together to show me whether any of their works has prevented that scale from becoming shorter and shorter until the end touches the beginning

to leave only one condition, the condition of a slave, as its outcome.[7]

Diderot's verdict on the Morellet's translation of Beccaria was substantively the same as Ramsay's. Morellet, he wrote in 1770, had effectively 'killed' Beccaria's book because he had turned it into a philosophical treatise.

> He did not see that there is a more or less rapid natural gradation among the feelings that arise in our hearts and, if you destroy this gradation, then calm suddenly follows fury and fury follows calm, without any movement to prepare for, or offset, these moral dissonances, causing the melody of feelings to disappear and the author to appear to be mad with a madness that I cannot share because I have not already been imperceptibly captivated.[8]

---

[7] Ramsay, *Lettre*, 434, 444. It is tempting, given his friendship with Richard Burke, brother of Edmund Burke, to compare Ramsay's treatment of the social hierarchy with the famous passage in Burke's *Reflections on the Revolution in France* [1790], ed. J. G. A. Pocock (Indianapolis, 1987), 67, describing 'the pleasing illusions which made power gentle and obedience liberal'.

[8] For Diderot's assessment of Morellet's translation, see Jean Pandolfi, 'Beccaria traduit par Morellet', *Dix-Huitième Siècle*, 9 (1977), 291–316 (at p. 312). On Morellet, Beccaria and Diderot, see too Cesare Beccaria, *Philosophie de la matière et philosophèmes matérialistes*, ed. Jérôme Ferrand (Paris, 2025), 28–30, 144–62 and, earlier, Paul Vernière, *Lumières ou clair-obscur?* (Paris, 1987), 287-92.

As in Hume's moral theory, calm passions could do more than strong feelings, but they relied for their existence on elaborate social hierarchies and subtle shades of meaning. By 1770, Diderot had already set out this version of the effects of the division of labour in an article on 'political economy' that he published in the *Encyclopaedia* in 1765 under the letter 'o' (for '*Oeconomie politique*') with the intention of refuting Rousseau's entry on '*Economie politique*' published ten years earlier under the letter 'e'.[9]

In the article Diderot drew heavily on an earlier examination of the subject of theocracy written by a now forgotten military engineer named Nicolas-Antoine Boulanger who had died some ten years before Diderot recycled many of Boulanger's ideas. Although Diderot did not supply an explicit explanation of the purpose of his identification of theocracy with political economy, the message of the article was contained in three main propositions. The first was that the distinction between divine sovereignty and human government was generic rather than particular either to Scripture or the history of the Hebrew republic. All human societies, Boulanger argued, echoing the thought of the seventeenth-century Neapolitan theologian Giambattista Vico but also his more sceptical contemporary Pierre Bayle, were vulnerable to natural disasters caused by volcanoes, earthquakes, fires or floods and all human societies pro-duced theocracies requiring the worship of the powerful but invisible divinities taken to be responsible for these unforeseen disasters.[10] In this

---

[9] On Boulanger and Diderot, see the entry on *Oeconomie politique* in Denis Diderot and Jean Le Rond d'Alembert, *Encyclopédie* [1765], 3rd ed. (Neufchâtel, 1779), vol. 23, 429–57. Boulanger's text was also printed as *Essai philosophique sur le gouverne-ment, où l'on prouve l'influence de la religion sur la politique* (London, 1788). For helpful commentary, see Christophe Salvat, 'Les articles 'OE/Economie' et leurs désignants', *Recherches sur Diderot et sur l'Encyclopédie*, 40–41 (2006), 107–26; Iolanda Anna Richichi, *La teocrazia: crisi e trasformazione di un modello politico nell'Europa del xviiie secolo* (Florence, 2016); and the two introductions by Antony McKenna and Pierre Boutin to Nicolas-Antoine Boulanger, *Oeuvres complètes*, ed. Pierre Boutin, 3 vols. [2006–2023], vol. 3, 9–13, 15–107. On Boulanger himself, see Paul Sadrin, *Nicolas-Antoine Boulanger (1722–1759), ou avant nous le déluge* (Oxford, 1986) and, classically, Franco Venturi, *L'Antiquità svelata e l'idea del progresso in N. A. Boulanger* (Bari, 1947).

[10] On these themes, see John Robertson, *The Case for the Enlightenment* (Cambridge, 2005), 201–55; Nathaniel Wolloch, *History and Nature in the Enlightenment* (Farnham, 2011).

light, assuaging or appeasing the gods was a natural human response to catastrophe but was also the cause of the emergence of a specialised set of qualified intermediaries to appease or assuage a previously nameless but increasingly personified set of threats (gods, in Boulanger's interpretation, were personifications of kings). From this perspective, theocracy preceded priestcraft but priestcraft itself would slowly lose its power as both its natural origins and the real causes of natural disasters came to be better understood.

The second proposition that Diderot extracted from Boulanger was a strong endorsement of Boulanger's treatment of the emotional side of the human response to natural disaster. Unlike Rousseau's concept of a presocial state of nature and of the accidentally socialising effects of catastrophe, Boulanger's conjectures presupposed the existence of human societies and highlighted the scale of human effort required to overcome the massive social dislocation arising from natural disaster. In doing this, he singled out a range of human responses to adversity that were radically different from anything to be found in Rousseau. Fire, flood and famine did not cause humans to come together, as Rousseau had written. Humans were together already and natural disaster would instead simply produce flight and cause humanity to seek refuge on safer ground. The new environment, however, was likely to be higher, dryer and more arid than earlier settlements had been and these new conditions called for a mixture of human effort, ingenuity and restraint to enable isolated and helpless individuals to face adversity together. Here too, this time as the third proposition, Diderot used Boulanger as a foil to Rousseau's account of natural disasters, sociability and, on Rousseau's terms, the line that began to be crossed when humans began to make comparisons. For Diderot, there was simply no crossed line because catastrophes generated the human qualities required for facing adversity.

Many years later, the early twentieth-century Franco-German cultural historian Bernard Groethuysen drew attention to the puzzle involved in explaining how and why the bourgeois virtues came to have such a positive status in France. Catholicism and absolutism, he argued, relied on two different images of the Deity. One set of images highlighted the majesty, splendour and power of God, while a second highlighted the humility, poverty and suffering of Christ. Neither, Groethuysen wrote, favoured the bourgeois virtues. Oddly, even in 1927, when he published his still thought-provoking book, neither Diderot nor Boulanger nor, still less, the concept of the bourgeois virtues that formed the core of Diderot's reply to Rousseau were parts of Groethuysen's examination of the origins of the bourgeois spirit in France and, with the exception of the work of Franco Venturi, this has remained the case ever since.[11] For Diderot and Boulanger, however, living together under adverse conditions called for cooperation rather than conflict, for prudence rather than prowess and for work and effort rather than striking gestures and heroic actions. These, according to Boulanger, were the qualities that had originated in the harsh but safe mountain sides to which humanity had retreated after the floods and the fires. Later, they spread to the valleys and the plains as humanity recovered and agriculture, trade and industry began to take hold. They were, in short, bourgeois not noble virtues. As Diderot later wrote in a range of further comments on Beccaria and his translator, they were virtues that relied on subtlety, shade and nuance rather than antithesis, dissonance and polarity.[12] In the theatre, they were the basis of what he called the *genre sérieux* or the serious type of drama that could arise from what he called 'perplexity and difficulties' and the strong moral choices they imposed on the ordinary actions that followed. These, Diderot explained, were the actions most common in life and the genre that took them as its object would be the most extensive and useful.[13]

[11] On these subjects, see Bernard Groethuysen, *Origines de l'esprit bourgeois en France* (Paris, 1927), 167–77. See too Sarah Maza, 'Bourgeoisie', in William Doyle (ed.), *The Oxford Handbook of the Ancient Regime* (Oxford, 2012), 127–40. For the sharpest version of Groethuysen's response to the surprising presence of bourgeois virtues in the theological, anthropological and political context of French Catholicism and absolute government, see Bernard Groethuysen, 'Introduction à la vie bourgeoise', *La Nouvelle Revue Francaise*, 14 (1926), 645–56.

[12] On Diderot's further views on Beccaria, see Pandolfi, 'Beccaria', referred to at fn. 4.

[13] Denis Diderot, *Entretiens sur le fils naturel* [1757], in Diderot, *Oeuvres*, ed. Naigeon, vol. 4, 185. On this aspect of Diderot's thought, see the editorial notes to the fullest modern edition of *Le fils naturel* in Jacques Chouillet and Anne-Marie Chouillet (eds.), *Diderot, Le drame bourgeois* (Paris, 1980) together with Alain Ménil, *Diderot et le drame* (Paris, 1995), 49–96; the chapters by Jürgen Siess, Michael O'Dea and Béatrice Didier in Marc Buffat (eds.), *Diderot, l'invention du drame* (Paris, 2000); Graham Ley, *From Mimesis to Interculturalism: Readings of Theatrical Theory before and after 'Modernism'* (Exeter, 1999), 52–107; and Franco Moretti, *The Bourgeois* (London, 2014), 72–3.

Diderot later went on to highlight the various types of moral evaluation involved in this modern mixture of social differentiation and emotional complexity in a short essay entitled *Regrets sur ma vieille robe de chambre* ('Regrets on Parting with my Old Dressing Gown') that was published in 1772 as a light but subtle commentary on the subject of luxury. More recently, because of what is now called the 'Diderot effect', the essay has become something like a model for studying the dynamics of consumption.[14] In the essay, Diderot showed that it was possible to think about the dynamics of consumption without having to make any direct association between consumption and such morally charged topics as inequality, luxury or the distribution of wealth. In the early eighteenth-century French concept of fashion's empire, the emphasis fell on fashion as an initially high-priced component of a chain linking products and product cycles to different types of market and market segments as new and expensive fashionable goods turned into more affordable staples when they trickled down the social hierarchy at different stages of the product cycle. In this newer concept, Diderot showed that the whole process relied less on social competition, conspicuous consumption and imitative display and more on a mixture of individual propriety, aesthetic judgement and a more generic capacity (highlighted by Hume) to discriminate between tastelessness and good taste.[15] Wealth, in this evaluation, could be admired or condemned but the judgement had more to do with the difference between refinement and vulgarity than with that between assets and income. Diderot, accordingly, made a radical revision to the fierce condemnation of the wealth of the Stoic philosopher Seneca that he had made in his youth.[16] In some contexts, he now recognised,

<hr>

[14] On the essay and its resonances, see Katie Scott, 'The Philosopher's Room: Diderot's *Regrets on Parting with My Old Dressing Gown*', *Oxford Art Journal*, 39 (2016), 185–216 and, with Kate Tunstall, a translation of Diderot's text in *Ibid*, 175–84. For the concept, see Grant McCracken, 'Diderot Unities and the Diderot Effect', in his *Culture and Consumption: New Approaches to the Symbolic Character of Consumer Goods* (Bloomington, 1988), 118–29.

[15] On fashion's empire, see Michael Sonenscher, *Work and Wages: Natural Law, Politics and the Eighteenth-Century French Trades*, new ed. (Cambridge, 2011), vii–xx.

[16] See Charles Vincent, '"Quelle si grande importance cette énorme fortune?" La curieuse palinodie de Diderot sur la richesse de Sénèque', *Recherches sur Diderot et sur l'Encyclopédie*, 54 (2019), 71–86. See too Stephane Pujol, 'La *Satire contre le luxe*

wealth was compatible with virtue. As Hume showed, liberality could be combined with propriety to neutralise social envy.

Diderot described the effects of this mixture by showing how it worked when he was given a new scarlet dressing gown by a famous French *salonnière* named Madame Geoffrin (famous, as will also be shown, as part of the background of the *sans-culottes*). The initial effect of the dressing gown was to make everything else look old and shabby and so, gradually, they were replaced. The resulting array of new acquisitions did not, however, add up to a better environment. It was, certainly, cleaner and shinier but it was no longer comfortable or pleasant. But there was still a measure of continuity between the old and the new because Diderot had kept a fine painting of a storm and its aftermath by his friend, the painter Claude-Joseph Vernet. The quality and familiarity of the painting not only helped to offset the discomfort produced by the shock of the new but also underlined the several different shades of value involved in luxury and the arts. Vernet's painting was, in a sense, luxury but its quality, location and content made it as much a part of a home as an old dressing gown once was. Putting the two together helped to explain why an ostentatious present from a well-to-do lady could help to disclose the nuances of feeling and different levels of significance involved in parting with an old dressing gown.

On this basis, the concept of the division of labour was compatible with several different versions of liberty as independence.[17] On Rousseau's premises, the division of labour was the real-life embodiment of the concept of a social contract because its existence was the key to the many contractual relationships underpinning a society predicated on the rule of law. Its contractual character fitted the many fiscal and financial resources required to maintain the distinctions between sovereignty and government, laws and administration, public institutions and private life that were central features of Rousseau's thought. On Hume and Ramsay's premises, however, the division of labour injected propriety and cooperation into arrangements that seemed otherwise to call for

de Diderot, ou le risque de contresens', in Elise Pavy-Guilbert and Françoise Poulet (eds.), *Contre le luxe (xviie-xviiie siècle)* (Paris, 2021), 381–400.

[17] On this theme, see Quentin Skinner, *Liberty as Independence: The Making and Unmaking of a Political Ideal* (Cambridge, 2025).

either authority or benevolence. Its reciprocal character added civility and polish to power and patronage and turned the emotions bound up with respect and self-respect into motivations as powerful as honour and shame or innocence and guilt. On these terms, it made individuality compatible with integration, variety compatible with culture and differences compatible with distinction. If the division of labour substituted market friendship for real friendship and soft power for power itself, it also ensured that both were compatible with political and social stability.

'Yes, Monsieur Rousseau', Diderot wrote dismissively in 1774. 'I much prefer refined vice dressed in silk to brute stupidity clothed in animal hide. I much prefer voluptuousness on soft palace cushions under gilded panelling to pale, featureless, hideous misery stretched out on soaking, infected ground to be met with fear on the face of another savage.'[18] By then, as he went on even more furiously to show in the *Essai sur les règnes de Claude et de Néron* ('Essay on the Reigns of Claudius and Nero') that was published in 1782, Diderot made it clear that he really did hate Rousseau.[19] Less than a decade separated this final settling of scores from the events of the French Revolution. But, independent of the personal venom, the tiny number of protagonists and the hyperbolic posturing, there was one reason why the end of a friendship still had a bearing on the events of the French Revolution and, more particularly, formed much of the initial context of the thought of the assortment of political actors and political commentators who came to be called Brissotins or Girondins between 1791 and 1793. It was, in fact, particularly visible in the thought of their eponymous figurehead Jacques-Pierre

18 Denis Diderot, *Réfutation suivie de l'ouvrage d'Helvétius intitule L'Homme*, in Denis Diderot, *Oeuvres complètes*, ed. Jules Assézat and Maurice Tourneux, 20 vols. (Paris, 1875), 2, 224, and in Denis Diderot, *Oeuvres*, ed. Laurent Versini, 5 vols (Paris, 1994), 1, 886. On the place of the passage in the cleavage between Rousseau and Diderot, but without Boulanger, see Louisa Shea, *The Cynic Enlightenment* (Baltimore, 2010), 100–1.

19 For this volley of abuse, see Diderot, *Oeuvres*, ed. Versini, vol. 1, 1029–36. On the Diderot-Rousseau conflict, see, famously, Jean Fabre, 'Deux frères ennemis: Diderot et Jean-Jacques', *Diderot Studies*, 3 (1961), 155–213, and Yves Citton, 'Retour sur la misérable querelle Rousseau-Diderot: position, conséquence, Spectacle et sphère publique', *Recherches sur Diderot et sur l'Encyclopédie*, 36 (2004), 57–95.

Brissot, who began his early legal and literary career as one of Diderot's and Helvétius's most committed followers.[20]

The reason with a bearing on the events of the French Revolution arose from the antagonistic assessments of the political thought of Thomas Hobbes made in the 1750s by Diderot and Rousseau. As Hobbes described them, there were two fundamental human motivations for society. One was for advantage, or utility, while the other was for what Hobbes called glory, or what Rousseau would call *amour-propre*. Both, Hobbes emphasised, were self-centred. 'All society', he wrote, 'therefore exists for the sake either of advantage or glory: i.e. it is a product of love of self, not of love of friends'.[21] Both Rousseau and Diderot took issue with this claim, but did so in different ways. Diderot accepted Hobbes's initial premise but, in keeping with his endorsement of Boulanger and his friendship with Hume and Ramsay, argued that commerce and the interdependence that it brought in its wake had the power to neutralise the selfishness that was the hallmark of Hobbes's system. As Diderot's friend, Claude Adrien Helvétius set out to show that Hobbes's starting point did not lead to Hobbes's outcome. 'Interest and want', he wrote in his *De l'homme* (or *Treatise on Man* in the contemporary English translation), 'are the principles of all sociability'.[22] Commerce, for Diderot, broke boundaries both between societies and states, but also between individuals. 'It is from thence', he wrote in a famous passage,

> that viewing those beautiful regions in which the arts and sciences flourish, and which have been for so long a time obscured by ignorance and barbarism, I have said to myself,: who is that hath dug these canals? Who is it that hath dried up these plains? Who is it that hath founded these cities?

---

[20] See James Burns, 'Jacques-Pierre Brissot: From Scepticism to Conviction', *History of European Ideas*, 38 (2012), 508–26.

[21] Thomas Hobbes, *On the Citizen* [1651], ed. Richard Tuck and Michael Silverthorne (Cambridge, 1998), 24. On Hobbes in the Rousseau-Diderot split, see Robert Wokler, 'The Influence of Diderot on the Political Theory of Rousseau', *Studies on Voltaire and the Eighteenth Century*, 132 (1975), 55–111. See also, but without Diderot, Christophe Litwin, 'Rousseau et l'activité démocratique moderne', *Ethique, politique, religions*, 26 (2025), 57–81.

[22] Claude Adrien Helvétius, *A Treatise on Man, His Intellectual Faculties and His Education* [1773], 2 vols. (London, 1777), vol. 1, section 2, ch. 8, 133. On Helvétius, see Sonenscher, *Before the Deluge*, 266–81.

> Who is that hath collected, clothed and civilized these people. Then I have
> heard the voice of all the enlightened men among them who have answered:
> it is the effect of commerce (*c'est le commerce, c'est le commerce*).[23]

Rousseau's approach was different. Ultimately, his response to Hobbes
was given the name of 'unsocial sociability' (*ungesellige Geselligkeit*) by
Immanuel Kant.[24] Unlike Diderot, Rousseau argued that the real problems began with love of friends rather than love of self because, as he went
on to demonstrate in all his published works, the latter was a product of
the former. In a reversal of Hobbes's initial assumption, Rousseau argued
that the concept of a self presupposed some sort of affective interaction
with others and that this other-directed activity superimposed *amour-
propre*, or love of self, onto the solitary and self-sufficient feeling of *amour-
de-soi-même*, or the care for oneself, that was part of natural life. The radical
social and emotional dependence produced by this addition meant that
humans formed local, particular and partial societies and gave these
societies their own different languages and cultures as well as their separate states, governments, economies and laws. In making this move,
Rousseau broke through the binary opposition between sociability and
selfishness that was part of Hobbes's legacy and gave the Hobbesian
binary the radically historical dimension that made sociability selfish
and, as Kant went on to assert, one of the underlying engines of human
history. As Rousseau pointed out, there was no necessary relationship
between needs, utility or even advantage and the human motivation for
society because, as the story of Robinson Crusoe helped to show, all three
of the former could be met without any prior requirement for social
interaction or society.

Society, however, was the source of *amour-propre*, meaning dependence
on others for a sense of self-worth or, as Hobbes had put it, 'glory'. Unlike
the physical needs or advantages associated with a purely natural self,
a self that was capable of *amour-propre* was a social self with a panoply of

<hr>

[23] Guillaume Thomas Raynal, *A Philosophical and Political History of the Settlements and
Trade of the Europeans in the East and West Indies*, 6 volumes, [1780], vol. 1, 3–4, as
cited by J. G. A. Pocock, *Barbarism and Religion*, 6 vols. (Cambridge, 1999–2015),
vol. 4, 236.

[24] On the concept and its relationship to Rousseau's thought, see Raymond Polin, *La
politique de la solitude. Essai sur J, J, Rousseau* (Paris, 1971), 1–34.

acquired and artificial capabilities including language, organised memory and general ideas along, most radically, with the concept of what Rousseau called a *moi* or an I. On these terms, this meant that the concept of a social contract was, in unequivocal contradistinction to Hobbes, an outcome rather than an origin because it was not a pact of submission but a model or a value of what a political society could be. In between, and also in contradistinction to the more conventional opposition between sociability and selfishness highlighted by Hobbes, this meant that there was a third possibility made up of arrangements compatible with both sociability and selfishness. In this alternative, the dynamics of *amour-propre* meant that humans were sociable, but sociable for competitively self-defeating reasons. This was why Kant called the resulting condition unsocial sociability. Its unsocial quality meant, finally and conclusively, that between Rousseau's social contract and its pre-social and individuated origins there was simply history, in all its variety, possibility and plasticity.

Diderot's solution to the Hobbes problem implied cooperation rather than competition, while Rousseau's solution implied the reverse. Both presupposed a state-based world, but the world that Diderot envisaged was a world tied to commerce, while the world that Rousseau envisaged was a world tied to states. For the one, commerce integrated; for the other, commerce divided. Although both visions of political society were compatible with the concepts of constituent power and the division of labour, it was less clear, as events between 1789 and 1792 were to show, whether they were actually compatible with each other. In Sieyès's usage, the concept of constituent power was singular, but the division of labour was plural. To his opponents, plurality had to prevail. Between 1789 and 1792, the difference between the two subjects and its bearing on the two related versions of the separation of powers, one vertical and the other horizontal, was magnified by two initially unforeseen problems. The first was the gradual disintegration of the French Empire, while the second was the unexpected magnitude of the French emigration. Both challenged the stability of the new regime and gave rise to deepening divisions over the viability of the new French constitution. As will be shown in the next chapter, argument over the various provisions of the constitution were also arguments over how best to respond to the problems of empire and emigration.

In this context, the ambiguities associated with the concept of constituent power turned into real antagonisms. In one rendition, constituent power was understood in largely causal terms and, in keeping with Ramsay's initial usage, was taken to be a constraint or limitation on political decision-making and choice. In another rendition, however, it was understood in more political terms and, in keeping with some interpretations of Sieyès's usage, was taken to be more like the concept of sovereignty and synonymous with a capacity for unconstrained political decision-making and choice. From a third perspective, however, the concept of constituent power was understood in more strongly moral terms and, in keeping with a more accurate rendition of Sieyès's usage, was taken to be a device to separate government from sovereignty and, by extension, one of the keys to electoral politics. Each of these three versions of the concept had different real-world implications and consequences. As these implications and consequences became increasingly apparent, they formed the political context of the flight to Varennes, or the event that took place on 20–21 June 1791 when the king and queen secretly left Paris but were captured at Varennes. By the autumn of 1791, the broad patriot coalition associated with the confiscation of church property, the creation of the *assignat* and the adoption of the civil constitution of the clergy had split into two antagonistic groups headed on the one side by Jacques-Pierre Brissot and his Girondin allies and on the other by Antoine-Joseph Barnave and his Feuillant allies. By the late summer of the following year, and after the events that unfolded between mid-June and mid-August 1792, it was clear that the Feuillants had failed.

CHAPTER SEVEN

The Failure of the Feuillants

The part played by the concept of constituent power in prolonging, multiplying or magnifying the divisions in existence in France before and after 1789 has not been given much historical recognition.[1] Between 1789 and 1792, however, it came to be used as a weapon in a number of concurrent conflicts centred on the consequences, whether actual or potential, of the disintegration of the French Empire and the growth of emigration from France. Through Sieyès, Ramsay's concept of constituent power was given a status that was similar to, but less foundational than, Rousseau's concept of a legislator. As Sieyès wrote in the draft Declaration of the Rights of Man that he presented to the National Assembly on 21 July 1789, constituent power was not required to constitute a nation or society but to constitute a government. This, initially, made its scope more limited than Rousseau's concept of a legislator. Its focus on government also made it possible for Sieyès to circumvent the two apparently intractable problems that Rousseau had highlighted in his *Social Contract*. The first was how a sovereign, whose will was general, could elect a government, whose will was particular. The second was how powers available to some, but not to others, as was the case with governmental powers, could still be considered to be legitimate powers. Rousseau's solution had been to argue that the sovereign would become a democracy and, therefore, a type of government. It could then do what

---

[1] Notwithstanding the insights in Rubinelli, *Constituent Power*, 18–22, 33–74. See also Nicolai von Eggers, 'Towards a Materialist Conception of Constituent Power', *History of Political Thought*, 39 (2018), 325–56, and Felipe Freller, 'Sieyès et Roederer, des autoritaires libéraux?', *Ethique, Politique, Religions*, 21 (2022), 133–59. See also Arnaud Le Pillouer, *Les pouvoirs non-constituants des assemblées constituantes. Essai sur le pouvoir instituant* (Paris, 2005).

governments can do and rightfully elect a government. Democracy, in Rousseau's rendition, was a transitional regime that could bridge the gap between inclusive sovereignty and elected government.

Sieyès's concept of constituent power made it possible to avoid these conceptual gymnastics but still deal with the two problems highlighted by Rousseau. By associating the concept of constituent power with a very literal interpretation of the idea of representation, Sieyès turned constituent power into something more like a microcosm acting for a macrocosm.[2] If it had something like the varied content of Ramsay's original property-oriented socially diverse concept, the purpose of Sieyès's version was simply to design the constitution of a government that, in time, would be ratified by the sovereign. By using the idea of representation as a mirror image, the aim of his move was to take much of the tension and potential for conflict out of the relationship between sovereignty and government. Sieyès made no reference to democracy in his concept of constituent power, but the concept was still nearer to Rousseau's idea of a legislator than it looks. As Sieyès wrote, it was not necessary 'for all the members of society to exercise constituent power individually' because they could place their confidence in representatives who would, however, 'assemble only for that objective, without themselves being able to exercise any constituted power'. On this basis, constituent power had a particular purpose and a particular status. It was not a government. Nor, however, was it a sovereign. At first sight, it was therefore, an ambiguous concept. Although it could be established by a sovereign, it could not assume powers belonging either to the sovereign or the government.

On this basis, constituent power was, therefore, something like a transitional mechanism, or a space – perhaps even a void – situated temporally and practically between sovereignty on the one side, which was unconstrained, and government on the other side, which was constrained. Much has been made of the putative void left by the demise of

---

[2] Compare to Bernard Manin, *Principles of Representative Government* [1996] (Cambridge, 1997), whose argument would be completed by including Sieyès's concept of constituent power. See also Antoine Chollet and Bernard Manin, 'Les postérités intellectuelles des *Principes du gouvernement représentatif*, *Participations*, 23 (2019), 171–92.

absolute royal sovereignty in 1789 and how it came to be filled by what, echoing Reinhart Koselleck, François Furet called a culture of democratic sociability.[3] It is worth emphasising, however, that if there was a void, it was created by design not default and filled not by a culture of democratic sociability but by an escalating sequence of arguments over the empire, the emigration, the assignat and the entitlements of citizenship. In these arguments, constituent power became a tactical weapon. It had to be part of a constitution but not have either the unlimited power that came with sovereignty or the limited power that came with government. This, Sieyès explained, was why it belonged to the very first chapter of the projected constitution 'to throw light on the means to form and reform all the parts of a constitution'.[4] From this perspective, constituent power meant designing the constitution of a government that could form and reform itself. It would be something like a fusion of Ramsay's historically oriented and property-based concept, coupled with Rousseau's insistence on the distinction between sovereignty and government. In this sense, it would be both a buffer and a bridge between a property system (Ramsay) and an electoral system (Rousseau) because its presence as part of the constitution would keep these two facets of political society separate, but connected. On this basis, constituent power would be the basis of party politics, government and opposition and a political society based on what Sieyès called 'electism'.

Between 1789 and 1792, the difficulties built into meeting this assignment were thrown into sharp relief. They arose not so much because of the number of potentially incompatible goals that the concept of constituent power was required to meet but because of the growing range of problems that it had to face. These, to list them summarily, began with the subject of the suffrage and the divisions between active and passive citizens and between eligible and ineligible candidates for election. That division spilled over into the subject of the composition and powers of the National Guard and, by extension, into the relationship between municipal authority and an armed militia on the one side and the

---

[3] Francois Furet, *Penser la révolution française* [1978] (Paris, 1983), 244–59.

[4] Emmanuel-Joseph Sieyès, 'Préliminaire de la constitution: reconnaissance et exposition raisonnée des droits de l'homme et du citoyen', *AP*, 8 (21 July 1789), 259.

National Guard and the regular army on the other. It spilled over too into the relationship between France and its colonies, giving rise to fierce and ultimately irreconcilable conflict between French settlers, French slaves and freed former slaves over the many different types of status and entitlement that they or their many different types of children or descendants were able to claim. These conflicts fed their way back into the fiscal and financial systems to raise questions about the relationship between the church and the state, the currency and the commercial system, the empire and the emigration and, ultimately, between constituting and constituted powers. Between 1789 and 1792 much of the membership of the National Assembly came to stand firmly on the one side, while the king, the court and successive ministries stood firmly on the other, but with the nation as the prize for both.

As the future Feuillant Adrien Duport pointed out in a speech to the National Assembly on 29 March 1790 on the principles of the judicial order, the concept of constituent power was part of a differentiated body of powers. It was impossible, he said, for all the powers to be established by the people and for the people. They had, instead, to be delegated. This, he explained, was why constituent power had representatives, legislative power had deputies, while executive power had a monarch. Judicial power, however, or the power to throw light on facts was not to be delegated because it could be exercised by the people themselves in trials by jury, as shown by Britain and the United States.[5] The terminological distinctions are worth highlighting because they indicate both the real differences and real difficulties built into the concept of constituent power. Constituent power, in Duport's usage, was exercised by representatives, presumably because it involved constituting the government of a whole nation and, in keeping with both the concept of representation and the original connotations of Ramsay's concept, called for matching the features of the government to be constituted to the features of society as a whole. Legislative power, on the other hand, was exercised by deputies, presumably because it called for these deputies to be accountable to the parts of society that had elected them. Sovereign power, interestingly, was absent from Duport's taxonomy.

[5] *AP*, 12 (29 March 1790), 416.

In Duport's usage the key difference between constituent power and other powers was comparable to the difference between a whole and its parts. A little more than a year later, on 7 April 1791, the concept was brought nearer to its earlier association with Rousseau's concept of a legislator but with more of an emphasis on the differences between the present and the future and between self-interest and self-denial. This time the author of the evaluation was Robespierre. 'A philosopher whose memory you have honoured and whose writings prepared the revolution and your work, once said', he told the National Assembly, 'that "to inspire more confidence and respect for the laws, the legislator should in a sense isolate himself from his work and emancipate himself from all those personal relationships that could bind him to the great interests he has to decide".'[6] As several accounts of the speech reported, the allusion was to Rousseau, although it is not particularly easy to find the passage that Robespierre appeared to quote in any of Rousseau's publications. Robespierre's aim, as he announced in his proposal, was to prohibit all members of the National Assembly from becoming ministers of the crown or from receiving any office, gift, commission, pension or income from the executive for four years after the completion of their mandate. The measure, in light of the imminent completion of the constitution and the end of the life of the National Assembly, was aimed at the many soon-to-be former members of the National Assembly. Current members were already barred from accepting a ministry by a decision by the Assembly in November 1789 that, it was said, was aimed particularly at Mirabeau.

Robespierre's insistence on the need to separate constituent power from ministerial power was amplified in an argument that began a month later on 16 May 1791 when Jacques-Guillaume Thouret, the head of the National Assembly's Constitutional Committee, introduced a debate on the ninety-nine articles covering the organisation and functions of the future Legislative Assembly. Many of the articles had already been decided by earlier votes, but Thouret introduced two that had yet to be approved. The first (article 6) stipulated that no occupation, profession or office could exclude citizens who met the conditions prescribed by the constitution for eligibility for election. The second (article 7) simply stated that 'members of the preceding legislature can be re-elected'. The article provoked an

---

[6] *AP*, 24 (7 April 1791), 621.

immediate intervention by Robespierre on a point of order. Before any decision could be taken, he said, the members of the present legislature had to be required to deliberate as citizens who were about to revert to ordinary life, or what Robespierre called 'the common class', rather than as potential members of the legislature that they were about to establish. Before there could be any discussion, he said, the National Assembly first had to decree that none of its members could be members of the next legislature. The point was then amplified by the future Girondin mayor of Paris Jérome Pétion. Its aim, he explained, was to establish whether a member of a constituting body could be elected to the next legislature.[7] Thouret replied, using the same terminology but rephrased the question. The real question, he said, amounted to deciding whether a body exercising constituent power could exercise that power in ways that limited the essential right of the people as sovereign to elect the representatives of their choice. For Thouret, sovereignty trumped constituent power. For Robespierre, however, constituent power – or, more accurately, the possible abuse of constituent power – could trump sovereignty. The discussion continued until 21 May, with several major speeches in favour of the original articles but finally, and by a large majority, the second of the articles proposed by Thouret was defeated. The new legislature would, accordingly, have no members drawn from the National Assembly.

A month separated this debate from the flight to Varennes on 20–21 June 1791 and, although the evidence is absent, it is hard not to think that the decisions by the National Assembly affecting the eligibility of its members to be re-elected or become ministers were not part of the context that encouraged Barnave and his allies to encourage or authorise the royal flight. As Mallet du Pan had commented earlier, the standard solution to a crisis adopted by the French monarchy was a *coup d'état* and, in addition to the chronological proximity of Robespierre's point of order to the flight to Varennes itself, there is also circumstantial evidence that suggests that it was projected to have a more ambitious outcome than has usually been assumed.[8] This evidence includes the abolition of noble

---

[7] *AP*, 26 (16 May 1791), 111, 112, 114.

[8] See, notably, Mona Ozouf, *Varennes: La mort de la royauté* (Paris, 2005) and, in parallel, Laurence Cornu, *Une autre republique: 1791 l'occasion et le destin d'une initiative républicaine* (Paris, 2005).

titles in June 1790, which eliminated the problem of transforming the huge French nobility into a British-style peerage. It also includes the convergence, after Mirabeau's death on 2 April 1791, between Sieyès's two-section legislature and Barnave's speculations about the beneficial effects on party politics of a two-chamber legislature. The convergence was certainly not complete because Barnave's speculations centred on intermittent elections to a lower house and an appointed life peerage to an upper house, while the divisions in Sieyès's two-section legislature were based solely on the difference between deliberating and deciding rather than any difference in the composition of the sections themselves. Nor, finally, was either project actually put into effect. Put simply, the flight to Varennes was envisaged as the first step in a process designed to reverse Robespierre and the National Assembly's interpretation of constituent power.

Robespierre's insistence on the need to prevent constituent power from interfering with the membership and policies of the future legislature was a product of a cluster of overlapping arguments over the electoral system, the fiscal system, the National Guard and the new French constitution that went back to 22 and 29 October 1789 when the National Assembly began to discuss the provisions of a new system of elections to replace the old estates-based system that had been overtaken by the events of June and July 1789. At the beginning of the discussion, there was a broad consensus in favour of adopting a distinction between active and passive citizens with only the former having the right to vote. In itself, the distinction was not controversial. As Rousseau pointed out in a note to his *Social Contract* referring to the entry on 'Geneva' in Diderot and d'Alembert's *Encyclopaedia*, there were five different classes of citizen in the Republic of Geneva, but only two were entitled to elect or be elected to all the offices of the republic.[9] Differences of age, place of birth, periods of residence or, more controversially, occupation, income or gender all had a bearing on the distinction. In keeping with this precedent, Sieyès echoed Rousseau. As he put it in a pamphlet published in September 1789 but written three months earlier, the introduction of an additional qualification, such as paying taxes equivalent to the local value of several days wages, could be an incentive to those initially unable

---

[9] Rousseau, *Social Contract* [1762], in Rousseau, *CW*, vol. 4, bk.1, ch. 6, 139 note.

to qualify for citizenship to make an effort to meet this relatively accessible requirement.[10] Although almost all of Sieyès's other constitutional proposals were rejected, the National Assembly opted to keep this distinction as the basis of the difference between active and passive citizenship and, more controversially, also introduced a further distinction between eligibility to vote and eligibility to be elected, with tax payments equivalent to the local value of three days wages remaining the criterion for the former, but with tax payments equivalent to a silver mark forming the criterion for eligibility for election, irrespective of local levels of wealth and poverty.

Although the latter qualification was ultimately dropped from the electoral provisions of the new constitution, it remained in place until 27 August 1791 or almost to the time of the elections to the new French Legislative Assembly in September 1791. This meant that the distinctions between active and passive citizenship and eligibility and ineligibility for election overlapped with the period covering the introduction and generalisation of the *assignat* and the formation and organisation of the French National Guard. The resulting concatenation of potentially incompatible subjects meant that what, in the context of Rousseau's Geneva, was designed to look like an incentive could look instead more like a barrier. There was no straightforward or seamless relationship between the *droit de commune*, the concept of a *milice bourgeoise* and either the idea of a right – possibly a natural right – to bear arms or, even more, to membership of a National Guard based, according to some, on the distinction between active and passive citizens. Adding the existence of the *assignat* to that distinction introduced an extra element of instability to both. From one perspective, the creation of the *assignat* complemented the incentive structure underlying the distinction between active and passive citizens. Buying nationalised property on favourable credit terms was designed to be an incentive to property owners to buy *assignats* and this, optimally, could be a source of stability to the *assignat*, an addition to the size of the tax base, a boost to the number of active citizens and, cumulatively, an inbuilt engine of prosperity. This, broadly, was the favourable scenario that Clavière envisaged and the reason for the

---

[10]   Emmanuel-Joseph Sieyès, *Quelques idées de constitution applicable à la ville de Paris, en juillet 1789* (Versailles, 1789).

parallel claim made in September 1790 by Adrien Duport that the Mississippi was now metaphorically to be found not in America, but France.

From another perspective, however, binding nationalised property to a state-generated currency and, in a further move, binding both to a volatile mixture of the fiscal and electoral systems amounted to creating so tight a nexus of incompatible ingredients that very little was needed to turn a virtuous circle into a doom loop. This, in the first instance, was an effect of connecting the distinction between active and passive citizenship both to the fiscal system and membership of the National Guard. If, from one point of view, it meant that the new French state would become a fiscal state because every citizen would have to be a taxpayer, it also meant, from another point of view, that the dominant form of taxation now had to be direct taxation, or taxation on property, products or income, rather than indirect taxation, or taxation on sales, transfers, transactions or consumption. As Condorcet warned in June 1790, switching from the former to the latter had the potential to disenfranchise whole swathes of the population. 'You have made the title of active citizen depend on direct taxation', he told the National Assembly, 'and, by doing so, tied financial laws to constitutional laws. A change in the former could alter the constitution, that precious benefit (*bienfait*) that we owe to your wisdom.' Converting 'some direct taxes into indirect taxes', he added, could change 'a free constitution into an aristocracy'.[11]

Condorcet's prognosis fed into a growing argument over the composition and organisation of the French National Guard that developed in November and December 1790. Here, what was at issue was the question of whether membership of the National Guard was limited to active citizens and, by extension, whether the Guard itself required a hierarchy of officers and a chain of command. To some, stipulations like these would turn a citizen militia into a standing army. 'The French National Guard', wrote the political journalist Louis-Marie Prudhomme in his periodical the *Révolutions de Paris* in November 1790, 'is the nation

---

[11] Marie-Jean-Antoine-Nicolas de Caritat, marquis de Condorcet, *Adresse à l'assemblée nationale sur les conditions d'éligibilité. 5 juin 1790*, reprinted in Condorcet, *Œuvres*, ed. Arthur Condorcet O'Connor and François Arago, 12 vols. [1847] (Hamburg, 1968), vol. 10, 77–91 (79–80 for the passages cited).

itself in arms. It is not, in truth, an institution. It is the natural state of mankind in society; it is the posture of a free people. There never has been any large or small association of free men that was not also its own national guard.' It was, Prudhomme asserted, a great mistake to think that the recent general taking up arms was an 'extraordinary novelty' calling for 'a new regime and extraordinary laws'. All that had happened was, simply, a return to 'our natural state'.[12] In this light, there was no need for an organised officer corps and, still less, any distinction between active and passive citizens.

Robespierre amplified on Prudhomme's argument in a widely circulated speech to the Jacobin club on 5 December 1790. In it, he coined the three-word slogan 'liberty, equality and fraternity' that continues to epitomise the French Revolution. Members of the National Guard, he announced, should have a badge announcing *Le Peuple Français* and, below it, *Liberté, Egalité, Fraternité.* The fusion, Robespierre argued, was a consequence of the fundamental compatibility between natural, civil and political rights. 'To be armed', he asserted, 'for one's personal defence is the right of every man. To be armed to defend the liberty and existence of the common fatherland is the right of every citizen.' It followed that every individual had a natural right of self-preservation and every citizen a right to membership of the National Guard. These rights overrode the distinction between active and passive citizens. They also gave the National Guard a different character from a standing army. Its officers should be elected and its members given financial support to pay for their uniforms and equipment. The model here were the militias of 'the free cantons of Switzerland' where, as Rousseau had described them, 'every inhabitant was a soldier but only when they have to be. Local drills and exercises were unpaid, but when members of the militia were on campaign they became real soldiers and were paid for their service by the state.'[13]

The range of evaluations of the relationship between citizenship, the currency and the National Guard was large and varied. Most fundamentally, however, they raised a question about the relationship between

---

¹² Louis-Marie Prudhomme, *Révolutions de Paris*, 72 (20–27 November 1790), 333–44 (here at p. 334).

¹³ Robespierre, *Oeuvres*, VI, 610–55 (here at pp. 617, 620–22, 626–27) and, on liberty, equality and fraternity, 643.

municipal government and the separation of powers. The result was a growing division within the broadly based patriot coalition that had emerged between the autumn of 1789 and the autumn of 1790, first in opposition to Mounier, the Monarchiens and a British-style mixed constitution, then in opposition to the Sieyès-Mirabeau proposal to apply Rousseau's Polish idea of gradated promotion to the new French electoral and administrative systems, and, thirdly, in opposition to the Necker–Bailly–Lafayette proposal to channel the sale of former church property through a combination of the municipality of Paris, a network of Parisian banking houses and a number of the larger municipalities of provincial France. In substantive terms, the divisions within the patriot coalition arose from arguments over the possible effects of the loss of empire and the growth of emigration on the financial and political stability of the new regime. Before 1789, many of the members of this broad coalition were opponents of slavery and the slave trade. By 1791, some of its members, headed by Barnave, were prepared to accept slavery abroad to preserve liberty at home, while others were not. These divisions were magnified by the way that the sovereignty of the nation was underpinned by the multiple militias established all over France during what came to be known as the *Grande Peur* (Great Fear), when rumours of a royal coup swept across most parts of the country in July and August 1789 and large numbers of the inhabitants of towns and villages armed themselves to protect their harvests and livestock from the rumoured threat. The tension was acknowledged in muted guise at the time of the *fête de la fédération* of 14 July 1790 when the anniversary of the events of 1789 was commemorated at a great Parisian public festival designed not only to celebrate the fall of the Bastille but also to symbolise the transformation of the many municipal militias into a single French National Guard. The pageantry of the occasion could not disguise the fact that the outcome of the revolution was predicated simultaneously on two different things. On the one side, there was a commitment to constitutional government and the separation of powers. On the other side, there were municipalities, militias and overlapping powers.

Sieyès himself had been quick to identify and respond to the problem. He made its implications clear in a pamphlet entitled *Quelques idées de constitution applicable à la ville de Paris, en juillet 1789* ('Some Constitutional Ideas Applicable to the City of Paris in July 1789'), written before the fall of the Bastille and published in September 1789. Paris, he emphasised, was certainly a commune, but the constitution of its future government called for a closer relationship between power that came from below and power that came from above than existing arrangements could provide. Integrating municipal government and their militias with the idea of the separation of powers called, he argued, for both a vertical and a horizontal separation of powers. The former would involve specialised responsibilities, such as a separation between the legislative, executive and judicial powers, or between civil and military power. The latter would involve devolved responsibilities or circumscribed jurisdictions such as those involved in a separation between municipal, departmental and national powers. Putting the two together, Sieyès argued, would produce a pyramid-like institutional structure, with power coming from below by way of taxation, elections and money and with power from above coming by way of legal authority, administrative decisions and, ultimately, force. The two were to be kept in place by the unusual combination of legislative and executive institutions that Sieyès envisaged as a constitution for Paris.

Under the provisions of this constitution, Paris would have a mayor, but the mayor would be the king, either the present king or, in a more distant future, one elected under the provisions of the system of gradated promotion. As mayor, the king would have a purely generic formal role by, for example, presiding over municipal assemblies, signing legislation, ratifying appointments and appearing at 'honorific representations'.[14] In this version of the king's two bodies, the king's virtual body would be matched by a real body or a mayoral lieutenant who would also be the officer presiding over the national legislature. Executive decisions would be made by a Regent elected by the primary assemblies and the Regent would, in turn, rely on a Provost of Paris for effective command of the Parisian militia. Every municipality, in keeping with this Parisian model, would have a Provost. As Sieyès described them, power from below would centre largely on money, while power from above would centre largely on force. Money would go upwards to enable the government to act, while force would go downwards to make the actions of government durable, consistent and predictable. There would, in short, be two types of

---

[14] On these details, see Emmanuel-Joseph Sieyès, *Quelques idées de constitution applicable à la ville de Paris, en juillet 1789* (Versailles, 1789), 27, 29, 33, 35–7.

separation of power, one that was horizontal and the other vertical, with both held together by money and force. If Sieyès changed much of his terminology between 1789 and 1799, the shape and structure of the institutions that he envisaged remained unusually consistent to these original specifications.

These speculations were blown aside by the events of October 1789 and the famous march on Versailles by large numbers of women from Paris on 5–6 October 1789 calling on the king, the National Assembly or the royal ministry to deal with an alarming spike in bread prices. The march on Versailles sharply exposed the ambiguity of the relationship between the *droit de commune* and the concept of the separation of powers because it was brought to a relatively peaceful conclusion when the marquis de Lafayette, the commander of the Parisian National Guard, took charge of the situation and, without authorisation from either Versailles or Paris, placed himself at the head of a detachment of the Parisian National Guard to escort the king and the National Assembly to what, *de facto*, became the new French capital. The resulting situation, epitomised by the ambiguous status of the National Guard within municipalities, cut across the hierarchy of elected and administrative offices that the National Assembly began to establish in 1789 and 1790. These began with municipalities, districts, sections, arrondissements and departments, all with their various relationships to national institutions, national ministries and the national legislature, but each also with their responsibilities for managing finances, enforcing the law, maintaining order, arranging elections and, after 1789, providing services previously supplied by the church. The many overlapping responsibilities of municipalities and their national guards, particularly in such big cities as Paris, Lyon, Bordeaux or Marseille, clashed visibly with established concepts of the separation of powers. 'Such', wrote Edmund Burke a year after the March on Versailles, 'is the character and disposition of the municipal society which is to reclaim the soldiery, to bring them back to the true principles of military subordination, and to render them machines in the hands of the supreme power of the country'. As Burke emphasised, the events of October 1789 underlined the ambiguous relationship between the civil and military powers. 'The municipalities', he wrote, 'by the necessity of their situation, and by the republican powers they have obtained, must, with relation to the military, be the masters, or the servants, or the confederates, or each successively; or they must make a jumble of all together, according to circumstances'. The range of scenarios confirmed the bleak diagnosis he made in an earlier passage. 'The military', he wrote, 'lays open the civil, and the civil betrays the military, anarchy'.[15]

Sieyès's system was designed to face this problem. As he emphasised in 1791 in the course of his public debate with Tom Paine, his system was pyramidal in structure, while the system that Paine envisaged was a platform that supported several different ministries or institutions. Paine's system was, therefore, compatible with a vertical separation of powers, but had less room for a horizontal separation of powers. Unlike the multiple levels built into Sieyès's system, Paine's system had little lying between its top and bottom levels. Sieyès called his own system a monarchy and Paine's system a polyarchy. Importantly, as Paine's own interest in a moderating or checking power helps to indicate, many of the opponents of Sieyès's system (meaning by 1791 much of the whole National Assembly) were more strongly committed to the concept of a second legislative chamber than Sieyès himself.[16] As one of James Harrington's admirers, a lawyer from Bordeaux named Joseph Saige, put it in his *Catéchisme du citoyen* ('Civic Catechism') of 1775, councils like the Senate at Rome, the Elders (*Gerontes*) in Sparta or the Sanhedrin among the Jews were all initially depositaries of executive power, while their kings were simply their presiding officers.[17] Although Sieyès advocated for a legislature divided into two sections, with one section discussing and the other deciding, the last word would belong, unequivocally, to the section that decided because there would, in fact, be no more than one decision. In a bicameral system, however, there would be two decisions and many opportunities for paralysis. The initial problem, however, was the huge French nobility and the difficulty of establishing an institution that would not, deliberatively or inadvertently, entrench the interests of all or part of the nobility within the new constitution. Usually, this

---

[15] Burke, *Reflections*, ed. Pocock, 189–90.

[16] On Paine's interest in a second chamber, see Angus Harwood Brown, 'The Pennsylvania Council of Censors and the Debate on the Constitutional Guardian in the Early United States', *American Journal of Legal History*, 64 (2024), 1–26.

[17] Joseph Saige, *Catéchisme du citoyen, ou éléments du droit public français* (Geneva, 1775), 17, 104 note 9.

problem has been described in terms of an argument between Anglophile advocates of a second chamber and Americanophile supporters of a Pennsylvania-style single legislature. Sieyès's preference for a single Harringtonian-style legislature made up of two sections – one responsible for discussing and the other for deciding – makes the argument more complicated. So too does the fact that several of his critics, including Paine, were not averse to a built-in checking mechanism, such as the Pennsylvania Council of Censors.[18]

There was, in short, more of a consensus in favour of a second chamber than has usually been recognised in French revolutionary historiography and, by 1791, more of a supporting tailwind from a number of different political figures. Initially, the impetus came from the comte de Mirabeau when, on 3 July 1790, he opened secret negotiations with the king and queen over the possibility of creating a new ministry. His aim was to use royal fear of the erosion of the monarchy's power to persuade the king and queen to align themselves quickly and decisively with his own visibly declining number of allies in the National Assembly because delay was likely to diminish the already dwindling body of support available to both sides. As Mirabeau wrote in a note to the court on 23 December 1790, the decline of royal power over the previous six months threatened to turn the monarchy into 'a phantom that, it might be believed, it was now possible to do without'. This, he acknowledged, was more likely to occur 'if the authors of the majority of the republican forms that have been adopted had an underlying idea (*arrière-pensée*) in laying the foundations of their work, and actually did believe in the possibility of a great democracy'.[19] But, he continued, even if they did not believe in it or, as was more probable, did not understand what they were doing, the demise of the monarchy was still likely to occur because 'the republican forms' adopted by the National Assembly were acutely vulnerable to the pincer-like pressure produced by the disintegration of the French Empire on the one side and the stream of emigration on the other.

It is not clear whether the new constitution that Mirabeau envisaged was intended to include a British-style House of Lords, an American-style Senate or a version of the two-sectional single chamber that Sieyès was to

[18] See Harwood Brown, 'The Pennsylvania Council of Censors'.

[19] Guy Chaussinand-Nogaret, *Mirabeau entre le roi et la révolution* (Paris, 1986), 174–5.

rehearse all the way through the French Revolution. Mirabeau died on 2 April 1791, but the secret negotiations that he initiated with the king and queen were taken over rapidly by Antoine-Joseph Barnave and his political allies in both the Jacobin club and the National Assembly because, until late July 1791, they still belonged to both. The outcome was the flight to Varennes and a botched attempt to overturn the constitutional innovations that Mirabeau had condemned and replace them by a two chamber legislature that, because of the different composition of each chamber, would house a British- or American-style system of party politics. In keeping with his earlier hostility towards Sieyès, Barnave advocated this two-chamber system rather than the two-section legislature advocated by Sieyès. 'In a word', he noted, 'the system of two sections is certainly a miserable puerility'.[20] Each section in Sieyès's system would, he objected, be elected in the same way, resulting in recurrent clashes and endless competition for legitimacy that would ripple through and finally destroy the whole system.

Barnave's alternative was a second chamber made up of life peers selected by the king from the existing elected legislature. Nominations to the second chamber would lead to intermittent local elections to replenish the membership of the elected chamber and these recurrent local elections would reinforce ministerial accountability and maintain competition between political parties. The unelected second chamber would, because of its life membership and its exemption from any electoral mandate or imperative to be accountable, have less incentive to be partial. Unlike what Barnave called the 'puerile' distinction between discussion and deciding built into Sieyès single legislature made up of two sections, the distinction between an elected chamber and a life peerage would be an innovation with real consequences. Recurrent appointments to the life peerage would enable popular parties to have their candidates elected to fill the resulting vacancies. More importantly, the existence of the life peerage would be an incentive to army officers to stand for election. There would, in short, be a place in France for someone like Washington and, more immediately, an opportunity to bind what Barnave called 'the principal army chiefs' to the cause of liberty and the constitution.[21]

---

[20] Antoine-Joseph Barnave, *Œuvres*, 4 vols. (Paris, 1843), 2: 38.

[21] Barnave, 'Système des deux chambres', in his *Oeuvres*, 2: 38–41.

Barnave did not refer to Lafayette or the National Guard in these speculations about a two-chamber system, but it is tempting to think that they, as much as the army itself, were the objects of what he called his political reflections. Elsewhere, he emphasised that it was 'indispensable' before establishing a bicameral legislature to reduce 'representative power' to what he called 'a single element' and establish a single legislative chamber for 'several years'. Although, he wrote, 'bicameralism' was 'the only reasonable and solid form of organizing the representation of the people in a large country', its establishment would be more secure when it was taken to be 'the solution to, and end of, the upheavals of the revolution'. Unless it was seen as a solution, bicameralism would be exposed 'almost infallibly to die from those same upheavals if it was attempted to establish it when the prejudices of the nation and the situation were opposed to it. If the instinct for equality was to rebuff it today, experience and love of order would establish it when equality no longer feels the same alarms.' Timing, Barnave wrote, was vital. Without it, the wrong experience of a second chamber could discredit one forever and leave 'the nation with no other remedy for anarchy than in absolute power'.[22]

Barnave's speculations can be taken as an indication of what the flight to Varennes was supposed to do. Had it succeeded, its outcome would have been a two-chamber legislature with a second chamber made up of an appointed life peerage and an elected first chamber designed to provide an entry point for emulators of George Washington or ambitious members of the National Guard like Washington's protégé Lafayette. It was, in one sense, a solution to the problem that Burke highlighted and, perhaps, a response to the problems of non-eligibility and re-election created by Robespierre's point of order of 16 May 1791. In another sense, however, it also created a different problem because the projected combination of an elected lower chamber and an appointed upper chamber made up of life peers meant creating a huge reservoir of royal patronage. From this perspective, Barnave's speculations form a context not only for thinking about the real aim of the flight to Varennes but also for thinking about the relationship between the failure of the Feuillants and, in the summer of 1791, the emergence of the *sans-culottes*. Patronage,

[22] Barnave, 'Introduction à la révolution française', in his *Œuvres*, 1: 113.

alongside party politics, was central to the system that Barnave envisaged. This, as will be shown in the next chapter, was why Barnave's opponents and, more broadly, opponents of the idea of a life peerage based on royal patronage began to call themselves *sans-culottes*.

In his posthumously published, but undated, notes on the French Revolution, Barnave made it clear that 'several years' would be needed before it was possible to establish the type of bicameral legislature that was compatible with the size and social and economic diversity of modern France and, at the same time, to leave behind the commitment to equality associated with the existing single-chamber legislature. By the summer of 1791, however, he had changed his mind. In the famous speech that he gave to the National Assembly on 15 July 1791, a day after the second anniversary of the fall of the Bastille and under a month after the flight to Varennes, he made it clear that everyone, as he put it, 'should feel that the common interest is that the revolution should stop'. The losers had to see that there was no going back, while the winners had to see that there was no going further forward. The question now raised by the national interest, Barnave said, was 'are we going to end the Revolution or are we going to begin it again?'[23] The warning underlying the question was a prelude to what was to come next. A day after he made his speech, Barnave and most of the other members of the Jacobin club seceded and, on 16 July 1791, established their new political society meeting in a former Feuillantine convent not far from the other former convent on the rue Saint-Honoré in Paris where the few remaining members of the Jacobin club continued to meet. The Feuillant secession left the Jacobins with a tiny residual membership headed by Brissot, Pétion and Robespierre. A day later, on 17 July 1791, it then had to face the consequence of what came to be known as the massacre of the Champs de Mars when a crowd summoned to sign a petition calling for the destitution and trial of the king was attacked by the National Guard under the command of Lafayette, leaving over fifty people dead and injured (contemporary estimates ran into the hundreds). The remaining Jacobin leadership now faced the possibility of prosecution under the provisions of the Le Chapelier law of 14 June 1791 prohibiting petitions by collective bodies. Although the law has come to be associated with the prohibition of trade unions and strikes, its initial

---

[23] *AP*, 28 (15 July 1791), 329–30.

targets were actually political associations and collective petitions, including the petition calling for the destitution of Louis XVI. By late July 1791, it looked as if Barnave's call to put an end to the revolution had succeeded.

Three months later, the situation had become less clear-cut. There were several reasons for this fast-moving sequence of events. In an immediate sense, they arose from the flight to Varennes and the vision of a constitutional monarchy, a bicameral legislature made up of elected representatives and life peers, and the vigorous system of party politics that Barnave clearly and consistently endorsed. In a more fundamental sense, however, they arose from the related problems of empire and emigration that, from the vantage point of Barnave and his political allies, amounted to the real threats to liberty. From their perspective, the possibility of the loss of empire and the growth of emigration magnified the already built-in threat to liberty from the landowners. Part of this diagnosis was supplied by Adam Smith and his claim, in *The Wealth of Nations*, that modern opulence was based on a precarious balance between town and country.[24] To Barnave, developments in France reinforced the problem. The post-revolutionary disintegration of the French Empire in the Caribbean reduced supplies of sugar, coffee, cotton, tobacco and rum. Prices rose; profits were squeezed; while substitutes became more difficult to find. As returns to industry and trade fell, more disposable income went on rent, particularly urban rent, because leases in towns came up for renewal more frequently than in rural areas. Although, as Barnave emphasised, there was no moral case for a slave-based empire, its existence could not simply be wished away because the disappearance of the colonial trade would have real economic consequences. As industry and trade dried up, the hegemony of the landowners would become more pronounced and the dependence of urban consumers on rural producers would grow. To Barnave, the end of empire might mean freedom in the Caribbean but, paradoxically, enslavement in France. Preserving liberty in France appeared, paradoxically, to call for preserving a slave-based empire abroad.

---

[24] Adam Smith, *An Inquiry into the Nature and Causes of the Wealth of Nations [1776]* (Oxford, 1976), bk. III, ch.1, 376–80.

The possibility of the loss of empire was a product of a decision by the National Assembly on 9 March 1790 to confer powers of self-government on France's existing colonies but to maintain the existing status of France's slaves. Most of the colonies and slaves were situated in the Caribbean, particularly in Martinique and Saint-Domingue, or what is now Haiti. The National Assembly's decision gave rise to fierce debate in France and more violent conflict in Haiti. There a settler insurrection in May 1790 precipitated a slave rebellion in November 1790. It turned into a war of liberation that lasted until 1804 and only came to a final end with French recognition of Haiti's independence in 1825. By the spring of 1791, it was clear that the war in Haiti had become entangled with the stream of emigration from France. As the emigration grew, the empire disintegrated and the condition of public finances continued to worsen, Barnave and his allies turned to a mixture of threats and promises to bring the emigration to an end and, in parallel, to assert that the preservation of the slave-based French Empire was now a reason of state. As Barnave told the National Assembly bluntly on 12 May 1791, 'the national interest and reason of state (*raison d'état*) cannot allow 600,000 men in a state of slavery to recover their liberty'.[25] One increasingly urgent reason for his assertion was that the growing stream of *émigrés* threatened to bring back the same problem from the other side. Losing the colonies was likely to cut off the supply of tax revenue from non-essential items of consumption, but so too was losing the tax base itself. Either prospect pointed towards greater reliance on tax revenue generated directly by landed property, and a vicious circle of higher taxation, rising cereal prices, and growing dependence by mainly poor urban consumers on largely rich rural landowners. If the British example showed that the balance of political power followed the balance of property, then the subjects of empire and emigration were two sides of the same coin. As Barnave began to insist, keeping the first and stopping the second really were reasons of state.

The problems generated by the overlapping subjects of the empire and the emigration began to become apparent on 28 February 1791, when the presiding head of the National Assembly's constitutional committee Isaac-René-Guy Le Chapelier gave the assembly a report on a decree on emigration that the committee had discussed. Le Chapelier (who six months later

---

[25] *Archives Parlementaires*, 26 (12 May 1791), 14.

became a member of the Feuillant club) was reluctant to read the actual text of the decree because, he informed the assembly, the committee had been divided over whether its provisions were constitutional. It soon became clear that the source of the division could be found in the second of its three, short articles. This stipulated that, were the decree to come into force, the National Assembly would appoint a three-man council to exercise, as the article in question put it, 'dictatorial power over the right to leave, and the obligation to return to, the kingdom'. Although Le Chapelier did not express his own views, it soon became clear that he, as well as Mirabeau, who spoke eloquently against the article, did not support the proposal. Mirabeau recommended dropping it altogether, and proposed that the assembly should pass on to the order of the day. There was noisy opposition, and the assembly decided finally to adjourn, rather than drop, the subject. By the time that it came back, Mirabeau was dead, and, on 20 June 1791, Louis XVI had tried, if not to emigrate, at least to move the royal government to somewhere outside Paris.

The problems deepened after the flight to Varennes, the secession of the Feuillants and the elections to the new Legislative Assembly in October 1791. On 2 October 1791, almost as soon as the new legislature had begun to sit, it began to discuss the emigration in a debate that continued into the second week of November. On 20 October, Mathieu Dumas, one of the five members of the committee that had taken over Mirabeau's secret negotiations with the king and queen (the others were Barnave, Duport, Lameth and Antoine-Joseph, formerly baron, d'André), proposed a decree ordering a court martial for any soldier who left his post without having first submitted his resignation. 'It is often said in this tribunal, where Montesquieu's shade is so often and so rightly remembered', Dumas told the assembly, 'that it may be necessary to draw a veil for a while over liberty, as it was customary to veil the statues of the gods'.[26] But, he continued, here referring back to Mirabeau's earlier opposition to the proposed use of 'dictatorial power' to put a stop to emigration, the need to

---

[26] *AP*, 34 (20 October 1791), 320. The phrase appears in Montesquieu, *SL*, Bk. 12, ch. 19. On its appearance in this context and, more generally, on the subject of the emigration, see Marcel Ragon, *La législation sur les émigrés 1780–1825* (Paris, 1904), 16. See also Manin, '*Un voile sur la liberté*', 221–86, and Karin Loevy, *Emergencies in Public Law: The Legal Politics of Containment* (Cambridge, 2016), 41–53.

maintain constitutional stability and political principle ruled out a more literal application of Montesquieu's metaphor. Five days later, however, the metaphor reappeared, but this time in a rather different sense. The speaker now was another prominent Feuillant, Charles-Emmanuel-Joseph-Pierre Pastoret (but an ally of Lafayette, rather than of Duport, Barnave and Lameth). 'On some occasions', he said, rehearsing Montesquieu's metaphor, 'it may be necessary to draw a veil for a while over liberty, as it was customary to veil the statues of the gods'. This time, however, Pastoret endorsed Montesquieu's recommendation. Rousseau, he added, citing book 3, chapter 18, of *The Social Contract*, had explicitly equated emigration to avoid serving one's country with desertion. Accordingly, Pastoret proposed a decree made up of six articles. The first two ordered the king's brothers, the comte de Provence and the comte d'Artois, to return to France within six weeks. Any soldier or public officer who had left his post after the king's acceptance of the constitution was to be deprived of his citizenship, but all other *émigrés* were to be invited to return to France within two months under the safeguard of the law. This carrot was accompanied by the threat of a future stick, since the sixth article of the projected decree left it open to the assembly to decide, on 1 January 1792, what to do with anyone who failed to obey its requirements.[27]

This shift of emphasis can probably be explained by the Pilnitz Declaration by the rulers of the Empire and Prussia of 27 August 1791 calling for armed intervention if Louis XVI was stripped of his crown. It put an end to the tactics adopted by Barnave and his allies immediately after the flight to Varennes. At that time, according to the notes made by Marie Antoinette, Barnave's first demand was to get the *émigrés* to come back. 'The king', she was told early in July 1791, 'can keep the throne with dignity, and obtain confidence and respect, only by obtaining great advantages for the nation'. These would consist, firstly, of the return of the princes and the *émigrés*, or at least some of them, and, secondly, of a declaration by the Holy Roman Emperor recognising the new French constitution and expressing his friendly and peaceful intentions towards the French nation.[28] By late October, particularly after the Pilnitz Declaration, it is likely that the

---

[27] *AP*, 34 (25 October 1791), 404–7.

[28] Alma Söderhjelm, *Marie-Antoinette et Barnave. Correspondance secrète (Juillet 1791–Janvier 1792* (Paris, 1934). 42.

prospects of delivery had evaporated. Barnave and his allies seem accordingly to have decided to switch tactics and opt for threats, rather than promises, either to get the *émigrés* back or to prevent others from leaving. Increasingly, it became usual to treat the *émigrés* as outlaws. On this basis, they deserved no more than summary justice and those of their relatives who remained at home would be treated as hostages. By March 1793, eighteen months after the flight to Varennes, and long after the failure of the Feuillants, the French republican Convention was presented with a proposal to revive the Roman republican practice of decimation.[29] Among those arrested as outlaws, lots would be drawn and one in ten would be put to death. By then, the empire had gone, leaving only the emigration susceptible to some sort of solution, even based on Terror. Continued emigration would mean that trade and industry would continue to go backwards, the deficit would grow, the *assignat* would fall and public and private credit would be strangled. By 1793, the switch of focus from preserving the empire to preventing emigration was complete.

Before the autumn of 1791, the strongest supporters of the *assignat* were Brissot, Clavière and their political allies. Irrespective of its potential long-term benefits, they claimed, its most immediate advantage was its capacity to prevent a catastrophic debt default and the economic disaster that a bankruptcy could cause. By late 1791, however, the emphasis changed. Where Barnave and his allies tried very hard to bring the *émigrés* back, Brissot and his allies began to try equally hard to keep the *émigrés* out. Bringing them back meant trying to maintain the financial stability that, among other things, would give them something to come back to. Keeping them out, on the other hand, meant removing the financial enticements that might bring them back. Clavière, accordingly, began to describe the nation's debt in a new and rather different way. Instead of arguing, as he had done earlier, that using the *assignat* was the best way to manage the many different financial instruments used by the nation to pay its assorted creditors, Clavière, in an article dated 25 November 1791, began to emphasise the distinction between what he called the 'constituted' and 'demandable' (*exigible*) debts. The first, consisting of perpetual or life annuities, remained a real obligation, but

---

[29] See, on this proposal, Ted W. Margadant, 'Provostial Justice and the *Hors la loi* Decree of March 19, 1792', *H-France Salon*, 11 (2019), 1–12, particularly at p. 7.

the second, consisting of debt arising from the abolition of venal offices, the suppression of feudal dues, the arrears of interest payments and anticipations of tax revenue, was no longer a matter of public faith. Trying to cover both sets of obligations, Clavière now argued, would lead to a massive rise in the issue of *assignats* and a further, more pronounced, devaluation of the currency. There was no alternative, he stated, to suspending payments on the *dette exigible*.

As the Feuillant *Journal de Paris* commented, this amounted to calling for a partial state bankruptcy.[30] In one sense, it could be said, it was simply a capitulation to reality and, as Clavière himself wrote, a recognition that the spiralling prices that continued deficit finance was likely to produce would destroy political stability. But in another sense, it was also a very public indication that there would be no financial carrots available to returning *émigrés*. For Clavière, finally, keeping the public faith took second place to politics and, by late 1791, politics required widening, not reducing, the breach with Barnave and the Feuillants. If this ruled out any further gestures towards trying to maintain urban expenditure on colonial and manufactured goods, it also eliminated any further need to try to use a mixture of inducements and intimidation to bring the *émigrés* back. With this breach in place, the only available constituency to which Brissot, Clavière and their allies could turn was a popular one. Without the resources of empire, or the expenditure of the *émigrés*, the one remaining pillar of the new regime had to be the people.

Brissot had already set out the argument in a speech to the Jacobin club on 15 July 1791, a day after the second anniversary of the fall of the Bastille and two days before the Massacre of the Champs de Mars. The king, he said, had to be tried. In similar circumstances, this had been the view of John Locke, Algernon Sidney, John Milton, Catherine Macaulay, William Blackstone and, most recently, Sir William Jones. Even if there was no trial, the constitution would have to be revised to

---

[30] Etienne Clavière, 'De ce qu'il faut faire dans l'état actuel des finances', *Chronique du mois*, 2 (December 1791), 4–30 (pp. 10–13, 18, 28–30). The description (rejected by Clavière) of his proposal as a national bankruptcy was published in issue 329, p. 1335, of the 1791 volume of the *Journal de Paris*. For a similar characterisation of Clavière's proposal, see the commentary in the pro-Feuillant *Ami des patriotes* described in Odette Dossios-Pralat, *Michel Regnaud de Saint-Jean-d'Angély, serviteur fidèle de Napoléon* (Paris, 2007), p. 89.

include an elected executive council to monitor and, if necessary, modify executive decisions. But, as Locke and even Blackstone had shown, the practice in Britain had been to establish a Convention specifically for the purpose of expelling and replacing a tyrant. Trying a king, Brissot continued, did not mean abolishing monarchy, as his Feuillant opponents claimed. Monarchy had continued to exist among the Jews even though the Sanhedrin was entitled to judge and condemn their kings. As Maimonides had written, kings of the line of David judged and were judged. The king could, accordingly, be tried. It was claimed, Brissot continued, that trying the king would provoke armed intervention by Europe's monarchs. If this was to happen, he argued, the revolution would be reinforced and the new regime made stronger. If France's enemies were to impose their power, they would force the French to establish the project of a two-chamber legislature, 'that hereditary senate that has always been the accomplice and pillar of despotism'. They would restore the nobility and, step by step, reinstate the Old Regime.

This, Brissot concluded, was why war was not to be feared. War might well be long and hard, but free nations could outlast soldiers and standing armies, as the American had shown both at Bunker Hill and over the course of the war for their independence. Once, Brissot argued, money was said to be the sinew of war. But, under the modern funding regime money ran out, leaving only free nations with the will and resources to face the hardships of a long war. All the European powers, from Britain to Spain and from Sweden to Russia, Brissot claimed, were either too exposed to their own domestic weaknesses or in thrall to their external enemies to be real threats to France. The oppressive nature of their militarised regimes meant, as the Germans had done in America, that the soldiers of France's enemies were more likely to abandon their rulers and enrol under the flag of liberty. 'The American revolution', Brissot concluded, 'gave birth to the French revolution and that revolution will be the sacred hearth from which a spark will fly to set fire to those nations whose masters now dare to approach her'.[31] There was, in short, a case for war modelled on French help to the American cause because, as it showed, a war whose aim was to secure liberty abroad as well as liberty at

---

[31] All these quotations are from Brissot's speech to the Jacobin club, reprinted in *AP*, 28 (15 July 1791), 338, 340, 341, 342, 343.

home was a winnable war. From the vantage point of Brissot's speech of 15 July 1791, the war declared by the first French republic on the rulers of Austria and Prussia on 20 April 1792 was a war that was long foretold. So too, from the same vantage point and within the same time horizon, was the emergence of the *sans-culottes*.

CHAPTER EIGHT

The *Sans-Culottes*

There was a closer relationship between the French declaration of war of 20 April 1792 and the emergence of the *sans-culottes* as a political force than is now apparent in modern scholarship on the French Revolution. In the nineteenth century, the ministry responsible for taking France to war, the ministry made up of the political figures subsequently labelled Girondins, was once known as the *sans-culotte* ministry.[1] As this designation implies, the *sans-culottes* were originally a Girondin creation. The name featured prominently in a highly programmatic pamphlet published under at least four different titles – all calling for the destitution of the king – that appeared in the names of the Forty-Eight Sections of Paris, the Commune of Paris, the 'true sovereign' of France and the Mayor of Paris until, finally, on 3 August 1792, or a week before the insurrection that overturned the French monarchy, the mayor himself and future Girondin leader Jérome Pétion presented the pamphlet in what amounted to an ultimatum to the Legislative Assembly. 'France', Pétion wrote, 'is divided internally into two very distinct parties, one called honourable men (*honnêtes gens*) and the other *sans-culottes*'. Both, he asserted, were ready to turn the kingdom over to the 'horrors of civil war'. But, he insisted, it would be a war with only one winner. All the passive citizens, he pointed out, or over 3,820,000 men, together with 1,680,000 less wealthy active citizens and a further 400,000 better-endowed active citizens, would support the *sans-culottes*. This meant that a single supporter of the *honnêtes gens* would be ranged against no less than fifteen supporters of the *sans-culottes*. Given this overwhelming force,

---

[1] See, for example, François-Auguste-Marie-Alexis Mignet, *History of the French Revolution from 1789 to 1814* [1824] (London, 1846), 128 and Georges Touchard-Lafosse, *Souvenirs d'un demi-siècle*, 6 vols. (Brussels, 1836), vol. 2, 262.

Pétion concluded, civil war was pointless. Instead, the party of *honnêtes gens* would have to join forces with the *sans-culottes* and face the common enemy, whether at home or abroad.[2]

Pétion's description of the balance of political forces in France was matched by one made by his close political ally Jacques-Pierre Brissot. If Sieyès oriented part of his intellectual and political allegiances towards the thought of Rousseau, Brissot did much the same towards Diderot.[3] Brissot was also very familiar with the earlier association between a *sans-culotte* and literary patronage. As he noted in his posthumously published memoirs, he had been imprisoned in 1777 for publishing a satirical pamphlet entitled *Le pot-pourri: étrennes aux gens de lettres* ('The Pot-Pourri: A Christmas Box for Men of Letters'), in which he had compared a solicitor's wife who kept a salon to a prostitute. He was familiar too with James Rutledge and the satirical play *Le Bureau d'esprit* that he published, centred on the story about Mme Geoffrin and her gifts of breeches to the men of letters who frequented her salon. He also knew Louis-Sébastien Mercier and his story about the satirical poet Nicolas Gilbert as the archetype of a *sans-culotte*. Gilbert had written a fierce attack on literary patronage entitled *Le Dix-Huitième Siècle* which, as Brissot acknowledged, was a more effective satire than his own *Pot-Pourri*. Before 1789, a *sans-culotte* was a writer without a patron. By 1792, however, for figures like Brissot and Pétion, the patron in question was the queen, while her clients were Barnave, his Feuillant allies and their endorsement of a second chamber made up life peers appointed by the king. This was patronage on a different scale and Brissot duly objected. His own Parisian section of Filles de Saint-Thomas, he told the Legislative Assembly on 5 August 1792, was 'divided into two parts: one, respectable, displaying a large number of patriots, or those designated by the name of *sans-culottes*, and the other gangrenous, made up of financiers, currency-dealers and speculators'.[4] It is not hard to guess where Brissot's allegiances lay.

---

[2] Jérôme Pétion, *Les Vœux du véritable Souverain exprimés à l'Assemblée Nationale au nom de la Commune de Paris sur la Déchéance du Roi* (Paris, 1792), 7. On the several versions of the pamphlet, see Frédéric Braesch, *La Commune du 10 Août 1792* (Paris, 1911), 144–5.

[3] See James Burns, 'Brissot', *History of European Ideas*, 38 (2012), 508–26.

[4] Mavidal and Laurent (eds.), *AP*, 47, 502. See also Ernest Mellié, *Les Sections de Paris pendant la Révolution française* (Paris, 1898), 115–16. On Brissot's earlier literary

These early invocations of the *sans-culottes* resurfaced some six months later in two different versions of a speech to the French Convention given by Maximilien Robespierre on 10 April 1793, attacking what he called 'a powerful faction', headed by Brissot, for 'conspiring with the tyrants of Europe to give us a king and a kind of aristocratic constitution'.[5] In the authorised version of the speech, published in the tenth number of his own *Lettres à ses commettants* (Letters to His Constituents), Robespierre accused Brissot and his allies of hiding their ambition under a mask of moderation and a spurious love of order.

> They called all the friends of the fatherland agitators and anarchists; even inciting real agitators and anarchists to make that calumny seem true. They showed themselves to be skilled in the art of covering up their criminal enterprises by imputing them to the people. Early on, they horrified citizens by raising the spectre of an agrarian law. They separated the interests of the rich from the poor; they presented themselves to the former as their protectors against the *sans-culottes*; they attracted all the enemies of equality to their party.[6]

In this version of his speech, it was Robespierre and his Jacobin allies who were the true protectors of the *sans-culottes*, while Brissot and his Girondin allies were the protectors of the rich. In a second version of Robespierre's speech, however, published at the same time in the *Logotachigraphe* (which, as its name implies, was meant to be a verbatim record), Robespierre was reported to have said exactly the opposite, namely that Brissot and his supporters had presented themselves not as the protectors of the rich against the *sans-culottes* but, instead, as 'the protectors of the *sans-culottes*' against the rich.[7] At different times, it could be said, both Brissot and Robespierre played the populist card.

career, see Jacques-Pierre Brissot and Nicolas-Francois Guillard, *Le Pot-Pourri: Etrennes aux gens de lettres* (London, 1777), 54–5, and Jacques-Pierre Brissot, *Mémoires*, ed, Claude Perroud, 2 vols. (Paris, 1911), vol. 1, 20, 104. On Gilbert, Rutledge and Mercier, see Sonenscher, *Sans-Culottes*, 17–21, 34–35, 59–61. 101–07.140, 227, 266, 270–73, 342–6.

[5] Maximilien Robespierre, *Œuvres*, 10 vols. ed. Marc Bouloiseau, Jean Dautry, Georges Lefebvre and Albert Soboul (Paris, 1958), 9: 376–416 (at p. 376).

[6] Robespierre, *Œuvres*, 9: 377–8.   [7] Robespierre, *Œuvres*, 9: 401.

Although they have come to be identified with the artisans and shop-keepers of urban France and the policies of maximum prices and market regulations promoted in 1793 and 1794 by the Jacobin part of the French Convention, the *sans-culottes* emerged as a political force much earlier and in an initially more satirical guise than modern historiography has assumed. They also had a more central presence in the dynamics of revolutionary politics than the same historiography has shown. That presence began to take shape in 1791 and 1792, rather than in 1793 and 1794, and did so in a context that had little to do with the urban trades and bread shortages usually associated with *sans-culotte* concerns. The context instead was formed by the flight to Varennes, the secession of the Feuillants from the Jacobin club and the massacre of the Champs de Mars. By July 1791, and in the aftermath of these events, the remaining membership of the Jacobin club was reduced to a tiny residual rump headed by Brissot, Pétion and Robespierre. Three months later, however, the Jacobin rump reinforced by a growing number of its provincial supporters had made a sudden and comprehensive comeback. In the most immediate sense, this was because its candidates were spectacularly successful in the elections to the Legislative Assembly and the municipality of Paris. In a more fundamental sense however it was, as Robespierre said, because of the initial association between Brissot, his allies and the *sans-culottes.*

Between the summer of 1791 and the summer of 1792 the phrase *sans-culottes* became the name of a political force and, as it did, its growing currency heralded the political renaissance of the Jacobin rump. That renaissance took place during the protracted sequence of elections in Paris, first to the Legislative Assembly, which began sitting on 1 October 1791, then to the administration of the department of the Seine, in which Paris was situated and, finally, to the municipal administration of Paris itself. These were organised electoral contests, with two semi-permanent political clubs meeting respectively in the chapel of the former Parlement of Paris and in a room adjoining the Cathedral of Notre-Dame and with each club drawing up rival slates of candidates and issuing advice and instructions about how to vote. The first organisation, known as the *Club de la sainte-chapelle*, supported the Feuillants, while the second, called the *Club de l'évêché*, supported the Jacobins. The *évêché* club carried the day in the Parisian elections to the legislature, while the *sainte-chapelle* club dominated the elections to the departmental administration.[8] The Jacobin rump, however, triumphed in Paris itself. Not only did Brissot and his allies win the Parisian elections to the Legislative Assembly in September 1791, they also in November 1791 had Jérôme Pétion elected to the office of mayor of Paris. The victory was sealed when, in March 1792, Brissot's allies became the king's ministers. This was the ministry once known as the *ministère sans-culotte*.[9] It was this ministry that on 20 April 1792 took France to war with what its proclamation called 'the king of Bohemia and Hungary' and, less than two months later, was dismissed by Louis XVI on 13 June 1792. A week later there was an organised insurrection in Paris calling for the recall of the now dismissed *sans-culotte* ministry. In it, a substantial crowd invaded the Tuileries palace and forced Louis XVI to put on a red Phrygian cap or *pileus*. According to one eyewitness, some members of the crowd could be seen carrying 'a pair of old black breeches carried on a pole with this comfortable inscription, *Libres – et sans-culottes* (Free – and without breeches)'. According to another eyewitness, the inscription actually read 'Tremble tyrants; we are the *sans-culottes*'.[10] The *sans-culottes* had arrived.

The *droit de commune* was, therefore, not the only subject to come back from the past to have a new and different political presence after 1789. Alongside the justification of a militia associated with the *droit de commune*, there were also justifications of a republic, justifications of the figure of a *sans-culotte* and, finally, justifications of civil war. Together, the new political salience of these three subjects underlined the failure of the

---

[8] On these organisations, see [François Boissel], *Adresse à la nation française. Peuple français, voici ta constitution* (n. p. n. d., but late 1791 from the content), 25–6. There is still a need to reconstruct the relationship between these clubs and the later Evêché committee of 1792–93. On the latter, see Henri Calvet, *Un Instrument de la Terreur à Paris: Le comité de salut public ou de surveillance du département de Paris (8 juin 1793–21 Messidor an II)* (Paris, 1941) and several of his earlier articles.

[9] Touchard-Lafosse, *Souvenirs d'un demi-siècle*, 6 vols. (Brussels, 1836), vol. 2, 262.

[10] John Moore, *A Journal during a Residence in France from the Beginning of August to the Middle of December 1792*, 2 vols. (London, 1793), vol. 2, 204–6. See also François-Emmanuel Toulangeon, *Histoire de France depuis la révolution de 1789*, 7 vols. (Paris, 1801), 2: 166 and Jean-Gabriel-Maurice Rocques de Montgaillard, *Histoire de France*, 9 vols. (Paris, 1827), 3: 92.

Feuillants. The first was associated with God's warning to the people of Israel about the dangers of having a king. The second was a New Year's Day custom followed over the seventeenth and eighteenth centuries by several generations of famous *salonnières,* from the seventeenth-century *salonnière* Madame de Sablière to Madame Geoffrin, of giving the men of letters who frequented their salons several ells of velvet fabric to be made into a pair of breeches or *culottes.* 'Never', as it was put in one early nineteenth-century account of patronage,

> was such a patron as Madame Geoffrin to those poets who sung her praises. She was so particularly nice in her taste that she complimented every such author with a new pair of velvet breeches as a Christmas box! It was calculated by one of her own coterie that no less than four thousand pairs of velvet breeches were worn out in the *poetical* service of that lady, who was resolved, at least, that the sons of Parnassus should never be *sans culottes.*[11]

The third and most recent of these subjects was a highly positive endorsement of civil war. Between 1789 and 1792, the three subjects were brought together to form the basis of an initially coherent, but subsequently fractured, political narrative. In this narrative, the line separating coherence from fracture was formed by a developing argument over the questions of slavery, empire and emigration that, cumulatively, fed into the subject of civil war. By early 1792, it was beginning to become clear that this last subject belonged not only to a large reservoir of historical precedents and moral examples but was also a more immediate and potentially catastrophic possibility. Some, like Diderot's younger acquaintance Antoine-Nicolas de Condorcet, were prepared to face its dangers. Others, like Diderot's long-standing collaborator Guillaume-Thomas Raynal, were not.[12] At different times and in different circumstances, many others, including Diderot's theatrical follower, the playwright Louis-Sébastien Mercier, did both. In this context, the centre of contention was formed by the figure of a *sans-culotte.*

---

[11]   Richard Ryan, *Poetry and Poets,* 3 vols. (London, 1826), vol. 2, 158.

[12]   On the difference, see Hans-Jürgen Lüsebrink (ed.), *L'Adresse à l'Assemblée Nationale (31 Mai 1791) de Guillaume-Thomas Raynal: Positions, Polémiques, Répercussions* (Paris, 2018), notably 284–85 on Machiavelli and civil war.

The emergence of the *sans-culottes* set the seal on the disintegration of the broad patriot coalition that had come into being in 1789 and 1790, first against Mounier and the Monarchiens, then against Necker and Bailly and finally against Sieyès and Mirabeau. That coalition was made up originally of figures as diverse as Barnave, Lameth, Duport, Condorcet, Pétion, Brissot, Danton and Robespierre, all now better known for their later conflicts than their earlier cooperation. Several of them had been members of *société des amis des noirs* (society of the friends of blacks) that had been established in 1788 and all of them were initially members of the Jacobin club or, to use its official name, the Society of Friends of the Constitution.[13] The disintegration of the patriot coalition was also the disintegration of the Jacobin club and, in place of the triumvirate centred on Barnave, Duport and Lameth, the triumph of the Jacobin rump centred initially on the new triumvirate of Brissot, Robespierre and Pétion. This new political grouping, dominated by figures who in 1793 came to be labelled as Girondins, was equipped with a political narrative that brought together the subjects of the Hebrew republic, salon society and the *sans-culottes* and amalgamated them with an unusually positive evaluation of civil war made most prominently by Mably and Mercier and based on the putative difference between ancient and modern civil wars. Where, they claimed, ancient civil wars had given rise to the end and dissolution of societies, modern civil wars led to their regeneration.

Initially, the emergence of the *sans-culottes* owed more to satire than civil war. The main exponent of the satire was a journalist and man of letters named Antoine-Joseph Gorsas. He was largely responsible for turning the words *sans culottes* into a signal of the differences between the Jacobins and the Feuillants and an emblem of the moral and political values that now divided them. Before 1789, Gorsas had specialised in art-criticism. He was the son of a shoemaker from Limoges who, after an education at the former Jesuit Du Plessis college in Paris, became the head of a private military school at Versailles (where, according to his enemies, he had run afoul of the authorities for darkly unspecified reasons).[14] Gorsas published his first

---

[13]   Marcel Dorigny and Bernard Gainot, *La société des amis des noirs 1788–1799* (Paris, 1998), 49.

[14]   See his own note on his earlier life in *Le Courrier de Paris dans les provinces et des provinces à Paris*, 10 (23 November 1789), 139.

work of art-criticism, the *Promenades de Critès au salon* (A Stroll at the Salon with Crites), in 1785. Despite its apparently neutral title (Crites was simply a Greek-like word for critic), the pamphlet was actually an extended exercise in satire.[15] It then had a sequel, a description of the following year's salon that Gorsas published in 1787 under the title of *La Plume du coq de Micille* (Mycillus's Cockerel's Feather). Here, Gorsas used the trick of treating the paintings and sculptures at the salon as if they were real people. He also gave himself the persona of another cobbler, this time named Mycillus, who managed to get into the salon because he owned a cockerel's feather that made him invisible (the idea came from Pythagoras, who believed that, in a previous life, he had been a cockerel belonging to Mycillus).[16]

Once inside the salon, Mycillus was welcomed by the busts of Cassandra, Racine, Bayard, Molière, the Marshal de Luxembourg and Saint Vincent de Paul before he began to assess the paintings and sculptures on display. These, it turned out, had views of their own, allowing Mycillus not only to describe what they said but also to add his own comments on their often rather curious pronouncements. In doing so, and just as Mycillus was in the process of returning a tiny lamb to the portrait of Mlle Dugazon by Mlle Vigée-Lebrun hanging next to her own self-portrait, he came across the statues of Racine, by Boizot, and Molière, by Caffieri, who, to the consternation of their neighbour Saint Vincent de Paul, were in the middle of a furious argument (which, Mycillus reported, was why Saint Vincent's posture in the bust by Stouf was said to look rather hesitant). The argument, he continued, would certainly have shocked the ladies on the wall nearby because it was about a pair of breeches (*une paire de culottes*). 'Give me back my breeches', Racine shouted. 'You can't have them', Molière shouted back.

> Be informed that the *History of the Royal Academy* and, moreover, the guide to this year's exhibition positively says, on page 46, line 6, word 7, including the comma and at the twelfth character of the line, that *Molière had a fine leg* and

---

15 For a recent edition, see Claude Thémiseul de Saint-Hyacinthe, *Le chef d'œuvre d'un inconnu*, ed. Henri Duranton (Paris, 1991).

16 For a version of the story, see François de Salignac de la Mothe Fénelon, *The Lives and Most Remarkable Maxims of the Ancient Philosophers [1726]* (London, 1726), 84–5.

that Mme Geoffrin had some fashionable breeches (*des canons à la mode*) made for me, simply to be able to show off my fine.

At that point, however, Molière suddenly fell silent. On closer inspection, it turned out that Caffieri had simply forgotten to add the relevant item.[17]

Gorsas was an unusually imaginative satirist. Between the summer of 1791 and the spring of 1792 he used his talent to highlight the differences between the Jacobins and the Feuillants by giving the word *sans-culotte* a highly charged set of social and moral connotations. In doing so, he turned the word into a synonym for the ordinary people of Paris, noting, for example, how a meeting of the Jacobin club early in January had approved of a proposal by the Legislative Assembly's committee on legislation concerning the distribution of money to provide relief to the *sans-culottes* and, early in February, commending the *sans-culottes* of Versailles for calling for public sessions of a club suspected of 'aristocratic' sympathies.[18] The shortage of sugar and other goods produced by the slave insurrection in Saint Domingo and the price-fixing riots that occurred in Paris in January and February 1792 added a new dimension to the term.[19] In late January 1792, Gorsas printed a letter from one of his correspondents, reporting that the price of materials in the hatting trade had rocketed by 30 per cent when a dozen or so major manufacturers in Lyon combined to buy up supplies in Paris, Rouen and Marseille.[20] The letter was a clear hint about what the real cause of the Parisian grocery

---

[17] Antoine-Joseph Gorsas, *La Plume du coq de Micille, ou aventures de Critès au salon, pour servir de suites aux Promenades de 1785* [1787], in René Démoris and Florence Ferran (eds.), *La peinture en procès. L'invention de la critique de l'art au siècle des lumières* (Paris, 2004), 285–369 (at pp. 332–3 for this episode). Thanks to Katie Scott for bringing this edition to my notice.

[18] *Courrier des LXXXIII Départements* (9 January, 4 February 1792).

[19] On these subjects, but without either Gorsas or Brissot, see, classically, George Rudé, *The Crowd in the French Revolution* (Oxford, 1959), 80–2, 95–8; William Sewell, 'The Sans-Culotte Rhetoric of Subsistence', in Keith Baker (ed.), *The French Revolution and the Creation of Modern Political Culture* (Oxford, 1994), 249–70; Colin Jones and Rebecca Spang, 'Sans-culottes, *sans café, sans tabac*: *shifting realms of necessity and luxury in eighteenth-century France*', in Maxine Berg and Helen Clifford (eds.), *Consumers and Luxury: Consumer Culture in Europe 1650–1850* (Manchester, 1999), 37–62. On the subject in France, see Audrey Provost, *Le luxe, les lumières et la révolution* (Paris, 2014).

[20] *Courrier des LXXXIII Départements* (26 January 1792).

riots might have been (Brissot, in his periodical, the *Patriote français*, published a letter explicitly stating that the sharp rise in sugar prices was the work, among others, of the pro-Feuillant deputy d'André who had apparently bought up 400,000 livres worth of sugar in Lille).[21]

The subject turned into a political dispute when, early in February 1792, the recently elected mayor of Paris, Jérome Pétion, published an analysis of the riots' causes and their possible political implications. In an open letter published in several newspapers, he claimed that they had been provoked to generate division within the popular cause. The 'numerous and prosperous class of the bourgeoisie', Pétion wrote, had 'made a scission with the people', opening up a breach whose only beneficiaries would be the enemies of liberty. There had, therefore, to be a revival of that union 'between the bourgeoisie and the people' that had once formed the 'union of the third estate against the privileged' or, as Gorsas himself put it, the union between the 'honourable artisan' and the 'honourable bourgeois' that had been the making of the revolution.[22] The letter produced a hostile Feuillant response. The poet, André Chénier, in an article published in the *Journal de Paris*, argued that if Pétion's diagnosis was right, then this was a reason to make the Jacobins pause for thought, since 'that class that he refers to as the bourgeoisie' stood midway between 'the vices of opulence and misery' or 'the prodigality of luxury and the most extreme need' and was, therefore, the real source of political stability.[23] According to the Feuillant *Gazette universelle*, Pétion's letter looked like a covert call for the enfranchisement of passive citizens. The periodical attacked his implicit assertion that the bourgeoisie could be distinguished from the people, noting that it was possible to make this distinction only if the term *bourgeois* was used to mean something different from that part of society legally entitled to take part in elections. If, the *Gazette* stated, Pétion meant that 'the people' was something other than those who enjoyed political rights by dint of their 'honest industry' and who, as members of the National Guard, were responsible for maintaining law and order, then he was practising the kind of dangerous demagoguery used by the Roman republican advocate

<hr>

[21] See the reply to it in the *Journal de Paris*, supplément 13 (9 February 1792), 165.
[22] *Courrier des LXXXIII Départements* (13 February 1792), 193–4.
[23] *Journal de Paris*, supplément 19 (26 February 1792), 3–4.

of an agrarian law Caius Gracchus (whose fate, it noted, was presently available for inspection in the tragedy of the same name).

Gorsas was quick to defend Pétion. It was difficult, he commented on 13 February 1792, to accept the assumption made by the *Gazette universelle* that passive citizens were the sole threat to law and order unless it was also assumed that 'it is the *sans-culottes* who engross metal coin, insult magistrates, commit arbitrary acts, protect ministerial corruption, favour the party of Coblenz or send articles ready-made to the *Gazette universelle*'.[24] He returned to the subject in the 22 February issue of the *Courrier* with a none-too-subtle modification of Pétion's examination of the relationship between the bourgeoisie and the people in the context of a further attack on the Feuillant-backed *Gazette universelle*. The Feuillants, Gorsas wrote, had made it look like a crime for the 'virtuous Pétion' to have said that 'it was necessary to distinguish the bourgeoisie from the people'. But Pétion had been right. The bourgeoisie, Gorsas continued, were 'a pile of financiers, legal bigwigs (*robins*), wholesale merchants, bankers, money-dealers, annuitants, and the major-domos (*intendants*) and dressing-room valets of former seigneurs'.[25] The people, on the other hand, consisted of 'men of letters, retailers, artists, craftsmen (*fabricants*), in short of all those whom the once-privileged caste called the *populace* and whom they now style as bare-footed rustics (*va-nu-pieds*), *sans-culottes*, etc.'.[26] The contrast between honest industry and *honnêtes gens* was sharp. It was matched, Gorsas emphasised, by two quite different visions of politics. While the people were wholeheartedly committed to the revolution, the bourgeoisie favoured 'a mixed government' where, 'with a little money and a talent for intrigue, they can be really *free*, namely the masters of every position and where, through corruption, disposing of all the favours of the court and the nation, they will be in a position to lead both'.[27]

Gorsas's claim that political differences arose from conflicting social interests provoked a hostile reply in a letter from a *bourgeois de Paris*, published as a *Supplement* to the pro-Feuillant *Journal de Paris* on 1 March 1792. After noting that Gorsas had placed men of letters at the

<hr>

24 *Courrier des LXXXIII Départements* (13 February 1792), 194–6.
25 *Courrier des LXXXIII Départements* (22 February 1792), 348.
26 *Courrier des LXXXIII Départements* (22 February 1792), 348.
27 *Courrier des LXXXIII Départements* (22 February 1792), 348–9.

head of the various parts of the people, the anonymous *bourgeois* pointed out sarcastically how apt his choice had been. While, he wrote, some men of letters might imagine that they were likely to find a place in any society in which honesty and ability were honoured, Gorsas had the peculiar insight to recognise that his talents were of a higher order. Here, the anonymous Parisian burgher turned the neologism that the word *sans-culotte* had become back to its original meaning. Gorsas, he wrote, was simply a hack writer who fitted all the specifications of Voltaire's earlier caricature in *La pauvre diable* (The Poor Devil) and, 'superior to the good Lafontaine, who received his breeches from Mme de la Sablière, you receive none from anyone, and walk out, proud of your nakedness'.[28] Gorsas's claim that merchants belonged to an aristocracy of the rich was, the author of the *Letter* concluded, both false and divisive (he himself, he emphasised, was a patriotic wholesale merchant). It turned a blind eye to exactly the kind of violation of property rights that had occurred during the Parisian grocery riots of January and February 1792. The effect of this further round of insults was to turn the new buzzword, *sans-culotte*, into the name of one side of an increasingly antagonistic political and economic divide. By the spring of 1792, the name had acquired most of the connotations usually associated with 1793 and the politics of the Year II of the first French republic.

Alongside this type of endorsement of the *sans-culottes* there were also a number of more recent and politically charged endorsements of the positive qualities of civil war. The most prominent had been made by the abbé Gabriel Bonnot de Mably in his *Des droits et des devoirs du citoyen* (Of the Rights and Duties of the Citizen), probably written in the 1760s but published only late in 1788 or early in 1789, six years after Mably's death.[29] 'Civil war', he wrote there, 'is sometimes a great good'. It was true, he continued, that civil war 'contravened the security and wellbeing that men envisaged in forming societies and can cause many citizens to perish'. But, just as it was sometimes necessary to amputate an arm or a leg to preserve the body, so a civil war was sometimes a benefit if society was exposed to die from gangrene or 'to avoid talking metaphorically, ran the risk of dying of despotism'. Some civil wars, Mably asserted, can 'ignite the

---

[28] *Journal de Paris*, 61, supplément 19 (1 March 1792), 2.

[29] Gabriel Bonnot de Mably, *Des droits et des devoirs du citoyen* [1789], ed. Jean-Louis Lecercle (Paris, 1972), at pp. 62–3, 68.

love of country, respect for law and the legitimate defence of the rights and liberty of a nation'. If Rome's civil wars were certainly pointless, this was not the case with the war of the United Provinces of the Netherlands against the domination of Spain's Philip II. 'I begin to find it strange', Mably concluded, 'that the oppressors of society have had the magical ability to persuade us that it is in our interest not to interfere with the progress of their usurpations and injustice and that civil war – for a people still virtuous enough to benefit from it – is somehow a greater scourge than the tyranny that menaces them'.[30]

The most emphatic endorsement of civil war appeared in the summer of 1792, a year after the flight to Varennes but at about the same time as the insurrection that took place in Paris on 20 June 1792 in response to the dismissal by Louis XVI of the so-called *sans-culotte* ministry formed less than four months previously by Brissot and his political allies. It had actually appeared many years earlier in a satirical novel entitled *L'an 2440, rêve s'il en fut jamais* (The Year 2440, a Dream if Ever There Was One) that was published in 1770 during the last, decaying, years of the reign of Louis XV (who died in 1774) by the dramatist, satirist and political writer Louis-Sébastien Mercier. 'In certain states', Mercier wrote, 'there is a time that can become necessary, a terrible, bloody time, but one that signals liberty'. Civil war, Mercier added, 'makes use of the most obscure talents', causing 'the most extraordinary men' to emerge and become able to take command.[31] He repeated the claim in 1787 in his *Notions claires sur les gouvernements* (Clear Notions of Government), backing it up by invoking the authority of the seventeenth-century English republican Algernon Sidney and did so again in 1792 in a further three volume compilation of his earlier articles published as *Fragments de politique et d'histoire* (Fragments of Politics and History) that included a very positive assessment of the sixteenth-century Catholic League.[32] 'In civil wars the destruction of the state is not to be dreaded', Mercier asserted. 'Notwithstanding that the people may be divided into

<hr>

[30] Mably, *Des droits et des devoirs du citoyen*, (Kell, 1789), 98–9.

[31] Louis-Sébastien Mercier, *L'An deux mille quatre cent quarante-quatre, rêve s'il en fut jamais* [1770], ed. Raymond Trousson (Bordeaux, 1961), ch. 36, at 330, note 3.

[32] Louis-Sébastien Mercier, *Notions claires sur les gouvernements*, 2 vols. (Amsterdam, 1787), 1, 196.

factions', he continued, 'it is far from being annihilated. It has, on the other hand, a superabundance of vital action.'[33] Civil war's legitimacy could be derived 'from necessity and strict justice' particularly where there were 'no alternative means available to the injured party' so that civil war became a form of action that was 'truly undertaken for the safety of the state.' Its effects, Mercier added, were rarely harmful. 'Nations emerge from these internecine debates in a redoubtable condition. Political enlightenment is more widespread; armed valour grows stronger with exercise. The very fury and violence of this kind of war makes it of short duration.'[34] Mercier connected an endorsement of civil war with a rejection of monarchy. He made this double evaluation in the course of issuing a warning about the dangers of combining royal with military power, particularly in the context of relying on foreign troops such as the famous Swiss guards. Here, God's warning to Samuel was still salient. 'Ah', Mercier wrote in his *Fragments of Politics and History,* 'how has it not been possible for peoples at all times to see how fearful the consequences of this horrible combination have been. Oh Samuel! How right you were to frighten the people who were mad enough to demand a *king* by presenting the most terrifying images of the innumerable calamities that go with royalty.'[35] By the summer of 1792, when Mercier republished his article, the scriptural warning was now an exhortation and encouragement.

Behind the escalating claims and counterclaims were the more durable and intractable divisions generated by the problems of empire and emigration. On 9 February 1792, the so-called *sans-culotte* ministry persuaded the Legislative Assembly to confiscate the property of *émigrés* and, with further legislation on 30 March–8 April 1792, to organise the process more thoroughly.[36] The two problems of empire and emigration played into

---

[33] Louis-Sébastien Mercier, *Fragments of Politics and History* [1792], 2 vols. (London, 1795), 2, 11–12 (I have modernised the translation slightly).

[34] Louis-Sébastien Mercier, 'De la ligue', *Chronique du mois* (July 1792), 58–80 (here at pp. 64–5). The same passage appears in Mercier, *Fragments of Politics and History*, 2, 341.

[35] Louis-Sébastien Mercier, *Fragments de politique et d'histoire*, 3 vols. (Paris, 1792), 3, 333.

[36] On these later measures, see Jean d'Andlau, 'Penser la loi et en débattre sous la Convention: le travail du comité de législation et la loi sur les émigrés du 28 mars 1793', *Annales historiques de la révolution française*, 396 (2019), 3–19.

a range of different characterisations of political economy. For Barnave and the Feuillants, political economy was, substantively, a matter of commodities and commerce. Trade relied on tradeable goods and tradeable goods depended on markets and prices. Prices, in turn, were signals of abundance or warnings of scarcity, heralding either prosperity or adversity as the ebb and flow of tax revenue generated the broader measures of trade and payments balances that drove the myriads of dispersed decisions underlying the quarterly or seasonal rhythms of industry and agriculture. No government could afford to ignore the information about power and prosperity that commerce and commodities supplied. No government, however, could also afford to ignore the disruption to commerce caused by the disintegration of empire and the disappearance of commodities. Although, as Raynal and Diderot had shown, commerce could supersede empire, as Adam Smith had shown, imperial collapse could disrupt commerce and undermine currencies based on tax revenue.

For Brissot and the future Girondins, political economy was, substantively, a matter of needs and reciprocity. Trade was required for both, but trade had as much to do with utility and humanity as with competition and advantage. As Brissot's friend and utilitarianism's founder Jeremy Bentham put it in a letter in 1781 describing a clergyman, Joseph Townsend, rector of Pewsey in the country of Wiltshire, this was what utilitarianism meant. 'He seems a very worthy creature', Bentham wrote,

> has been a great deal abroad and has a great [deal] of knowledge; his studies have lain a good deal in the same track with mine. He is a utilitarian, a naturalist, a chemist /a physician/, was once what I had like to have been, a methodist: and what I should have been still had I not been what I am, as Alexander if he had not been Alexander (I am wrong in the story but never mind) would have been Parmenio,

a name that Bentham later changed to 'Diogenes'.[37] Utilitarianism fitted the broader aspirations of the antislavery campaign that both Brissot and Bentham supported. It also fitted the broader ideal of international cooperation that, again, both Brissot and Bentham supported.

---

[37] Jeremy Bentham to George Wilson, 24 August 1781, in Ian R. Christie (ed.), *The Correspondence of Jeremy Bentham*, (London, 1981), vol. 3, 57.

This joint preoccupation with antislavery and international relations was the basis of a broader and less competitive version of political economy that, as was the case with the *Société des amis des noirs*, straddled the circles associated with both Brissot and Bentham. One of its watchwords was a passage from an energetic attack on slavery entitled *An Essay on the Treatment and Conversion of African Slaves in the British Sugar Colonies* that was published by another British clergyman, named James Ramsay, vicar of Teston in Kent, in 1784. 'By giving man one simple origin', Ramsay wrote,

> by bestowing on him a common nature, a foundation was laid for the ultimate reunion of mankind, as well now in improved social life as in futurity, a reunion intended to take place in time under the then-promised connecting head of the creation, and particularly rendered practicable in a unity of laws, government and worship by this universal equality established among the various families which keeps the way open for the equal and gradual improvement of their common nature.[38]

The passage was picked up and given a French summary in a book entitled *La cause des esclaves nègres et des habitants de la Guinée, portée au tribunal de la justice, de la religion et de la politique* (The Cause of the Black Slaves and Inhabitants of Guinea at the Tribunal of Justice, Religion and Politics) that was published in 1789 by a Protestant pastor named Benjamin Sigismond Frossard who later became part of the circle that aligned the supporters of Brissot and Robespierre against the followers of Barnave and Lafayette in the silk-producing city of Lyon.[39]

If slavery went with empire, humanity and utility went with trade, reciprocity and social interdependence rather than with states, competition

---

[38] James Ramsay, *An Essay on the Treatment and Conversion of African Slaves in the British Sugar Colonies* (London, 1784), 207. On Ramsay, see Folarin Shyllon, *James Ramsay: The Unknown Abolitionist* (Edinburgh, 1977), and Christopher Leslie Brown, *Moral Capital: Foundations of British Abolitionism* (Chapel Hill, 2006), 228–30, 243–53.

[39] Benjamin Sigismond Frossard, *La cause des esclaves nègres et des habitants de la Guinée, portée au tribunal de la justice, de la religion et de la politique*, 2 vols. (Lyon, 1789), vol. 2, 207. The passage is cited in Robert Blanc, *Un pasteur du temps des lumières: Benjamin-Sigismond Frossard (1754–1830)* (Paris, 2000), 107, but misattributed to the better-known follower of Fénelon Andrew Michael Ramsay rather than to James Ramsay.

and political power. Where once, according to the British politician William Pitt the elder, America was conquered in Germany, so now, according to Brissot and Clavière, would liberty in France be conquered in America? At its most ambitious, the future that both envisaged would be a world that could accommodate trade, but one in which trade would be based on a more clearly differentiated set of natural economic endowments, and, more importantly, where trade would be free, not simply in the negative sense of being unimpeded but also in the stronger sense of being voluntary and reciprocal, rather than simply necessary and competitive. From this point of view, the monetisation of the assignat supplied a peaceful way to remove the distortions generated by France's overreliance on industry, trade and public debt. France, as Clavière viewed it, was both an agricultural and a trading nation.[40] With these as the features of its economy, it could rely more heavily on the skill-intensive manufacturing industries of the Swiss or Dutch republics for its import of manufactured goods, and, in the longer term, on the additional resources supplied by a further, westward extension of the whole, now economically rebalanced, international system, as the American economy came to complement its European counterpart. Then, as Clavière and Brissot wrote in their co-authored book on France and the United States, American agriculture would underpin the growth of French manufacturing industry, to form an alliance based on real common interests.[41]

This was the gamble underlying Brissot's campaign for a war. There were many reasons for the success of his campaign, not all of them confined to Paris, or even entirely to France.[42] The reaction to the Pilnitz Declaration by the rulers of Prussia and the Holy Roman Empire of 27 August 1791; the hostile clusters of *émigrés* on France's northern and eastern borders; the violence in Avignon known as the massacre of La Glacière of 16 October 1791 when dozens of opponents of the more-orless legal annexation of the Papal enclave were put to death; the slave

---

[40] The description can be found in Etienne Clavière, *Dissection du projet de M. l'évêque d'Autun. Sur l'échange universel et direct des créances de l'état contre les biens nationaux* (Paris, 3 July 1790), 75.

[41] Etienne Clavière and Jacques-Pierre Brissot, *De la France et des Etats-Unis* [1787], ed. Marcel Dorigny (Paris, 1996), 45–70.

[42] On the wider international setting, see Timothy Charles William Blanning, *The Origins of the French Revolutionary Wars* (London, 1986).

insurrection in Saint-Domingue; the sugar shortage that it produced; and the inflationary spike in prices produced by the collapse in the supply of colonial goods, all played their part. So too, however, did the neologism that the name *sans-culotte* had become. It did so because it played into the political situation produced both by the conflict between the Jacobins and the Feuillants after the massacre of the Champ-de-Mars and by the perceived threat to French external security represented as much by the alarming longer-term military implications of the depreciation of the *assignat* as by anything actually done by the rulers of Prussia and the empire. In this sense, the rush to war in the winter of 1791–92 owed less to military delusion than to a bleaker assessment that the longer a war was postponed, the more unstable French public finances might become, and, consequently, the more difficult it might be to win a war later rather than sooner, particularly in the absence of the Franco-British alliance that, almost to the last, Brissot and his supporters hoped might occur.[43] In this sense, the war was not so much a gamble on the pro-French sympathies of the Belgians or on the patriotism of the French army command as, more desperately, a more clear-headed assessment of the scale of risk built into the future and a gamble on the possibility of short-term triumph over the more certain prospects of long-term disaster.

Once underway, Brissot envisaged broadening of the war to a global scale. 'It is necessary to promote this revolution in Spain and in America at the same time', he informed his friend and political ally the Venezuelan General Francisco Miranda in November 1792, 'Miranda will soon put an end to the miserable quarrels of the colonists, he will soon bring the turbulent whites to reason and he will become the idol of the coloured people. Then, with what ease will he not be able to revolutionize the colonies that the Spaniards possess in the West Indies or on the American Continent?'[44] But as the war progressed – often badly – during the winter of 1792–93, both the connotations of the word *sans-culotte* and the object

---

[43]   On these hopes, see A. N. F^7 4774^{70}, dossier Pétion; Marcel Reinhard, 'Le voyage de Pétion à Londres, 24 Octobre–11 Novembre 1791', *Revue d'histoire diplomatique* (1970), 1–60; and Albert Goodwin, *The Friends of Liberty. The English Democratic Movement in the Age of the French Revolution* (London, 1979), 186–8.

[44]   William Spence Robertson, *The Life of General Miranda*, 2 vols. (Chapel Hill, 1929), vol. 1, 128. On Miranda, see John Maher (ed.), *Francisco de Miranda: Exile and Enlightenment* (London, 2006).

of allegiance to which the word referred began to change comprehensively. By the time of the publication of the authorised version of Robespierre's speech on 10 April 1793, the Girondins were described as protectors of the rich against the *sans-culottes*, while Robespierre and his Jacobin allies had become protectors of the *sans-culottes* against the rich.

By then the war had become a war for the world after the trial and execution of Louis XVI on 21 January 1793 and the French declaration of war against Britain on 1 February 1793. It was, initially, a catastrophe marked by desertions, betrayals and threats of defeat when first General Lafayette in August 1792 and then General Dumouriez in April 1793 went over to the enemy. It also, however, turned the *sans-culottes* from a street-centred, section-based political presence into a military and administrative force that, institutionally and financially, became part of the embryonic government of the new French republic. This transformation was largely the work of Robespierre and his Jacobin allies. It was a transformation that borrowed many of the tactics and organisational initiatives that Pétion, Brissot and their Girondin allies had used between the summer of 1791 and the spring of 1792 to recapture the political initiative in Paris from Barnave and the Feuillants. But, where Brissot, Pétion and the Girondins had relied on Paris as the means to take back France from the Feuillants in 1791–92, Robespierre, Saint-Just and the Jacobins relied on France and the provincial membership of the republican Convention as the means to take back Paris from the Girondins in 17993. In 1791, a *sans-culotte* was a Parisian version of a salon-society joke. By 1793, a *sans-culotte* had become a symbol of the French republic.

The most famous version of that symbol was, according to its author, an answer to 'the impertinent question' *What Is a Sans-Culotte?* The 'impertinent question' was actually the title of a wallposter headed *Mais! Qu'est-ce qu'un sans-culotte?* ('But, What Is a *Sans-Culotte?*') that was published by Antoine-Joseph Gorsas at the time of Robespierre's speech to the Jacobin club in April 1793 attacking Brissot and the Girondins for misrepresenting the *sans-culottes* and their relationship of the rich and the poor in the new French republic. The answer amplified on Robespierre's definition. A *sans-culotte*, it asserted, was

> a man who goes everywhere on his own two feet, who has none of the
> millions you're all after, no mansions, no lackeys to wait on him, and who

lives quite simply with his wife and children, if he has any, on the fourth or fifth floor. He is useful, because he knows how to plough a field, handle a forge, a saw, a file, to cover a roof, how to make shoes, and to shed his blood to the last drop to save the republic.[45]

But the original answer that the Girondin-supporting Gorsas gave to his own question matched Robespierre's identification of a *sans-culotte* as the creation of political demagoguery but, in opposition to Robespierre, Gorsas gave the populist slur a different evaluation. 'A *sans-culotte*, a *sans-culotte*', he wrote, 'well, since I have to tell you, today's *sans-culotte* is a *sans-culotte* who has fine breeches but wants still to get hold of the breeches of those who do have breeches so as not to give a thread or a penny or even any breeches at all to those poor devils who have no breeches, the *sans-culottes*'. The description simply reversed Robespierre's evaluation. Where Robespierre described the original promoters of the *sans-culottes* as demagogues and opportunists, Gorsas applied the same accusation to their more recent supporters. A *sans-culotte* in 1793 was, he wrote, a '*sans-culotte postiche*', a fake *sans-culotte* and a 'pseudo-Diogenes' whose demagogic rise to revolutionary prominence concealed a very shady past.[46]

These clashing characterisations can be taken as a measure of the political conflict that came to a head between the summer of 1792 and the spring of 1793. At its heart was a struggle for control of Paris and, by extension, France. One indication of what was at stake in that struggle was the transformation of the *Marseillaise*, the military anthem created by Rouget de Lisle in the summer of 1792 to accompany the detachment of the Marseille National Guard on its march to Paris to take part in what had become the annual commemoration of the fall of the Bastille. By this time, however, the *fête de la fédération* had become considerably more than a Parisian affair. Its membership now encompassed deputations or *fédérés* from the whole republic brought together in Paris partly to face the invading enemy, but also, as Pétion indicated, to face down the enemy at home. By 3 August 1792, when Pétion published his threatening pamphlet, the situation had developed into a three-sided trial of strength.

---

[45] I have used the translation in Gwyn A. Williams, *Artisans and Sans-Culottes* [1968], 2nd ed. (London, 1989), 19, 57. For the original French document, see Walter Markov and Albert Soboul, *Die Sansculotten von Paris* (Berlin, 1957), 2.

[46] [Antoine-Joseph Gorsas], *Mais! Qu'est-ce qu'un sans-culotte?* (Paris, n. d.).

On the one side, there was the court and its beleaguered ministry trying to recover its authority after the dismissal of the *sans-culotte* ministry and the *sans-culotte* invasion of the Tuileries palace of 20 June 1792. On the other side were the Girondin members of the former *sans-culotte* ministry, with their presence in both Paris and the Parisian Jacobin club. Between the two, as had been the case a year earlier, there was a tiny Jacobin rump, headed this time by Robespierre and his allies. In 1793, in a reversal of what had been the case a year earlier, it gradually took control of Paris and the rest of France.

CHAPTER NINE

Robespierre and the Politics of the Terror

Retrieving the forgotten evidence of the relationship between the Girondins, the *sans-culottes* and the short-lived *sans-culotte* ministry that took France to war on 20 April 1792 makes it possible to throw new light on the revolution of 10 August 1792. This was the revolution that led to the fall of the French monarchy, the end of the constitutional regime established in 1791 and the proclamation of the first French republic on 5 September 1792. It was also, as in 1789, a mixture of what was expected, but did not happen, and what was unexpected, but really did happen. The part that was expected, but did not happen, was encapsulated by Pétion's muted ultimatum to the Legislative Assembly on 3 August 1792 with its evocation of Britain's Glorious Revolution of 1688 and its none-too-hidden message about how a determined legislature could dismiss a discredited king. The one that was unexpected but really did happen was the armed conflict between the king's Swiss guards and the federated companies of the Parisian and provincial National Guards that took place in the grounds of the Tuileries Palace on 10 August 1792. This unexpectedly violent episode was quickly followed by news of the military defeats of the French army at the battles of Longwy and Verdun on 23 August and 1 September 1792 and, a day later, by the gruesome prison massacres that took place in Paris between 2 and 6 September 1792. The whole sequence of events meant that instead of an organised process of regime change carried out under an existing legislature as in Britain in 1688, the revolution of 10 August 1792 resulted in the unforeseen problem of establishing a republican government without a republican constitution or an identifiable constituent power. The scale of the problem forms a context both for measuring the significance of the trial and execution of Louis XVI on 21 January 1793 and for developing a fuller explanation of its relatively long-drawn-out political aftermath in the Jacobin–Girondin conflict that encompassed most of France for much of 1793. With these chronological adjustments in place, it is possible to piece together more of the mixture of political and conceptual improvisation, expediency and creativity involved in what came to be called the period of the Terror of 1793–94. Put summarily, that mixture involved using Girondin means to reach Jacobin ends.

With the exceptions of the king and the court, the revolution of 10 August 1792 had no obvious winners or losers. The resulting political and constitutional hiatus produced an accelerated replay of the debate on a future constitutional Convention that had taken place a year earlier, in August and September 1791, when the National Assembly came to the end of its life and was about to submit its draft constitution for royal ratification. That debate revived the subject of constituent power because it centred on the question of whether the need to revise the constitution meant that the existing draft should make provision for periodic constitutional conventions, perhaps beginning in 1800 and continuing at intervals of thirty years as also envisaged by Thomas Jefferson in the United States. The idea had its supporters, among both the remaining members of the Jacobin club and also among future members of the Feuillant club who opposed Robespierre's use of the concept of constituent power to prohibit the election of members of the National Assembly to its Legislative successor. As its critics pointed out, however, the range and variety of subjects required to provide for these future conventions seemed to entail so many decisions over their possible frequency, size, composition, remit and relationship to other institutions and constituted powers that adopting the provision amounted to trying to establish a future version of the present assembly without knowing what it would have to address.[1] By the late summer of 1792, however, what a year earlier was deemed to be an impossible assignment had become an unavoidable requirement.

Its most immediate outcome was a new round of elections to municipal, departmental and national office. This time there were no restrictions on eligibility either to vote or be elected (although women and domestic servants continued to be excluded). In other respects, however, there was considerable continuity in terms of both the number of former

---

[1] For the main contributions, see *AP*, 30, 36–66. 95–107.

members of the National and Legislative Assemblies elected to the Convention and the part played by organised political societies, particularly the Évêché club, in drawing up lists of candidates and presenting their credentials to their various local or national electorates. As Robespierre later indicated inadvertently, the distribution of votes in these elections was largely even because, in different ways, all sides brought the *sans-culottes* into their campaigns. In one sense, this meant that Pétion's appeal of 3 August 1791 for an alliance of *sans-culottes* and *honnêtes gens* had been successful. In another sense, however, it also meant that the differences between Jacobins and Girondins were largely limited, at least in 1792. It is easy to forget, for example, that Brissot was the author of a pamphlet entitled *Recherches philosophiques sur le droit de propriété considéré dans la nature* ('An inquiry into the right of property in nature') that was published in 1780 and was as hostile to the inegalitarian effects of private property as anything published by Robespierre. Later, in November 1791, one of Brissot's English acquaintances made a point of using Jérome Petion's visit to London to send Brissot a copy of the equally critical *Essay on the Right of Property in Land* by a philosophy professor at the University of Aberdeen named William Ogilvie. There is, in short, no reason to look for long-standing or deep-seated differences between Jacobins and Girondins. They were driven instead by the tactics, opportunities and calculations that they adopted cumulatively and divergently, but, for both, with the survival of the republic at stake.

One indication of the initial overlap was the election in October 1792 of a doctor named Nicolas Chambon de Montaux to the office of mayor of Paris in succession to his better-known predecessor Jérôme Pétion who, in his turn, was elected to the Convention. Although he is no longer famous, Chambon was the author of a large treatise published in 1787 on the means, as its title announced, to make hospitals more useful to the nation (*Moyens de rendre les hôpitaux plus utiles à la nation*). It was, in part, a reply to two pamphlets on charitable and philanthropical reform published respectively by Turgot's admirer and biographer Pierre-Samuel Dupont de Nemours and a less well-known architect named Claude Philibert Coquéau (who was later executed on 8 Thermidor of the Year II, the day before Robespierre was overthrown). Both pamphlets emphasised the limited responsibilities of the state for the welfare of its members and took issue with the putative charitable obligations of hospitals and comparable public institutions such as those associated with the English Poor Laws. Chambon, however, took the opposite tack. 'Those legislators who had thought about sociability most wisely and had laid its foundations most firmly', he wrote, 'made benevolence a duty'. Property rights were certainly consecrated by established usage and a consent usually taken to be general, but it remained the case that everyone born had a share in the products of the land and could, 'according to the system of foreign legislators', appropriate what they judged to be necessary for their needs and preservation. Here, the reference was to the natural jurisprudence of Samuel Pufendorf buttressed, however, by Saint Paul and his injunction to work to be able to have what could be given to those in need. For much of the eighteenth century, this combination of Pufendorf and Saint Paul was sometimes known as 'socialism'.[2]

Between the time of the elections to the Convention and the office of mayor of Paris in September and October 1792 and the debates on the constitution of the first republic in April and May 1793, the overlap between Girondins and Jacobins on property, sociability and morality turned into acrimonious conflict. One indication of the scale of the transformation was a change in the connotations of the concept of a federation. In 1790, the concept was associated with the idea of the *droit de commune* because the *fête de la fédération*, or festival of federation, held in Paris on 14 July of that year to commemorate the first anniversary of the fall of the Bastille was designed to be a public celebration of the union that made the many French communes a single French nation and their many different militias a single National Guard. Sieyès coined a special word, *adunation*, to describe the resulting combination of the many and the one. By the summer of 1793, however, calling for a federation had become a crime. By then, the concept of a federation was associated with the revolt headed by Brissot and his Girondin political allies against Paris and the authority of the French Convention. Among those deemed to be suspects, according to article 2 of the famous Law of

---

[2] Nicolas Chambon de Montaux, *Moyens de rendre les hôpitaux plus utiles à la nation* (Paris, 1787), 15–17, 23–4, 25–6. On Chambon, see Joseph Génévrier, *La vie et les œuvres de Nicolas Chambon (de Montaux)* (Paris, 1906). On socialism and Pufendorf, see Sophus A. Reinert, *The Academy of Fisticuffs: Political Economy and Commercial Society in Enlightenment Italy* (Cambridge, MA, 2018), 6, 8–11, 269, 285–8, 298, 352, 377–9.

Suspects passed by the Convention on 17 September 1793, were 'those who by their conduct, relationships, statements or writings have shown themselves to be partisans of tyranny or federalism and enemies of liberty'.[3] The switch from 'federation' to 'federalism' was matched by a comparable switch in evaluations of street demonstrations before and after 1793 and, in particular, of the part played by the *sans-culottes* on the days that they occurred. In 1792, a *sans-culotte* could be taken to be a synonym of a *fédéré* because both could be identified with street demonstrations, popular campaigns and membership of a militia or an *armée révolutionnaire*. By the end of 1793, however, the two labels had become antonyms because a *fédéré* was now likely to be a criminal, while a *sans-culotte* was likely to be a participant in a sectional assembly, the administration of a *commune* or a member of a revolutionary committee or tribunal. A *fédéré* was an enemy of the republic, but a *sans-culotte* was now part of the republic and, on Robespierre's insistence, would be paid for what this involved.

Where once, according to Adrien Duport, in 1791, the *assignat* was the cement of society, society, according to Robespierre in 1793, now had to be the cement of the *assignat*. By then, his conception of a republic had come to centre on what he called popular economics (*l'économie populaire*). He set out the concept forcefully in his speech on the new French republic's constitution on 10 May 1793. What weight, he told the Convention, could be attached to the idea of equality of rights 'if the most imperious of all laws, necessity, forces the major (*la plus saine*) and most numerous part of the people to renounce public affairs'. It followed, he argued, that everyone who lived from their work should, like all public officials, be indemnified for attending public meetings. These, too, should be genuinely public. 'A splendid and majestic building, open to 12,000 spectators', Robespierre said, 'should be the site of sessions of the legislative body'. Ensuring that all public debates and decisions were underpinned both by a real popular presence and an institutionalised popular tribunal were, he emphasised, the only ways to turn 'the virtue of the people and the authority of the sovereign into the necessary counterweight to the passions of the magistrate, and government's tendency

---

[3]   The text can be found under its date in the Baudouin Collection of the University of Chicago: https://artfl-project.uchicago.edu/collection-baudouin.

towards tyranny'. As he put it in his conclusion, 'in this way you will have solved the still unresolved problem of popular economy (*l'économie populaire*)'.[4] Two days later, on 12 May, he repeated the call, this time in the context of a speech advocating the establishment of a popular republican militia, or an *armée révolutionnaire*, made up of *sans-culottes*. As he had emphasised in an earlier speech, its members would not wear braid breeches. 'He who has braid breeches (*culottes dorées*) is the born enemy of all *sans-culottes*.' Nor, he now said, could genuine *sans-culottes* be expected simultaneously to handle 'trowels and arms'. They would instead form 'a reserve army' that would remain in Paris, and be paid by the public treasury.[5] Both proposals, for a fully paid Parisian *sans-culotte* militia and for a 40-sous-a-day indemnity for participating in public life, were put into effect six months later, in September 1793.

At first sight, Robespierre's concept of 'popular economics' looks similar to the concept of a closed – or complete – commercial state set out later by the German philosopher Johann Gottlieb Fichte in his *Der Geschlossene Handelstaat* in 1800. A version of the same idea had, however, been anticipated in a number of comments on the properties of public credit published by the playwright Louis-Sébastien Mercier with the aim of giving Rousseau's moral and political thought greater real-world applicability. Rousseau, Mercier wrote, 'whose severe morality' made him the 'enemy' of '*capitalists, financiers and bankers*', did not have a monetary theory. He had, therefore, not been able to see how money, the naturally available means to 'free land from its sterility, trade from its limits and workers of every kind from their fatal idleness', could be supplemented by the additional monetary and financial resources gener-ated by public credit. This 'science, new in so many regards', Mercier argued, was one of the keys to future prosperity and political stability.[6] Its fundamental principles had been established by the Scottish financier John Law. If, Mercier claimed, Law had been in the position of his more

---

[4] Maximilien Robespierre, speech to the Convention, 10 May 1793, reprinted in his *Oeuvres*, vol. 9, pp. 503 (on the size and appearance of a legislative building), 506–7 (on indemnifying the people). On his earlier call for an indemnity, see Robespierre, *Oeuvres*, vol. 7, 689.

[5] Robespierre, *Oeuvres*, vol. 9, 490, 514–15.

[6] Louis-Sébastien Mercier, *De Jean-Jacques Rousseau, considéré comme l'un des premiers auteurs de la révolution* (Paris, 1791), 79–81, note 1.

recent counterpart Jacques Necker, 'you would have seen the great man correct his plans, set himself all at once at the head of the revolution and march majestically towards immortality'.[7] The claim matched a striking comment on public credit that Mercier had made in 1787. If, he wrote then, a state was able to maintain the credit of an artificial currency (*une monnaie factice*), 'it would no longer have need for taxes or finance'. But, he added, for this to be possible, 'the state would first have to be isolated'. Once this was the case, the artificial currency could perform all the functions of metallic money more efficiently and, since the source of the money supply would now be entirely domestic, there would be no need to rely on exports, particularly the export of subsistence goods, to acquire hard currency. The result would be a virtuous circle in which the artificial currency would 'fertilise land that is susceptible to prodigious increase' and, 'on this marvellous hypothesis', both the state and members would be winners. The 'secret', Mercier wrote, was to find a way 'to isolate a kingdom'.[8]

One way to do so was to cut it off from the outside world. Another, however, was to bring the outside world into the inside of the republic and turn foreign trade into domestic trade. Robespierre, famously, opposed the Girondin campaign for war. 'No-one', he told the Jacobin club on 2 January 1792, 'likes armed missionaries'.[9] But, after the war began, Robespierre was uncompromising on the need to win because, he argued, it was a war that had the potential to end war. Here, two features of Robespierre's thought were particularly salient. The first was a muted, but consistent, set of claims about the part played by providence in human history. The second was his concept of a revolutionary government. These two aspects of his thought complemented one another and chimed too with the idea of money as a medium of exchange that, if foreign trade became domestic trade, would turn competition into reciprocity by bringing needs and justice into closer alignment.

The combination of a providential theory of history and a revolutionary theory of government supplied the motivation and

---

[7] Mercier, *De Jean-Jacques Rousseau*, 81, note 1.

[8] Louis-Sébastien Mercier, *Notions claires sur les gouvernements*, 2 vols. (Amsterdam, 1787), vol. 2, 347–8.

[9] Robespierre, *Oeuvres*, vol. 8 (2 January 1792), 81.

means to outflank the Girondins. The motivation was relatively new but many of the more practical means were already available because they relied on a number of ideas and arguments produced by the Feuillants and Girondins during the previous three years that were used subsequently to justify the serial denunciation, organised intimidation and summary punishment that in 1793 and 1794 became the hallmarks of Jacobin rule. In the new context of the first French republic, they enabled Robespierre and his Jacobin political allies to capture the political initiative from Brissot and his Girondin political allies and take the question of the king's fate from out of the hands of the nation by transferring it to the recently elected membership of the French republican Convention. The trial of the king soon became a model of the mixture of legal procedure and a foregone conclusion that came to be followed in proceedings against suspects. As has been indicated, the first ingredient of this mixture owed something to a passage from Montesquieu's *The Spirit of Laws* of 1748 in which he had written that in some dangerous circumstances it was necessary to draw a veil over the Statue of Liberty and temporarily suspend the rule of law. The second was more explicitly Roman in origin because it involved the Roman military concept of decimation, or the idea that, irrespective of innocence or guilt, one individual in ten would, in the French language version the idea, be put to death *pour encourager les autres.* The third ingredient complemented the other two. It was centred on the concept of an outlaw or someone outside the law and who was therefore in a condition beyond the formalities and procedures that made the law lawful.

In 1793 all three of these ideas crystallised into what both its supporters and opponents called the principles of revolutionary government. They became current in the context of the threat to financial and political stability represented from 1790 onwards by the disintegration of the French Empire and the growing stream of emigration by opponents of the new constitution. After the events of 10 August 1792, Robespierre and his political allies took them over and, in this new context, used Girondin ideas to outflank the Girondins and occupy the ground once occupied by the original exponents of those ideas. They supplied the means, in the first instance, to convict the king without having to refer his status or conduct to the judgement of the nation, the people, the *sans-culottes* or, still less, the largely unknown membership of French rural society. Their availability made it possible to transfer the concepts of necessity, decimation and an outlaw from the *émigrés* to the monarchy and from the monarchy to the growing number of allegedly treacherous, disloyal or incompetent administrators now grouped together under the broader rubric of a suspect. Shortly after Robespierre's fall on 9 Thermidor Year II (24 July 1794), this expanding conceptual compound came to be defined as 'a system of terror' in a speech delivered to the Convention on 11 Fructidor II (28 August 1794) by the former Jacobin leader Jean-Lambert Tallien. Tallien, however, was not actually the author of his own speech. Its real author was Sieyès's political ally Pierre-Louis Roederer and its conceptual content was probably supplied by Sieyès himself.[10] That content centred on a distinction between fear and terror and, by extension, on the difference between the rule of law and the concept of decimation. As Tallien presented this difference in his speech, fear galvanises, while terror paralyses. Fear, he argued, has the motivating power to promote prudence and avoid harmful actions. Terror, however, simply ruled out the capacity to act. It was decimation in all but name. As Tallien described it, terror produces suspicion and suspicion gave rise to increasingly atomised isolation. Fear, as Hobbes had famously argued, promotes political integration. Terror, on the other hand, promotes social disintegration. From this perspective, Robespierre's system was radically self-defeating.

Its initial effect, however, was to eliminate the possibility of any political exploitation of the king's fate by Brissot and his Girondin allies by consigning the trial to the Convention and, behind it, the members of the Jacobin club. Its more substantive and durable effect was the oxymoron made up of the two, usually incompatible, components of the concept of a revolutionary government.[11] The phrase was certainly used in a pamphlet published in

---

[10] For the speech, see Jean-Lambert Tallien, *Discours pronounce à la Convention nationale, dans la séance du 11 Fructidor, l'an 2 de la Republique, sur les principes du gouvernement révolutionnaire* (Paris, 1794), notably pp. 6–9, on the distinction between fear and terror and their different consequences. On the real authorship of Tallien's speech see Pierre-Louis Roederer, *Notice sur ma vie*, in his *Oeuvres*, 7 vols. (Paris, 1854), vol. 3, 288, and, more fully, Ami-Jacques Rapin, 'The First Conceptualization of Terrorism: Tallien, Roederer, and the "System of Terror" (August 1794)', *Journal of the History of Ideas*, 82 (2021), 405–26.

[11] On the concept, see Hervé Leuwers, 'Construire une nouvelle catégorie politique: Robespierre et la théorie du gouvernement révolutionnaire', in

April 1793 by a member of the Jacobin club named François Boissel, but it was Robespierre who gave the concept its definitive rendition in his famous 'Report on the Principles of Revolutionary Government' issued on what was once Christmas Day 1793 but was now 5 Nivôse of the Year II of the first French republic. 'The theory of revolutionary government', Robespierre announced,

> is as new as the revolution that has brought it. It cannot be found in books written by political writers who did not foresee that revolution. Nor can it be found in the laws of tyrants who, content to abuse their power, have no interest in seeking its legitimacy. The phrase, to the aristocracy, is either a subject of terror or a term of abuse. To tyrants, it is a scandal and to many people it is an enigma. It has to be explained to all to enable at least the good citizens to rally to the principles of the public interest.[12]

Robespierre's explanation was quite detailed. A revolutionary government was not entirely the same as the old Roman republican concept of a dictatorship. A dictatorship involved the temporary suspension of a constitution and the abrogation of the rule of law to respond to an emergency. Here, however, there was no constitution to suspend and this gave the nature and purpose of a revolutionary government a more foundational quality than a dictatorship. Its purpose was to found a republic in place of a monarchy. This meant that it had many enemies among the supporters and clients of the Old Regime, but, without a constitution, that it also had no established laws and procedures to deal with them. Rousseau, in his *Social Contract*, had emphasised that virtue was required in every law-governed society because every citizen sometimes had to subordinate self-interest to the rule of law. Robespierre took Rousseau one step further. Under a revolutionary government, he asserted, virtue had to stand in for the law. Without virtue, there would no more than suspicion and the work of foundation would be impossible.

Elsa Forey, Jean-Jacques Clère and Bernard Quiriny (eds.), *La pensée constitutionnelle de Robespierre* (Paris, 2018), 183–98.

[12] Maximilien Robespierre, *Rapport sur les principes du gouvernement révolutionnaire fait au nom du Comité du Salut Public* (Paris, 1793), 2. On Boissel's pamphlet, see François Boissel, *Les Entretiens du Père Gérard, sur la constitution politique et le gouvernement révolutionnaire du peuple français* [1793], ed. Pierre Antoine Courouble (Toulon, 2007).

The politics of virtue had to match the politics of suspicion to enable the republic to reach safe haven and establish the rule of law. As Robespierre described it, virtue was more than the self-denial involved in accepting the rule of law. It was an active and generous quality most visible among the people. 'All the vices', he wrote, were fighting on the side of the tyrants. 'The republic has only the virtues on its side. The virtues are simple, modest, poor, often ignorant, and sometimes crude. They are the apanage of the unfortunate and the patrimony of the people.'[13]

The name 'revolutionary government' was, as Robespierre indicated, very new. Its content – as he indicated in his description of the virtues – was considerably older. Robespierre was an unusual political thinker. The combination of Rousseau and religion that is so visible in his public pronouncements has made it difficult to avoid emphasising the one at the expense of the other. The key to both, however, was Robespierre's use of providential history to justify revolutionary government. This meant that the subjects of providence, divine inspiration and Christology were as much a part of Robespierre's politics as the more familiar, Rousseau-inspired, subjects of virtue and the general will because, put summarily, the first set of subjects supplied a moral foundation for the second. The Festival of the Supreme Being that Robespierre organised in the spring of 1794 was, in this sense, a public celebration of an abiding commitment. As Robespierre emphasised repeatedly, without providence, divine inspiration and Christ, virtue and the general will were no more than empty words superimposed upon arbitrary human choice. Political morality, he insisted, called for something more than purely human choice. It required a real bedrock of rational certainty based on the mixture of knowing and feeling involved in recognising Christ as the one truly providential human. Religion, accordingly, had a recurrently positive presence in the sequence of theologically oriented pronouncements that Robespierre made over the course of his life. There was the surprisingly strong endorsement of the life and career of the very devout bishop of Amiens Louis-François-Gabriel d'Orléans de la Motte (notorious for the part that he played in the trial and execution of the chevalier de la Barre) that Robespierre included in his eulogy of the writer Jean-Baptiste-Louis Gresset in 1786. 'Thanks to your virtues', he wrote, 'we could have

---

[13] Robespierre, *Rapport*, 10.

believed that one of those saintly bishops who once gave lustre to Christianity in its cradle had come back to life to console an exhausted religion and reaffirm a tottering piety' (in the manuscript version, the praise was even more extended, with a stronger emphasis on the bishop's charity, and commitment to the poor).[14] There was his clear identification of a patriot king as a vehicle of providence in his *Mémoire* on behalf of Louis-Marie-Hyacinthe Dupond in 1789. There was his unequivocal and controversial claim that the death of the Emperor Leopold II at the time of the Declaration of Pilnitz in the autumn of 1791 was, literally, a sign of divine providence. Despite a volley of accusations of superstition and obscurantism (*capucinades*) from his Girondin critics, Robespierre refused to back down.[15]

In his speech to the Jacobin club of 25 March 1792 on the subject of the impending war with Austria, Robespierre set out an unequivocal endorsement of providence as the moral guarantee of what the French Revolution had achieved and the further guarantee of what it was destined to fulfil. The speech underlined the breach that had opened between Robespierre and Brissot and, more broadly, between what became Girondin support for the war and Jacobin opposition to it. As Robespierre described it, the war was a trap set by the king and the court and a result of the earlier failure by the National Assembly to deprive the king of all trace of a royal

[14] Robespierre, *Oeuvres*, 1, 79–152 (p. 139 for the passage on d'Orléans de La Motte, and pp. 107–8, for the manuscript version). On the earlier career of the bishop of Amiens, see John Rogister, *Louis XV and the Parlement of Paris* (Cambridge, 1995), 52–8.

[15] On this aspect of Robespierre's politics, see Bernard Quiriny, 'Robespierre, la République et le Royaume de Dieu', in Michel Ganzin (ed.), *Pensée politique et religion* (Aix-Marseille, 2017), 261–76; Mircea Platon, 'Robespierre's *Eloge de Gresset*: Source of Robespierre's Anti-*Philosophe* Discourse', *Intellectual History Review*, 20 (2010), 479–502, and his 'Physiocracy, Patriotism and Reform Catholicism in Jean-Baptiste-Louis Gresset's Anti-*Philosophe* Enlightenment', *French History*, 26 (2012), 182–202; William R. Everdell, *Christian Apologetics in France, 1730–1790* (New York, 1987), 246–62; Jonathan Smyth, *Robespierre and the Festival of the Supreme Being: The Search for a Republican Morality* (Manchester, 2016), 13; Hugues Petit, 'Religion et terreur chez Robespierre', in Germain Sicard (ed.), *Justice et politique: La Terreur dans la révolution française* (Toulouse, 2021), 81–91; and, more fully, Joseph Waligore, 'God's Mighty Arm Makes the French Victorious: The French Revolutionary Deists Who Believed in Miracles', *Historical Reflections*, 50 (2024), 43–63.

veto. That failure, he asserted in an earlier speech to the Jacobins on 11 January 1792, was a failure to take up 'one of those unique opportunities in the history of revolutions that providence presents to men and that they cannot neglect with impunity'.[16] That neglect now meant that the Legislative Assembly faced an impossible choice between action and inaction because either course would play into the hands of the court. Inaction would cause military and political collapse and restored royal power. Action would place the initiative in the hands of the executive and give the king an opportunity to restore royal power. Long before the war began, Robespierre predicted that it would turn into a catastrophe. In this respect, his guidance came from Mably rather than Fénelon.

Providence, Robespierre argued, had supplied a unique opportunity to establish liberty. 'History, reason, everything tells us', he informed the National Assembly in April 1790, 'that nations have no more than one moment to become free. For us, that moment has arrived. You are those who eternal providence has destined to take advantage of that moment for the regeneration and well-being of peoples.'[17] In keeping with this insistence on an opportunity that could be lost, Robespierre argued consistently from 1789 onwards in favour of using public finance to enable every citizen to play an active part in public life. From one point of view, the argument was simply a rehearsal of other, more widely voiced calls to provide travel and attendance allowances for the many, often long drawn-out, electoral meetings that were a feature of public life after 1789.[18] But from Robespierre's point of view, using public funds in this way had a more ambitious moral and political objective. It was, he claimed, the real alternative to Sieyès's idea of representative government and the only way to secure full and continuous political accountability. Coupled with the principles underlying the attenuated right to private property that he set out in his draft Declaration of the Rights of Man of 10 May 1793, and the programme of redistributive taxation that, he envisaged, would be tied to the new, republican system of public

---

[16] Maximilien Robespierre, *Oeuvres complètes*, vol. 8 (Paris, 1954), 104.

[17] Robespierre, *Oeuvres complètes*, vol. 6 (Paris, 1950), 310.

[18] For an example, see Malcolm Crook, 'Citizen Bishops: Episcopal Elections in the French Revolution', *Historical Journal* 43 (2000), 955–76 (958).

education, it would give formal equality a real substance.[19] 'Despotism', he was reported to have said in August 1791, was preferable to what he called 'absolute representative government', where, he continued, the nation was no longer free nor, in any real sense, even in existence.[20] The 'bizarre system of absolute representative government', he repeated in October 1792, was 'the most unbearable of all despotisms' because it had 'no counterweight in the sovereignty of the people'.[21]

He had, he asserted in his famous attack on Dechristianisation on 21 November 1793, been a 'fairly poor Catholic' ever since his time as a student but he had never been 'a cold-hearted friend or unfaithful defender of humanity'. If God did not exist, he continued, echoing Voltaire, 'he would have to be invented' because 'the idea of an incomprehensible power that is the terror of crime and support of virtue' was a feeling shared by the common people of 'Europe, the universe and the French people'. Worship of that power was, in this simple sense, the foundation of morality and the basis of popular sovereignty.[22] Securing the sovereignty of the people meant, in the first place, recognising and overcoming the threat to its existence and, in the second place, identifying and reinforcing its real foundations. Importantly, and as in Rousseau, the threat to sovereignty came from the government or, as Robespierre put it, 'the passions of the magistrate, and government's tendency towards tyranny'. In the constitutional hiatus that followed the revolution of 10 August 1792, the government was a democracy and every member of the administration was a magistrate. But the multiplication of magistrates was a particular problem in the context of the war, the need to requisition supplies and the effects of requisitions on the availability and prices of subsistence goods. The resulting situation meant bringing price inflation under control by imposing a general maximum on the prices of subsistence goods and a broader range of essential commodities. But, as

---

[19] On these subjects, see Michael Sonenscher, 'Property, Community and Citizenship', in Mark Goldie and Robert Wokler (eds.), *The Cambridge History of Eighteenth-Century Political Thought* (Cambridge, 2002), 489–91.

[20] Robespierre, speech to the National Assembly, 10 August 1791, in Robespierre, *Oeuvres*, vol. 7, 615.

[21] Robespierre, *Lettres de Maximilien Robespierre à ses commettants* (19 October 1792), in Robespierre, *Oeuvres*, vol. 5, 19.

[22] Robespierre, *Oeuvres*, vol. 10, (Paris, 1967), p. 197.

Robespierre's political ally Louis-Antoine Saint-Just pointed out to the Convention on 10 October 1793, establishing a maximum was no more than an unavoidable necessity. Putting a ceiling on prices, he asserted, would simply benefit the rich because they had the financial resources to take advantage of the price freeze. It would also have the perverse effect of increasing the purchasing power of the agencies responsible for acquiring war supplies and, by making it easier for them to buy up supplies, would put an even tighter squeeze on popular consumption.[23] In this sense, the effects of imposing a maximum on prices pulled strongly against the need to maintain the unity of the democracy and made it more urgent to prevent the abuse of power by the republic's many magistracies. In itself, the maximum would magnify, not reduce, economic and political divisions.

This was why the same conception of democracy as magistracy became the premise of Saint-Just's call to make the republic's 'provisional government' revolutionary until an eventual peace settlement. 'The laws', he said, 'are revolutionary, those executing them are not'. This, he continued, meant that 'government is a perpetual plot (*une conjuration perpétuelle*) against the present order of things'. Ministers made appointments to offices (*emplois*) and their appointees did the same. The result was that government had become 'a hierarchy of errors and outrages'. If, Saint-Just asserted, 'one was to examine with severity the men administering the state, remarkably few of the 30,000 individuals employed would be those for whom the people would vote'. The present state of the government, he argued, ruled out constitutional rule. 'In the circumstances in which the republic finds itself, the constitution cannot be established. It would be turned by itself into ashes. It would become the guarantor of outrages on liberty because it would not have the violence needed to repress them.' This, Saint-Just concluded, was why 'you cannot hope for prosperity unless you establish a government that, restrained (*doux*) and moderate towards the people, will be terrible towards itself, because of the energy of its own internal relationships. It must press down (*peser*) on itself, not the people.'[24] In a democracy, if the magistracy went wrong,

---

[23] Louis-Antoine Saint-Just, *Oeuvres*, ed. Michèle Duval (Paris, 1984), 523.

[24] Saint-Just, speech to the Convention of 10 October 1793, also in *AP*, 76, 313, 315. For two further examinations of the complex conceptual compound involved in

everything went wrong. On these premises, the prime suspect of the law of suspects was, in fact, the government itself.

The other side of this suspicion of office and authority was trust in the *communes* and the virtues that they housed. Here too Saint-Just complemented Robespierre. 'The sovereignty of the nation', he wrote in his essay on a constitution for France in April 1793, 'resides in the communes'.[25] The essay and its accompanying constitutional proposals underscored the switch from endorsing a federation in 1790 to condemning federalism in 1793. As Saint-Just emphasised, the unity of the nation was paramount. To secure it, the constitution that he presented to the Convention would have a single, 341-member legislature elected for a period of two years by a unitary electorate made up of men aged twenty-one or over who could vote for anyone aged twenty-five or over. Although the electoral assemblies of the communes would be the basis of elections, the names and number of votes of those who topped the polls at the communal level would be tallied at the two higher levels formed by the arrondissements and departments. Those elected would not, therefore, represent particular departments or fractions of the population because the legislature itself would be made up of those with the highest number of votes within the nation as a whole. From this perspective, the system that Saint-Just envisaged was a scaled-up version of a republican city-state such as Machiavelli's Florence. Alongside a legislature that was the French equivalent of a Swiss or Italian great council, Saint-Just also envisaged a small council, this time elected for a three-year term. Unlike the national legislature, it would be elected on a departmental basis and would, accordingly, have as many members as there were departments. Its role and responsibilities would centre on the oversight and implementation of

justifications of Terror, see Anne Simonin, *Le déshonneur dans la république* (Paris, 2008) and Jean-Christophe Gaven, *Le crime de lèse-nation: histoire d'une invention juridique et politique (1789–1791)* (Paris, 2016) and also, more generally, see the fine review essay by Anne Simonin, 'Actualité de la terreur. L'apport des émotions à l'étude de la Révolution française', *Annales HSS*, 77 (2022), 673–701, and, earlier, Bronislaw Baczko, *Ending the Terror: The French Revolution after Robespierre* [1989] (Cambridge, 1994), together with his 'The Terror before the Terror? Conditions of Possibility, Logic of Realization', in Keith Michael Baker (ed.), *The Terror* (Oxford, 1994), 19–38.

[25] Saint-Just, *Oeuvres*, 427.

laws passed by the legislature and the enforcement of ministerial account-ability. It would, as Saint-Just described it, be a kind of intermediate power. It would have particular responsibility for monitoring the per-formance of military commanders appointed, however, by the national legislature. The executive itself would be made up of nine ministers, each responsible for their respective departments, but with no collective iden-tity, activity or accountability.

Saint-Just's constitutional proposals were the opposite of those pre-sented to the Convention by Brissot, Condorcet and the Girondins. Their proposals, he wrote, contained 'more precepts than laws, more powers than harmony, more movement than democracy'. It consisted, he con-tinued, of 'a *federative* representation that makes laws and a *representative* council that executes them'. Its outcome, he claimed, would be a legislature that would be divided and weak because its members were accountable primarily to the departments that elected them and a council that would be united and strong because it would develop a common interest against ministerial particularity. 'A council and ministers are two separate and heterogeneous things', Saint-Just asserted. 'Put them together and the people will need gods for ministers because the council will make the ministers inviolable and the ministers will leave the people with no guarantee against the council.' In a decade or two, he warned, liberty would be lost. 'The vision of the future that comes to mind is one of an executive power that is master of the republic and with liberty denuded of all sanction.'

The problem, Saint-Just argued, was a product of the Girondin concept of the general will. 'The general will', he explained, 'described properly and in the language of liberty is formed by the majority of individual wills collected individually without external interference. The law, thus formed, necessarily secures the general interest because if each will is based on each interest, the majority of wills gives rise to that of interests.' On these terms, the general will was plebiscitary all the way through. To Saint-Just, the Girondin concept was 'intellectual' and turned the general will into something 'purely speculative' resulting more in 'views of the mind than the interest of the social body'. Under the aegis of the imagin-ation, he continued, 'everything is altered and loses its natural form, creating as many liberties as the eyes create figures in the clouds'. The 'true principle' of the general will was 'the material will of the people' because this 'stimulated will' had the goal of 'securing the active, not the passive, interest of the greatest number'. Rousseau, 'in establishing the general will as the principle of laws, who wrote with his heart and wished the world all the good that he could only say', Saint-Just concluded, 'would never have dreamt that it could have a principle external to itself'.[26]

Much has been made of the difference between direct democracy and representative government in accounting for the Jacobin phase of the French Revolution. In the light of Saint-Just's constitutional proposals, it is worth asking whether this was the difference that mattered. What in fact mattered for Saint-Just was not the difference between representation and democracy but the difference between two distinct forms of representation. One was singular and national, while the other was plural and federal. Saint-Just endorsed the first, while Sieyès endorsed the second. In a superficial sense, Saint-Just's concept of representation was similar to Sieyès's concept of *adunation*. In both cases, the emphasis fell on the unity of the representative rather than on the variety and multiplicity of those represented. But where unity in Sieyès's system was formed by a single head of state, unity in Saint-Just's system was formed by a single national legislature and an electoral system designed deliberately to overcome local and social division. Unity for Sieyès came from the top-down; unity for Saint-Just came from the bottom-up. Both, it could be claimed, took their intellectual cue from Rousseau, but where Saint-Just (like Robespierre) took Rousseau to be a sociability theorist, Sieyès (like Kant) took Rousseau to be an unsocial sociability theorist.[27] These two different starting points gave rise to two different concepts of political society with, in the case of the first, the emphasis falling on the cohesion of community and, in the case of the second, the distinctions involved in individuality.

The differences applied initially to the subject of war. Before 1792, Sieyès endorsed the concept of a professional army, while Robespierre, echoing Rousseau, endorsed the idea of a citizen militia and applied the

---

[26] The passages are quoted in order from Saint-Just, *Discours sur la constitution de la France*, 24 April 1793 (Paris, 1793), 11, 13, 14, 15.

[27] Compare to Julien Boudon, *Les Jacobins: une traduction des principes de Jean-Jacques Rousseau* (Paris, 2006).

idea first to the National Guard and then to the subject of an *armée révolutionnaire*. The setbacks and uncertainties of the war that began on 20 April 1792 quickly caused these distinctions to disappear and, when they did, the resulting amalgamation formed a militarised solution to the problem of the relationship between the civil and military powers that Burke had highlighted. The amalgamation of the regular army and the civilian militia had already begun to take shape in the immediate aftermath of the flight to Varennes. On 21 June 1791, the National Assembly authorised the creation of battalions, of what were called 'national volunteers', from the National Guard to serve alongside the standing army. The process accelerated after the war began. On 4 July 1792, the Legislative Assembly issued a proclamation that the fatherland was in danger (*la patrie en danger*) and, a week later, authorised the enlistment of an additional 50,000 troops. Well before the establishment of the two most famous committees of the Convention, the Committees of Public Safety and of General Security, the Convention established a Committee of General Defence on 1 January 1793. On 23 August of that year, the Committee of Public Safety and the Convention established the system of conscription that remained in place for almost a generation. By then, it was no longer usual to associate the *sans-culottes* with satire and the streets. As Robespierre now insisted, they were an emblem of the nation in arms. In a superficial sense, the rise and fall of the *sans-culottes* matched the switch from Girondin to Jacobin political domination. More fundamentally, it matched the switch from Sieyès's to Saint-Just's version of representation.

The parallels and differences between Sieyès and Robespierre applied, more broadly, to their respective treatments of work. Monarchy is maintained, Saint-Just wrote, for as long as half the people work and the other half adopt thrift instead of virtue. 'The French monarchy perished', he continued, 'because the rich class disgusted the other of work. The more work or activity there is in a state, the more that state is strengthened.' Any division between those who worked and those who did not created opportunities for patronage, favours and advantages. Under a 'popular government', he asserted, magistrates had no favours or patronage to offer and, because they could not corrupt anyone, mores and manners could take root more readily. With a popular government, everyone was free and everyone worked.[28] For Sieyès, work mattered too. It did so, however, not so much to fortify community as to promote freedom. For Saint-Just, work gave rise to social integration. For Sieyès, with his watchwords *jouir plus, travailler moins*, work gave rise to individual emancipation. Ultimately, as Diderot (echoing Hume) had shown, utility mattered to both. But, for Sieyès, as for other largely German-speaking readers of Rousseau, the *Marseillaise* had qualities that went beyond utility. The problem of establishing a political system compatible with all three evaluations was one of the legacies of the French Revolution.

[28] Saint-Just, *Discours*, 10. Although Saint-Just's concept of an institution was not at issue, see also Arnaud Le Pillouer, *Les pouvoirs non-constituants des assemblées constituantes. Essai sur le pouvoir instituant* (Paris, 2005).

CHAPTER TEN

The War for the World: Social Science and Imperial Power

By the summer of 1794, the store of examples, precepts and precedents that was available from the past had partly permeated the present. The concept of a *droit de commune* that was used to underpin the fall of the Bastille and the establishment of the National Guard went on to be used to assert the political entitlements of the network of communes in Paris and provincial France and justify the rival claims of Paris over the provinces or the provinces over Paris at the height of the conflict between Jacobins and Girondins in 1793. The idea of a Hebrew republic that once stood either for a combination of divine sovereignty and civil magistracy or for absolute monarchy and its Monarchomach alternatives was later invoked not only to justify the civil constitution of the clergy as a closer approximation to the original church but also to question the compatibility between the monarchy and a republic and, echoing Tom Paine, to highlight the old, but now new, salience of democracy to the modern age. The figure of a *sans-culotte* that was initially applied satirically to the world of salons, urbanity, the queen and the court was associated subsequently with the entitlements of industry, the precariousness of poverty and the power and presence of the politically excluded both at home and abroad. The existence and survival of the first French republic established by the insurrection of 10 August 1792 and the French military victory at Valmy on 20 September 1792 had, after two further Parisian insurrections on 31 May and 5 September 1793, come to be identified with evocations of the Roman republic, the politics of necessity and justifications of Terror as the order of the day.[1] By the winter of 1794–95, one

---

[1] For a fine, but neglected, collection of essays on Rome's presence before and during the French Revolution, see Mouza Raskolnikoff, *Des anciens et des modernes* (Paris, 1990).

of the few genuine innovations of the whole period – the *assignat* and the paper currency that came to bear its name – had lost almost all of its original value, and trapped within the competing imperatives of the empire, the emigration and the electoral system, the new engine of equality fell gradually, then rapidly, into total disuse. Only the division of France into eighty-three departments stood as a largely abstract and administrative monument to the end of the Old Regime and the events of 1789. By the summer of 1794, Saint-Just's private note to himself that the revolution was frozen was a fairly literal description of how things had become.[2]

A more fiercely disabused description of the situation in that summer came from Joseph Cambon, the president of the French republican Convention's committee of finance and one of the growing number of Robespierre's increasingly vocal critics. 'How', he was reported to have said in 1794,

> will you be able to deal with what you have to deal with? Guillotine! How will you be able to pay for the immense costs of your fourteen armies? Guillotine! How will you pay for the maimed, the mutilated and all those who have a right to demand assistance? Guillotine! How will you be able to amortize your incalculable debts? Guillotine, guillotine, and guillotine again![3]

As Cambon clearly intended, it was not an enticing formula and was also likely to be self-defeating. The insurrection that produced the events of 9 Thermidor of the Year II (27 July 1794) and gave rise to Robespierre's fall was followed by a further, far more chaotic settling of accounts than the guillotine could supply. There were street fights in Paris, murders in former royalist or federalist zones of support in southern, eastern and western France, and deep divisions among the surviving membership of the Convention and its committees over the direction and content of future policy. The gravity of the situation was magnified by a harvest failure and a winter that was far more severe than anything that had

---

[2] Louis-Antoine Saint-Just, *Oeuvres complètes*, ed. Charles Vellay, 2 vols. (Paris, 1908), vol. 2, 508, and, for commentary, see Ferenc Feher, *The Frozen Revolution: An Essay on Jacobinism* (Cambridge, 1988) and, subsequently, Ferenc Feher (ed.), *The French Revolution and the Birth of Modernity* (Berkeley, 1990).

[3] On the pronouncement, see Henri Wallon, *Histoire du tribunal révolutionnaire de Paris*, 6 vols. (Paris, 1880), vol. 5, p. 290.

occurred in 1788–89. Three large popular insurrections in Paris on 1 April, 21 May and 5 October 1795, calling in the case of the first for the implementation of the constitution of 1793 and, by the time of the third, for a restoration of the monarchy, turned the future of the first French republic into a very open unsettled question.

The question hung over the new political arrangements established after Robespierre's fall. The Constitution of 1795 with its provisions for a five-man executive Directory, a two-chamber legislative system made up of a Council of Five Hundred and a Council of Ancients and a proliferating panoply of administrative agencies made the new French regime look like a revival of the older mixed or balanced system advocated earlier by Mounier and the Monarchiens. It also, however, made it look like those existing in Britain and the United States, the two countries with which France was actually or potentially at war. As the war continued, so too did the question about the long-term prospects of the Directory and its ability to avoid defaulting either into a restored monarchy (as was also sometimes predicted of the United States) or into further civil violence. Two developments, however, became the basis of an answer. The first was the sheer scale of the warfare in which France was involved. The second was the collapse of the *assignat* in 1795. The first development raised the prospect of a fully militarised society, comparable in size and centralised power to imperial Rome but subject as well to the vicissitudes of transfer-ring authority from one military leader to the next, which, as Montesquieu argued, played a significant part in the decline and fall of the Roman Empire. The second development raised the even more alarming prospect of no society at all, as harvest failure was magnified by hyperinflation and political fragmentation was reinforced by the first signs of social collapse. The different types of threat represented by these two developments gave rise to a new range of assessments of the intellec-tual legacy of the eighteenth century, centred partly on the still opaque content of Montesquieu's *The Spirit of Laws*, partly on the new subject of political economy, and partly on the thought of Jean-Jacques Rousseau.

The concept that came to encompass this mixture of retrospective assessment and prospective policy was *science sociale*, or social science. Underlying the term was a more substantial and durable division over whether the concept referred to morality or politics and, by extension, over whether, in light of the Jacobin experience, it could identify where and how to set limits on state power. Behind this division was a deeper question about whether social science was simply a new name for what, earlier, was called natural jurisprudence or the law of nature and nations or, more substantively, whether it could add a new content into those earlier names. This latter question arose because social science seemed to rely more fully on claims about the relationship of human physiology, gender differentiation and, more problematically, human diversity to the sexual and emotional foundations of society than those available in the famous seventeenth-century treatises of natural jurisprudence of Grotius, Hobbes, Pufendorf and Locke. It was less clear, particularly in the context of the Napoleonic wars, whether this new range of subjects meant that social science was designed to underpin or overcome the politics of a divided world. The arguments that arose over these radically different assessments made the subject of social science one of the more durable components of the range of competing questions and answers carried forward from the French Revolution into the nineteenth century. One indication that it really could be distinguished from natural jurisprudence was a new, largely secular, approach to the nature of the family and, in particular, to the origins and nature of what came to be called the bourgeois family. In this largely Rousseau-inspired setting, thinking about the family became as much a matter of physiology, emotions and gender as of sacraments, law and property.

The growing range of questions and answers surrounding the concept of *science sociale* also arose from discussions of the joint bearing of the thought of Rousseau and Sieyès on the politics of the French Revolution and, in parallel, from a revival of interest in the thought of Etienne Bonnot de Condillac and his brother Gabriel Bonnot de Mably as authors of a more morally capacious and economically egalitarian alternative to the social and political arrangements associated with the thought of Rousseau and Sieyès. The resulting juxtaposition of the thought of Rousseau and Condillac on the philosophical side and of Sieyès and Mably on the political side ensured from the start that what came to be called *idéologie* meant something both like and unlike what it still means now. In one guise, ideology meant simply the study of ideas. In another guise, however, it meant something more like explaining or unmasking illusion or uncovering realities hidden by mistaken beliefs. The uncertainty surrounding the content and implications of ideology fed into the concurrent uncertainty over the concept of social science. Together, they meant that if many assessments of the intellectual legacy of the eighteenth century were sometimes critical or hostile, they did not add up to a putative end of enlightenment.[4] Instead, they meant that much of the speculation about the future that preceded the events of 1789 continued to be rehearsed in a modified idiom and, more substantively, with a modified range of concepts.

In this context, it was not so much a range of subjects from the past that came to have a bearing on the significance and future possibilities of the French Revolution as the subject of the French Revolution itself. This was most immediately visible in the new connotations given to the concept of a revolution. By 1830, it was clear that, in asking whether the events of 1789 were a revolt rather than a revolution, Louis XVI had made a category mistake. It was also apparent in the new array of largely secular connotations given to words that end in -ism. Instead of Catholicism, Protestantism, Calvinism or Jansenism, there was now Jacobinism and Royalism, followed shortly by industrialism, utilitarianism, socialism, liberalism, romanticism, nationalism and communism. There was also a more specialised range of new names for old subjects, such as *macrobiotics* for the study of reform or the process of bringing societies back to moral and political health, *technology* for the study of mechanised techniques and *cybernetics* for the study of the dynamics of international politics or, as it later came to mean, the art of turning initially separate things into integrated components of managed organisations such as firms, states and, potentially, a whole world system.[5] Only then, after developments like these, did the old religious concept of enlightenment begin to

---

[4]   Compare to Richard Whatmore, *The End of Enlightenment* (London, 2023).

[5]   The term 'macrobiotic' was coined (as *Makrobiotik*) by Christoph Wilhelm Hüfeland, *Die Kunst das menschliche Leben zu verlängern* [1797], translated as *The Art of Prolonging Life* (London, 1853), xi–xii. Cybernetics and technology appear in André-Marie Ampère, *Essai sur la philosophie des sciences* (Paris, 1834); see also Michele Kennerly, 'Cybernetics in the Republic', *History of Human Sciences*, 36 (2023), 80–102. Thanks to Béla Kapossy and Anthony Lanz for alerting me to these developments. On technology (but without Ampère or cybernetics), see Eric Schatzberg, *Technology: Critical History of a Concept* (Chicago, 2018), 1–15, and Arthur M. Melzer, Jerry Weinberger and M. Richard Zinman (eds.), *Technology in the Western Political Tradition* (Ithaca, 1993).

give way in the nineteenth century to the more historically bounded concept of *The Enlightenment* together with the more programmatic or pejorative connotations generated by the addition of the definite article.

This mixture of continuity and discontinuity was particularly visible in the concept of social science itself. As the periodical *L'Historien* (edited by the economist and former member of the French National Assembly Pierre-Samuel Dupont de Nemours) reported in its issue of 10 December 1795, the decision by the newly established French Institute to add the 'analysis of sensations and ideas', 'morality' and 'social science and political economy' to the established subjects of philosophy, history and geography complicated the new institution's intellectual remit. 'We confess', *L'Historien* commented,

> that we do not have a very clear idea of the difference between *social science* and *political economy*. All that we can imagine is that the scholars responsible for cultivating the one or the other may be able to establish a subdivision, and think of political economy as social science applied to administration and to legislation on agriculture, manufacturing, trade, public works, navigation, taxation, or all the means required to make families subsist and nations prosper.

Although the Institute's plan appeared to indicate that social science was intended to go alongside legislation, all the subjects associated with social science, *L'Historien* pointed out, were not exactly 'alien' to the subject of legislation. This seemed to suggest, the periodical reported, that 'the authors of this classification must have understood *social science* to be the law of nature and nations, and restricted *legislation* to the section on constitutional legislation in which they placed it, even though this latter seems, itself, to belong to the science of political economy'.[6] These uncertainties, the article concluded, showed how difficult it was to classify human knowledge and how much more was still needed to clarify their relations.

Behind the uncertainty was a deeper division that became visible in the related concept of ideology. This division arose from the way that the respective treatments of the imagination by Rousseau and Condillac were carried through into two different versions of the concept of social

---

[6] *L'Historien*, 19 (19 Frimaire an IV/10 December 1795).

science. The differences arose from two different accounts of the origin of language. For Condillac, languages grew out of signs which, in turn, were a product of a need to communicate needs. For Rousseau, needs isolated, while desires integrated. Desires were generated by the mind rather than the body and by the imagination rather than sensation. As Rousseau described it, the imagination made it possible to think and feel about things that, in a straightforwardly natural or material sense, did not really exist, such as a society, a state or a self, because things like these had a value and affective presence that was sometimes more powerful than their physical properties. As, on the other hand, Condillac described it, the imagination was at once less powerful, because it was common to both animals and humans, but also more treacherous because it could turn imagined subjects into simulations of reality. Condillac gave the process the name of 'realisation', a name that he probably took over from the thought of the early eighteenth-century German philosopher Gottfried Wilhelm Leibniz, who used the term to explain how, as he put it, 'eternal truths' that 'have their existence in a certain absolute or metaphysically necessary subject, that is, in God', were made available as impressions, perceptions and ideas so that, as Leibniz explained, 'those things which would otherwise be imaginary are realized, to use a barbaric but graphic expression'.[7]

For Condillac, humans did the opposite because, unlike God, they could not distinguish their truths from eternal truths. On this basis, realisation amounted to claiming that partial, human truths were absolute, eternal truths. Condillac went on, accordingly, to argue that memory, with its capacity to store, arrange and retrieve the signs produced by sensations, supplied the means to counter the effects of realisation. As he presented it, memory supplied the distinctions and judgements that the imagination could not supply. From this perspective, social science was an analytical science. It relied on making critical assessments of abstract concepts by

---

[7] Gottfried Wilhelm Leibniz, 'On the Ultimate Origination of Things' [1697], in G. W. Leibniz, Roge Ariew, and Daniel Garber, (eds.), *Philosophical Essays* (Indianapolis, 1989), 152. For a helpful summary of the Rousseau-Condillac discussion of language and its origins, see Paul Janet and Gabriel Séailles, *Histoire de la philosophie: les problèmes et les écoles* [1887], 3rd ed. (Paris, 1899), 248–50. See also Avi Lifschitz, *Language and Enlightenment: The Berlin Debates of the Eighteenth Century* (Oxford, 2012), 39–48 (particularly p. 47, n. 25).

using the resources of language and memory to deconstruct the clusters of signs and sensation on which the concepts themselves relied. Rousseau's treatment of the imagination was different because, he argued, it was an acquired rather than a purely natural capacity. It did not arise at birth, but started to make its presence felt at the onset of puberty when sexuality and sociability began to overlap. On Rousseau's terms, the imagination was a gendered faculty right from the start. If, as he emphasised, it was the key source of the self because it supplied the reflexive capacity that turned *amour-de-soi-meme*, or care for oneself, into *amour-propre*, or care for one's status, its origins in the physical differences between male and female sexuality made the resulting self a gendered self.

These differences were carried through into differences within ideology and social science. Condillac's analytical treatment of the imagination, memory and knowledge was adopted most fully by one of the most prominent Ideologues and Thomas Jefferson's friend Antoine Louis Claude Destutt de Tracy, while Rousseau's more gendered treatment of the imagination became the basis of the famous study of the *Rapports du physique et du moral de l'homme* ('Physical and Moral Relationships in Mankind') published in 1805 by Condorcet's brother-in-law Pierre Jean Georges Cabanis. Neither was a slavish imitator of their respective precursors. Destutt de Tracy's interests fell more strongly on the compound quality of signs and their aggregates than Condillac had indicated, while Cabanis's interests fell more strongly on the physiological causes and effects of the emotions than Rousseau had done. In this respect, Cabanis was closer intellectually to Sieyès, Condorcet, Pierre-Louis Roederer and Jean-Baptiste Say, together with Condorcet's widow, Sophie de Grouchy, and her physiologically oriented and gendered commentary on Adam Smith's *Theory of Moral Sentiments*. Destutt de Tracy, on the other hand, was closer to their more rationally oriented critics. In this respect, the differences between Cabanis and Destutt de Tracy were as marked as those between Rousseau and Condillac. 'Of all the writers to have said things about women', Cabanis commented, 'Jean-Jacques Rousseau seems to me to have best unravelled their natural inclinations and understood their true destiny'. He 'painted nature with an inimitable veracity', Cabanis wrote, later rehearsing Rousseau's observation that, with puberty, the imagination became 'the dominant faculty' in humans.[8] Nothing like this type of claim appeared in the works of Destutt de Tracy.

The gulf between Rousseau and Condillac that gave rise to different versions of ideology and social science was paralleled by the gulf between Rousseau and Mably that was carried through into different assessments of the relationship between domestic politics and international relations. These differences centred on three main subjects. The first, and least controversial, was the subject of the nobility. The second, and more controversial, was the subject of the state and the question of the type of political society to which a new, reformed nobility would belong. The third, and most controversial, was the subject of property, trade and finance. The three subjects lay at the heart of the differences between Rousseau and Mably before the French Revolution. They remained at the heart of the differences between critics and supporters of the empire that was proclaimed in 1801, less than three years after the military coup organised by Sieyès on 9 November 1799 (18 Brumaire Year VIII) that brought Napoleon Bonaparte to power. The most visible evidence of the differences underlying these three subjects was the strong endorsement of the empire headed by Charlemagne that was a feature of Mably's thought. As Mably described it, Charlemagne's empire was the archetype of an extensive system of republican government, headed by 'a prince who was simultaneously a philosopher, a legislator, a patriot and a conqueror'.[9] It was a republic not only because, as in Rousseau, the term could be applied generically to almost any political society but also because, under Charlemagne, the monarch was not the sovereign.

The constitutional core of this version of a republic was a revived and more stable version of the ancient republican assemblies of the Franks. Under Charlemagne's aegis, and as the French people came to 'possess a very extensive territory', each county of the empire came to depute a dozen representatives every autumn to a closed meeting on the *Champ de Mars* followed, in May, by a general assembly of the bishops, abbots,

---

[8] Pierre Jean Georges Cabanis, *Rapports du physique et du moral de l'homme* [1805], in Pierre-Jean-Georges Cabanis, *Œuvres philosophiques*, 2 vols. (Paris, 1956), vol. 1, 299, 226 & 176 (in order of citation). On Destutt de Tracy and Condillac, see, for example, the adulatory footnote in his *Projet d'élements d'idéologie* (Paris, 1801), 127–8.

[9] Gabriel Bonnot de Mably, *Observations sur* l'histoire *de la France [1765]*, in his *Oeuvres*, vol. 1, p. 221.

counts, lords and deputies of the people, sometimes deliberating separately, sometimes as a single body, so that, as Mably put it, 'there can be no doubt that the legislative power resided in the body of the nation', with the king as its executive head.[10] The outcome was a huge territorial republic made up of myriads of largely self-governing units. In it centralisation would give way to decentralisation and government would revert to something more like the combination of a royal executive and a decentralised network of estate- and commune-based legislatures that had existed before the Bourbon ascendancy and the rise of absolute government. It also meant that the new Napoleonic nobility would be based on service rather than inheritance and that the assortment of titles, running from prince to baron of the empire, that was established in 1806 and ratified in 1808 would belong to individuals rather than families or lineages. To become hereditary, special application would have to be made to establish, and finance, a *majorat,* or what in English law was something like a perpetual trust.[11] In flat contradiction to Montesquieu's earlier controversial endorsement of venal office, the Napoleonic nobility meant that the connection between money and honour would, finally, be broken.

Importantly too, the size and scale of this new version of Charlemagne's republican empire meant that foreign trade would become domestic trade and, consequently, that trade would begin to lose the competitive edge built into the struggle between separate states for economic and military survival. Reinforcing economic reciprocity and limiting economic competition meant that there would be more room for redistributing resources at home and for international arbitration and adjudication abroad. In the case of the first, Mably made no secret of his endorsement of Harrington's vision of a modern version of the Hebrew republic. In the case of the second, Mably also emphasised that the law of nations was 'but a slender safeguard to each particular society'.[12] It had, therefore, to be reinforced by a positive system of durable alliances. This

[10] Mably, *Observations,* in his *Oeuvres,* vol. 1, p. 229.

[11] On the Napoleonic nobility, see Jean Tulard, *Napoléon et la noblesse d'Empire* [1979], new ed. (Paris, 2003), particularly pp. 85–105.

[12] Gabriel Bonnot de Mably, *Phocion's Conversations or the Relation between Morality and Politics* [1763] (London, 1769), 142.

was why Mably entitled his very successful commentary on the modern, post-Westphalia, treaty system *Le Droit public de l' Europe*, or 'The Public Law of Europe'.[13] The potential for the existence of this international system meant that there had to be a powerful, but just, state (one not wedded to the illusory maxim that money was the sinew of war) to uphold the system's stability, just as the Spartan republic had done in the ancient world. Mably's vision of equality and merit at home and justice and arbitration abroad is said to have appealed greatly to Napoleon.[14]

There was real common ground between Mably and Rousseau's concepts of nobility. Both were merit based and non-hereditary. As has been shown in an earlier publication, Rousseau, with his proposal to create a Court of Honour as a solution to the problem of duelling, established the initial idea for what became the Napoleonic Legion of Honour.[15] But Charlemagne was not a presence in Rousseau's system. Nor was the idea of a republican hegemon as the key to international stability visible in his thought. Rousseau certainly gestured towards the idea of a federation, but it was a federation made up of separate states comparable in this respect to the NATO-like alliance advocated earlier in the eighteenth century by Charles Irénée de Castel, abbé de Saint-Pierre, that Rousseau discussed in two separate examinations of Saint-Pierre's thought. As Rousseau described it, Saint-Pierre's project for perpetual peace looked as if it was a chimera, but its insistence on the inviolability of state boundaries, irrespective of differences in size, endowments or levels of economic development, made it possible to reformulate the idea of a federation as a variation on the balance of power. With fixed boundaries, states would have to grow from within but, with limited domestic resources, they would also have to trade. Trade, however, would be more than a matter of large single markets with convergent prices for goods and services as Mably, echoing his brother Condillac's *Le commerce et le gouvernement considérés relativement l'un à l'autre* ('Commerce and Government Considered in Relation to One Another') of 1776, envisaged. Separate states would mean potentially different trade and payments balances as well as

---

[13] Gabriel Brizard, 'Eloge historique de l'abbé de Mably', [1787], reprinted in Mably, *Oeuvres*, 15 vols. [Paris, 1794–5], (Aalen, 1977), vol. 1, p. 99, note b.

[14] Frédéric Masson, *Le Sacre et le couronnement de Napoléon* (Paris, 1908), 63, 78.

[15] Sonenscher, *Before the Deluge*, 15, 78–9, 81, 84, 86–7, 91, 96; *Sans-Culottes*, 161–4.

potentially different trade policies and tariffs that would then have to be offset by fiscal and monetary adjustments. Rousseau acknowledged and accepted all these constraints, particularly in his posthumously published works on Poland and Corsica. Money, accordingly, would have to be more than a simple measure of value or a medium of exchange. These two functions were certainly adequate for a large single market, but, as Rousseau recognised, money also had to function as a reserve currency, or capital, if it was to meet the needs of international trade and payments balances. Gold was the usual reserve currency because it was accepted everywhere, but it was also possible to envisage the use in domestic transactions of other currencies, including an artificial currency like the new French franc, provided that they maintained their value by means of a positive tax-take, positive trade and payments balances, and positive oversight by a central bank like the newly established Banque de France.[16]

The divergences between Mably, Condillac and Rousseau meant that the foundational properties of both social science and ideology were fissured from the start. The implications of Rousseau's thought were picked up and amplified not only by Sieyès but also by Jean-Baptiste Say, Cabanis, Roederer and much of the more physiologically oriented section of the Ideologue cluster. The same applied to the implications of Condillac and Mably's thought and amplified its resonance within much of the more socially and intellectually oriented section of the same Ideologue cluster. The differences among the Ideologues did not exhaust the distinctions. If Mably's followers could endorse a large, relatively centralised republic, while Rousseau's followers could endorse a large central bank, some of Napoleon's strongest admirers rejected both a centralised republic and a central bank but still endorsed the qualities and status of a single leader. It was a position that applied particularly to Charles Fourier, the first advocate of the right to work. France, he warned, 'will not always have a ruler *of such outstanding greatness*', but would still have to face the lethal combination of commerce, inequality and sexual exploitation driving modern civilisation. As one of Fourier's followers, the Franco-Peruvian author of the *Peregrinations of a Pariah* Flora Tristan later wrote, the problem with Napoleon was that

---

[16] On the Banque de France, see Crouzet, *La grande inflation*, 527–59 and Jean Bouvier, *Un siècle de banque française* (Paris, 1973).

he was a man.[17] The real solution to the problem of modern civilisation would be a female Bonaparte.

Long before Flora Tristan, however, another solution had been rehearsed. This one appeared in a pamphlet entitled *La Voix du citoyen* (The Voice of the Citizen) that was published early in 1789 as the political deadlock that preceded the fall of the Bastille began to take hold. Its author, Charles-François Lebrun, had been an advisor of the French chancellor René-Nicolas de Maupeou in the last great demonstration of royal authority in France in 1772 and now presented his pamphlet as a warning about what could happen if it was impossible to find a solution to the monarchy's financial problems.[18] Instead of a royal *coup*, Lebrun wrote, there would be a popular *coup* that, finally, would end up with what Lebrun called a legal despotism or, as he implied by publishing his pamphlet again in 1814, something like the empire established by Napoleon. In 1789, however, when he first published his pamphlet, he began by predicting that the representatives of the nobility and the clergy at the forthcoming Estates-General would refuse to accept fiscal equality, leaving the Third Estate alone to address the problem of the debt. But the Third Estate might well refuse to do so and could then precipitate a bankruptcy whose effects, Lebrun emphasised, would be catastrophic. A bankruptcy would either destroy public power, leaving no social ties and no nation at all, or, if France did manage to survive, its weak and divided state after the collapse of public credit would make it the most insignificant of all European powers.[19] But in this extremity, Lebrun concluded, patriotism would come into its own and, taking up the ancient republican maxim that the public safety should be the supreme law (*salus populi suprema lex esto*), would do whatever was necessary to preserve the French state. It would sacrifice the nobility and the clergy to the

---

[17] On Fourier and Napoleon, see Charles Fourier, *The Theory of the Four Movements*, eds. Gareth Stedman Jones and Ian Patterson (Cambridge, 1996), 207 and, on the right to work, 192, 262–3, 263–70. On Flora Tristan, see Máire Fedelma Cross, *The Letter in Flora Tristan's Politics, 1835–1844* (London, 2004), 98.

[18] On Lebrun, see Louis Laisney, 'Un Normand qui a influé sur les destinées de la France de Louis XV à Louis XVIII. Charles François Lebrun (1739–1824)', *Revue du département de la Manche*, 15 (1973), 121–240, and the introduction to Charles François Lebrun, *Opinions, rapports et choix d'écrits politiques* (Paris, 1829), v–xv, 3–168.

[19] Lebrun, *La voix du citoyen* (Paris, 1789), 83.

'tumultuous equality' of democracy. And if democracy was to fail, France would still find a way to ensure that it was not effaced from among the European powers. A 'determined *leveller*' would emerge from within the Third Estate and found a new constitution on the ruins of the old (Lebrun, who had spent some time in England, deliberately used the English-language word).[20]

This new constitution would set the true scale of society's needs and fix the true level of taxes. Not content with the destruction of the nobility and the clergy, this 'audacious leveller' would summon the citizenry to even greater liberty and prosperity. But he 'would lack the authority needed for his beneficent views'.[21] At every step, perpetual meetings would distract the people from industry, agriculture and commerce, generating a general desire (*voeu général*) to entrust him with all public power. A 'legal despotism', Lebrun asserted, would ensure that 'our common chains would be riveted to the trunk of legislation', allowing a new kind of monarchy to rise up on the ruins of the old social order.[22] The parallel between the prediction and the actual course of events was sufficiently close for Lebrun to republish his pamphlet in 1814, supplemented by a two-page preface saying that 'the reasonable and liberal hopes' expressed in 1789 were now soon to be realised.[23] It was, it could be said, Lebrun's final verdict on the French Revolution even if it was not the last announcement that the revolution was over to be made in the nineteenth and twentieth centuries. By the time that it was republished in 1814, Lebrun's call for a legal despotism had begun to pass into the category of speculation about the future that was soon to be consigned to the oblivion of the past.

[20] Lebrun, *Voix*, 84.   [21] Lebrun, *Voix*, 85.   [22] Lebrun, *Voix*, 85.

[23] Lebrun, *Voix* (Paris 1814), ii. For continuation of this type of speculation, see Antoine Madrolle, *La Sagesse profonde et l'infaillibilité des prédictions de la révolution qui nous menace, démontrée par l'accomplissement littéral des nombreuses prédictions de la révolution qui nous est arrivée* (Paris, 1828) and, later, his *Tableau de la dégénération de la France, des moyens de sa grandeur, et d'une reforme fondamentale dans la littérature, la philosophie, les lois et le gouvernement* (Paris, 1834).

CHAPTER ELEVEN

Conclusion: The Legacy

In a loose sense, it is not particularly hard to make a list of the several possible legacies of the French Revolution. The Declaration of the Rights of Man may have lost its gendered undertones but it has lived on more resonantly than the later, more historically grounded, Declaration of the Rights of Nations presented to the Convention by Henri Grégoire, bishop of Blois, in 1793 and 1795. For Grégoire, the latter was a reply to the former. 'Reason', he asserted in introducing its text, 'has passed judgement both on those extravagant individuals who talked of a universal republic and on those deceitful men who made a profession of loving men set at a distance of two thousand years or two thousand leagues to avoid having to be just and good towards their neighbours. Systematic, de facto cosmopolitanism is mere moral or physical vagabondage.'[1] As Grégoire's now largely forgotten declaration was designed to suggest, the tension between universalism and imperialism has not gone away. Nor, in a related sense, has Robespierre's concept of a revolutionary government. It too has lived on either as an aspiration for a new start or as a warning about what transitions can be. The moral ambiguity surrounding both sets of concepts goes some way towards indicating how hard it still is to reconcile morality, history and politics. In addition, and in a more straightforward sense, large parts of the legacy of the French Revolution still remain to be explored. It is not clear, for example, what kind of connection there might have been between the largely forgotten *droit de commune* invoked in 1789 and the insurgent, but still self-defensive,

---

[1] For the text, see Guillaume N. Lallement, *Choix de rapports, opinions et discours prononcés à la tribune nationale depuis 1789 jusqu'à ce jour*, 21 vols. (Paris, 1818–23), vol. 15, 230–9. For commentary, see Sonenscher, *Before the Deluge*, 177–8.

Paris Commune of 1871 as well as the place of the concept of the *droit de commune* within the broader history of the National Guard in both France and the United States over much of the nineteenth century. There is also a history still to be written of the figure of the war veteran in Restoration France and the array of images, arguments and entitlements that, beginning with the work of the poet and *chansonnier* Pierre-Jean Béranger, helped to turn the legacy of the first modern conscript army into one of the major forces of modern politics not only in nineteenth-century France but also, for example, in Germany, the United States, Russia, Israel and Zimbabwe in the twentieth and twenty-first centuries.

In a more immediate sense, Lebrun's vision of a 'determined *leveller*' armed with an ability to deal with a crisis was one of the more abiding legacies of the French Revolution. As Bonapartism, Caesarism or Boulangism, it remained alive for long into the nineteenth century. Even the version of French socialism associated with Claude-Henri de Saint-Simon and Prosper Enfantin, with its emphasis on the idea of a leader as 'the living law', continued to resonate to this fusion of morality, power and popular politics. A second and equally recognisable version of the legacy of the revolution also appeared in the nineteenth century. 'The history of modern France', wrote the Cambridge academic Goldsworthy Lowes Dickinson in 1892, 'is the history of the Revolution of 1789'.

> That Revolution is not yet completed; 1793, 1799, 1814, 1830, 1848, 1851, 1870, are so many dates of its advance and recoil. Becoming transformed itself in the process of transforming France, it has been gradually defining in practice its own theoretic ideal, limiting itself by the act of realization, and substituting for its airy vision of Utopia the solid and measurable structure of the Third Republic. That that Republic is not the term of the process will probably be admitted by anyone who has studied the history of parties and ideas in France, but it is the present halting-place and the present verdict of the facts on the scope and achievement of the movement of which it is the latest expression. With the Revolution, then, must begin, as with the Third Republic it must end, a book whose endeavour is to render intelligible the history of modern France.[2]

---

[2] Goldsworthy Lowes Dickinson, *Revolution and Reaction in Modern France* (London, 1892), p. 3. I have modernised the punctuation on the basis of the third, 1927, edition, here at p. 17.

The words, written towards the end of the nineteenth century, can still look familiar in the early twenty-first century because, although the Third Republic is now the Fifth Republic, they could have been written by François Furet, Lucien Jaume or Marcel Gauchet. Not much, it seems, has changed.

A third, equally familiar, version of the legacy of the revolution appeared three years after the publication of Lowes Dickinson's book. It was published in 1895 by the Italian Marxist Antonio Labriola in an article commemorating the fiftieth anniversary of the publication of *The Communist Manifesto*. Humanity, he wrote, has only one history but, given humanity's immensity, variety and duration, it was not really possible to identify the laws underlying its formation and development. Bourgeois society, however, was another matter. It was a whole society that, like feudal society, had an entirely self-standing set of characteristics. It was, Labriola wrote, 'a society that transforms all the products of human labour into commodities by means of capital, a society that presupposes or creates a proletariat and brings with it the restlessness, anxiety and uncertainty of continuous innovation'. These characteristics could be identified in many different times and places but, Labriola asserted, they were all laid out together within a single historical event at the time of the French Revolution. 'That great revolution', he wrote, 'offers the most dizzying and intense example of historical action that can ever be known and this makes it, therefore, the most instructive school of sociology (*la plus grande école de sociologie*)'.[3] The French Revolution, Labriola concluded, was a microcosm of human history, even though the phrase *révolution bourgeoise* (bourgeois revolution) only became current long after it began. As it was put by one of Labriola's contemporaries, Max Weber, it was an 'ideal type' of what a revolution could be. Alternatively, as the French Revolution was described on the basis of a more hostile evaluation of the dynamics of democratic politics, made by another of their contemporaries, a combative Catholic sociologist

---

[3] Antonio Labriola, 'En mémoire du Manifeste du parti communiste', *Le devenir social*, 1 (1895), 225–52, 321–44, 335–6, reprinted in his *Saggi sul Materialismo Storico* (Rome, 2000), 33–88. On Labriola, see Fernanda Gallo, *Hegel and Italian Political Thought: The Practice of Ideas, 1832–1900* (Cambridge, 2025), 99–108, 220–40, 247–8.

named Augustin Cochin, 'the rats were already there, well before the cheese appeared'.[4]

Much has been said, particularly in the twentieth century, about the question of whether, or how far, any of these characterisations of the French Revolution have been historically accurate or heuristically useful. A more illuminating question, raised at about the same time as these assessments by Dickinson, Labriola, Weber and Cochin, was the more fundamental question of why the French Revolution was given such enduring historical significance and why, whether positively or negatively, it could continue to carry so powerful a moral charge and so divisive a political presence. One set of answers to this second type of question focussed on the intractable quality of the issues that, well before the French Revolution, set Diderot against Roussseau. Each could accuse the other of moral and political hypocrisy because each also had a plausible case to make. For Diderot, the formal equality involved in states, governments and the rule of law was no match for the real inequalities generated by property, inheritance and cumulative social advantage. For Rousseau, the kind of community produced by morality, justice and social equality was no match for the power of governments, the imperatives of competition and the politics of necessity. From either perspective, the world as it is seems to call either for more power or more morality.

For Diderot, Rousseau's claim that the very existence of human society amounted to a kind of Fall was doubly disingenuous. It overstated the human capacity for self-sufficiency on the one side and underestimated the scale of resources required for political survival in a competitive world on the other. On Diderot's terms, Rousseau's thought magnified, not minimised, inequality. For Rousseau, Diderot's claim that the reciprocities built into human society amounted to an antidote to empire, inequality and injustice was also doubly disingenuous. It overstated the human capacity for self-government on the one side and underestimated the scale of moral cohesiveness and financial resources needed to establish and maintain real political independence in a world made up of states, competitive markets and volatile financial systems. On Rousseau's terms,

---

[4] For further discussion, see Michael Sonenscher, 'The Cheese and the Rats: Augustin Cochin and the Bicentenary of the French Revolution', *Economy and Society*, 19 (1990), 266–74.

Diderot's thought heralded anarchy, not order, and promised despotism not liberty because it had no institutional capacity to manage the imperatives of emergency or the politics of crisis government. Only in the early twentieth century, with the thought of Georg Jellinek and Max Weber in Germany and Maurice Hauriou in France, did it begin to become clear that the choice was not binary. As Hauriou put it, modern states had to house both a property system and an electoral system because the distinctive attribute of modern states was that the two systems were separate but connected. This, as Jellinek indicated, was why modern states had to be seen as things with two sides and, as Weber emphasised, why the two sides made up of the property system and the electoral system had to rely on both bureaucracy and charisma.

A second set of answers focussed on the number of unresolved issues left over from the French Revolution in both France and the wider world. There was, most immediately, the problem of legitimating the restored French monarchy not only in terms of the rights and powers of Louis XVIII versus those of the French nation and its members but also in terms of the size, composition and entitlements of those eligible to vote or be elected. There was also the question of the relationship between the Napoleonic nobility, the nobility of the Old Regime and the nobility of the Restoration. Behind these immediate problems were the broader problems of the relationship between the post-revolutionary French state and the post-revolutionary French church and, equally intractably, the relationship between France, Britain and the largely disintegrating Portuguese, Dutch, Spanish and Ottoman Empires in Africa, Asia and the Americas. As these problems began to take their toll, what was envisaged initially as a Fénelon-inspired Holy Alliance against Bonapartist despotism turned into a Metternich-dominated Holy Alliance against national self-determination, popular government and political reform.[5] As Dickinson (and, later, Furet) rightly emphasised, these issues remained unsettled at least until the establishment of the French Third Republic and, in the case of votes for women, until the establishment of the French Fourth Republic.

[5] Isaac Nakhimovsky, *The Holy Alliance: Liberalism and the Politics of Federation* (Princeton, 2024).

In a more durable and deeper sense, there was also the problem of the huge scale of property transfers that had taken place during the period of the French Revolution and Napoleonic wars. It raised many potentially intractable questions of retribution and restitution that remained alive for long into the nineteenth century. One set of questions applied to the property that was confiscated from the church or from noble and other *émigrés*. They centred on the competing claims of the current and former owners of the property and on whether the solution to these antagonistic claims was to opt for retribution, restitution or compensation. None of these options was painless. All of them indicated that the problematic relationship between constitutional government and public debt that Hume had highlighted in 1752 was as much a part of modern politics as of the politics of the Old Regime. The difficulties and dilemmas involved in opting for some mixture of restitution, retribution or compensation played into the furious argument over what was called the *milliard des émigrés* (or the *émigrés*' billions) in the years before the revolution of 1830, which then turned into a further argument over the putatively covert influence of the famously wealthy *deux cent familles* (two hundred families) in the years before the revolution of 1848. Opting for restitution meant either confiscating land presently owned by the purchasers of nationalised property or adding to state expenditure by buying them out. Opting for compensation for former noble or clerical landowners still meant adding both to state expenditure and the burden of taxation. Every course of action appeared to entail adding to the size of a public debt already inflated by the reparations payments imposed by the victorious allied powers after the Battle of Waterloo. It was not hard, in this light, to claim that the new regime was simply the Old Regime, or that the old aristocracy had become the new plutocracy or, particularly after 1830, that where property and inequality were concerned, Robespierre was right.

From this perspective, the aftermath of the French Revolution was as subject to the logic of interactive causation as its pre-revolutionary counterpart. As in 1789, politics after 1815, 1830, 1848 or 1871 were exposed to the pressures generated by changing economic circumstances, rising bourgeois aspirations, developing institutional weaknesses, mounting international pressures, faltering political legitimacy, growing ideological criticism, lingering religious antagonisms, increasing class conflict or an emerging public sphere. Tocqueville underlined the point in 1856.

Appearances notwithstanding, he wrote, the new regime was actually the Old Regime, armed with the authority of administrative law and the power of a centralised state.[6] But, as in 1789 too, there were also ideas and the part that ideas could play in adding something extra to the logic of interactive causation. Here, it could be said, this part of the legacy of the French Revolution was genuinely unprecedented. It was visible, for example, in the new cult of the war veteran, popularised in France by the poet and singer Pierre-Jean Béranger, celebrated in Britain by a proliferation of newly established brass bands and spreading over subsequent centuries throughout the world from the United States to Russia and Zimbabwe. It gave rise, particularly in the German-speaking parts of Europe, to a number of new and different ways of thinking about history, one that could include things thought to be possible, but which never actually happened, together with things that were unexpected, but which really did occur. Towards the end of the nineteenth century, this way of thinking about history became part of an imposing distinction established by the German philosophers Wilhelm Windelband and Heinrich Rickert between what was said to be nomothetic – or subject to causal laws or mechanisms, as is the case in the physical, chemical or biological sciences and their many derivatives and offshoots – and what was said to be ideographic – or what is not, or not entirely, subject to causal laws or mechanisms because they are, recognisably, singular, particular, separate or distinct.[7] There have, for example, been many revolutions but there is still only one French Revolution and not only because of the dates. In fact, in the case of the French Revolution, the dates are part of the singularity, because the 14 July 1789, 9 Thermidor Year II or 18 Brumaire Year VIII have a more than purely chronological significance and a place alongside the many other things that made the French Revolution what it was, from the Marseillaise to the *Tricolore* and from the prose of Sieyès to the music of Rouget de l'Isle or the paintings of Jacques-Louis David.[8]

---

[6] For amplification, see Michael Sonenscher, *After Kant: The Romans, the Germans, and the Moderns in the History of Political Thought* (Princeton, 2023), 487–90.

[7] Heinrich Rickert, *Science and History: A Critique of Positivist Epistemology* (Princeton, 1962) and his *The Limits of Concept Formation in Natural Science* (Cambridge, 1986), including the introduction by Guy Oakes, vii–xxx.

[8] For the significance of a date, see Colin Jones, *The Fall of Robespierre: 24 Hours in Revolutionary Paris* (Oxford, 2021). On David, see, recently, Norman Bryson,

This, to end this short book at the point at which it began, is why ideas matter. Bringing ideas into history makes it possible to bridge the gap between singularity and generality more fully and completely than can otherwise be done. The point was first made by the German philosopher Johann Gottlieb Fichte in the context of a lecture course on the significance of the French Revolution entitled *The Characteristics of the Present Age* that he published in 1806, a year before Hegel published his *Phenomenology of Spirit*. Although Fichte published his lecture course before Hegel published his book, it is tempting to think that Fichte was getting in his retaliation first. In his lectures, Fichte coined the term 'facticity' to describe the things that give history its peculiar content.[9] The term was designed to highlight the radically factual character of history because, as Fichte knew, words that end in 'icität' in German or 'icity' in English are used mainly to indicate the compressed essence of a thing, such as in 'authenticity', 'simplicity' or 'multiplicity'. Facticity, in Fichte's usage, was a word like this. History, in this light, was factual all the way through and it was this quality that gave it its facticity. 'This rule', Fichte wrote, 'that we can accept as proved only so much of the earlier fact as is absolutely necessary for the comprehension of the now-existing fact, is to be taken strictly'. Facticity, he emphasised, ruled out conjecture. 'In all sciences', he continued, 'and particularly in history, it is of greater importance to understand how much we do not know than to fill up the void with fiction and conjecture'.[10] To Fichte's modern editors, the comment was aimed at the conjectural histories produced by the eighteenth-century philosophers Christian Wolff and Moses Mendelssohn, although it could, equally plausibly, have been aimed at Rousseau or, perhaps in anticipation, at Hegel.

Hersilia's Sisters. Jacques-Louis David, Women, and the Emergence of Civil Society in Post-Revolution France (Los Angeles, 2023) and Sébastien Allard (ed.), *Jacques-Louis David* (Paris, 2025).

[9] On facticity, see François Raffoul and Eric Sean Nelson (eds.), *Rethinking Facticity* (New York, 2008), particularly the chapter by Theodor Kisiel.

[10] Johann Gottlieb Fichte, *The Characteristics of the Present Age [1806]* (London, 1844), Lecture IX, in Fichte, *Popular* Works, 2 vols. (London, 1889), vol. 2, 151, and in Fichte, *Le caractère du l'époque actuelle [1806]*, ed. & trans. Yves Radrizzani (Paris, 1990), 149.

Facticity for Fichte was, nonetheless, more complex than it might seem because the baseline for the existence of history was a hypothetical society named as Normal People. The name has often been taken to mean something morally normative, but this was not entirely what Fichte meant by the name. His point, instead, was simply to indicate that independent of time, place, culture and history, a human could normally be identified as human (as is still the case with, for example, a French *école normale*, meaning a school that is not technical, legal or theological because its only attributes are that it is a school and follows the norms that make a school a school). The people who Fichte described as normal had, accordingly, all the characteristics of the inhabitants of Rousseau's state of nature because they were solitary, silent and self-sufficient. As Fichte put it, 'there was no history among the Normal People and there is no history of them'. History began when something disrupted the uninterrupted sequence of facts built into this eternal present. 'History', Fichte wrote, 'takes cognizance only of the new, the wonderful, or that which can be contrasted with what comes before and what comes after it'.[11] There were, in short, facts, but there were also facts that could be contrasted to those that came either before or after. These facts had a value or a significance and this extra quality was as factual a matter as the facts themselves. It gave them, however, a capacity to inject value and significance into the passage of time and this, Fichte emphasised, was where history began. 'Now', he wrote, 'for the first time could the process of the free development of the human race begin and with it, history, the record of the unexpected and the new which accompanies such a process'.[12]

Fichte made this claim about history as the medium housing the free development of the human race in the context of a course of lectures intended to show why the French Revolution mattered both for the present age and for posterity. His interest in trying to understand and explain the mixture of routine and rupture involved in thinking about history was matched in the work of several of his contemporaries. To the royalist Louis de Bonald, something like the same mixture supplied

---

[11] Fichte, *Characteristics*, in Fichte, *Popular* Works, vol. 2, 148, and in Fichte, *Le caractère de l'époque actuelle*, ed. Radrizzani, 144.

[12] Ibid.

a basis for thinking about the differences between religious societies, commercial societies and authentically political societies. To the advocate of industrialism Claude-Henri de Saint-Simon and to the apostle of sociology, his dissident disciple Auguste Comte, the mixture supplied a basis for thinking about organic, critical and positive ages in human history. The parallel was more obvious in the work of Georg Wilhelm Friedrich Hegel, both in his *Phenomenology of Spirit* and in his later, posthumously published, lectures on world history. Although there were real similarities between all these conceptions of history, Fichte's distinction between facticity and conjecture was later picked up and used against some of Hegel's more conjecturally or teleologically oriented followers, first by the mid-nineteenth-century German philosopher Hermann Lotze and subsequently by Lotze's admirers Wilhelm Windelband and Heinrich Rickert.[13] In their publications, Fichte's distinction between facticity and conjecture fed into their distinction between the nomothetic and the ideographic but came gradually to be overwritten by a further set of distinctions made initially by one of Rickert's students, a philosopher named Emil Lask in a doctoral thesis entitled 'Fichte's Idealism and History' published in 1902, and, subsequently, by two of Lask's university friends and intellectual associates, the future Marxist philosopher György Lukacs and the future Nazi philosopher Martin Heidegger. Cumulatively, these examinations of Fichte's coinage 'facticity' remain one of the more significant legacies of the French Revolution. They contain almost all the conceptual resources still to be found in historical writing in more recent times.

Fichte's initial insistence on history as 'the record of the unexpected and the new' or something that 'takes cognizance only of the new, the wonderful' and 'comes between and can be contrasted with what comes before and what comes after' helps to throw fresh light not only on these later philosophical developments but also on the history and historiography of the French Revolution itself. Fichte's point was that history was – or is – this mixture of novelty and causality. Both parts of the mixture add

---

[13] For an illuminating examination of this line of thought, see Claude Piché, 'Hermann Lotze et la genèse de la philosophie des valeurs', *Les Etudes Philosophiques* (Issue 4, 1997), 493–518. On Hegel and history, see Richard Bourke, *Hegel's World Revolutions* (Princeton, 2023).

up to facticity. Without the novelty, there is simply causality, or causation all the way through. Without the causality, there is simply novelty, or conjecture all the way through. History, however, has both. This, Fichte also emphasised, meant that both the novelty and the causality had to be identified and explained. If everything was new and wonderful, then, logically, everything was already always old and familiar. But if everything was already old and familiar, then, equally logically, causation encompassed everything. Facticity, however, encompassed both. It did so in ways that, by definition, were sometimes new and wonderful but sometimes old and familiar. On Fichte's terms, this meant that history was a kind of palimpsest, made up of myriads of layers of both sides of facticity.

This, finally, is why ideas matter. Bringing them into the picture makes it possible to integrate fact and value, routine and rupture, the ordinary and the extraordinary, into a single narrative. There is no need here to go into a more detailed description of Fichte's explanation of how the two sides of facticity could be distinguished from one another while, at the same time, being parts of the same fact. All that is required at this juncture is to see that the distinction between facts and values can be applied quite readily to the same thing. Dinner, for example, is different from breakfast even though both are meals, food, nutrition, calories or diet. Fichte's explanation of how the same things could have different meanings, significance or values followed this line of thought because it had a great deal to do with freedom and with the different labels that can be attached to things. This meant, as Fichte went on to show, that freedom and facticity were two sides of the same coin because, however intermittently or unpredictably, freedom was connected to value. Facticity had something to do with evaluation as well as experience, making both value and experience parts of the subject matter of history. As Fichte also showed in his more analytically philosophical publications, freedom does not have a determinate content of its own because, if it did, it would become indistinguishable from causation. Most parts of history, however, have a largely causal content, from food and diet to laws and governments, even though some parts, surprisingly, do not. For Fichte, freedom established a distinction between causation and creation that would not otherwise be there. Freedom was, in short, a limiting concept. It imposed a limit on both creativity and causality by drawing a line between the magic of creativity and the routine of causation. Once there, it enabled the two to coexist.

This, to rehearse the initial point of this essay for the very last time, is why ideas matter. Fichte's coinage, facticity, captures something of the tension between values and causes that was involved in the frequently violent events of the French Revolution. Both are facts but facticity encompasses them both. Sometimes values overlap with causes producing either causation or speculation all the way though. Sometimes, however, the two fall apart and become separate and ordinary narrative, like ordinary politics, reaches its limits. This is why it is worth finding out about ideas. They have as much to do with creation as causation, with evaluation as much as experience and with possibility as much as actuality. Although they are part of events, they can be overtaken by events. They can point to the future, but be pulled out of the past. They can supply a precedent, but can create the unprecedented. Louis XVI was not a patriot king, but was once taken, notably by Maximilien Robespierre, to be a possible patriot king. Kings, according to Saint-Just, do not reign innocently but, as many of his contemporaries knew, the Hebrew judge Samuel made the point first. This is also why contexts count. It helps to know that the system of election that Sieyès called a system of gradated promotion had a pedigree in Rousseau's thought. It also helps to know that the early nineteenth-century socialist slogan about replacing the government of men by the administration of property was coined in 1772 by one of Sieyès's contemporaries, the comte de Chastellux, who, in his *De la félicité publique* (or 'An Essay on Public Happiness' as the contemporary English translation was entitled), also made a point of emphasising that in the modern, as against the ancient world, everything was done by means of representation.

Ideas provide clues to contexts and contexts, in turn, help to make the ideas more precise. Jacques-Pierre Brissot was not a *sans-culotte*, but still set out to win the allegiance of people who, before they came to be called *sans-culottes*, were once called *bourgeois de Paris* and, it was said, were entitled to a *droit de commune*. Inversely, many of those later called *sans-culottes* were, according to one of the original progenitors of the name, the journalist and satirist Antoine-Joseph Gorsas, actually fake *sans-culottes*. Maximilien Robespierre was, as he said, a poor Christian, but could still see that something about Fénelon's Christology meant that more than a cult of reason was required to secure a general will. Napoleon Bonaparte was not Charlemagne, nor even a determined *leveller*, but part of the history of the French Revolution turned on the possibility that labels like these had the potential to create something new and different from things as they were. Fichte's concept, facticity, was designed to capture this extra level of value and significance. Importantly, however, it was also designed to identify and explain both sides of the mixture of experience and evaluation, or causation and creation, that the concept implied. On these terms, there are no shortcuts. There is simply history, with its abiding injunction to find out more about events and ideas, not only, but certainly also, in the French Revolution.

adunation, 183

Aiguillon, Emmanuel Armand de
Vignerot du Plessis, duc d', 67

Alembert, Jean Le Rond d', 16, 139

amour-de-soi-même
in Rousseau, 130, 207

amour-propre
in Rousseau, 130, 207

André, Antoine-Joseph, baron d'
and negotiations with court, 153

Anglophiles
and Americanophiles, 147

Argenson, René-Louis Le Voyer,
marquis d', 96

armées révolutionnaires, 7, 184

army,
and Ségur ordinance, 89
conscript, 215
reform of, 89, 90, 98, 102

Artois, comte d', 154
and memorandum of the princes, 92

assignat, 8, 101, 109, 132, 140, 184
and citizenship, 135
and Clavière, 111
emissions of, 112
monetization of, 175
origins of, 112
supporters of, 155

Aubert de Vitry, François-Philibert, 106,
107

*Jean-Jacques Rousseau à l'Assemblée
Nationale*, 106

Babeuf, François-Noel (Gracchus), 10

Bailly, Jean-Sylvain, 108, 111, 165
and church property, 109, 110

Bancal des Issarts, Jean-Henri, 98

bankruptcy, royal, 33

Barnave, Antoine-Joseph, 100, 132, 165,
174
and Adam Smith, 151
and bicameral legislature, 139
and emigration, 154
and flight to Varennes, 138
and life peerages, 148
and Marie Antoinette, 148
and Sieyès, 100
and trade, 173
as client of Marie Antoinette, 160
on *assignat*, 113
on emigration, 152
on empire and emigration, 151
on Sieyès, 148
on slavery, 152
secession from Jacobins, 150

Barruel, Augustin, 18

Bastille, fall of, 6, 20, 31, 99, 178
and *fête de la fédération*, 143

Bayle, Pierre
and Boulanger, 123

Beccaria, Cesare, 121

Bentham, Jeremy, 17, 173

Béranger, Pierre-Jean, 215, 220

Bernardin de Saint-Pierre, Jacques-Henri

    and Rousseau, 119

bicameralism

    Barnave on, 149

Boissel, François, 59

Bolingbroke, Henry Saint-John, viscount,

    62

    and patriot king, 57

Bonald, Louis de, 222

Bonaparte, Napoleon, 225

    and Sieyès, 74

Bonneville, Nicolas, 98

Bordeaux, 64

Bossuet, Jacques Bénigné, 62

Boulanger, Nicolas-Antoine, 16

    and Diderot, 123

bourgeoisie

    characterisations of, 168

    Chénier on, 168

    Gorsas on, 169

    Pétion on, 168

breeches, 20, 108, See *sans-culottes*

Brienne, Etienne Loménie de, 4

Brissot, Jacques-Pierre, 64, 129, 132, 177,

    225

    and *assignat*, 113

    and Bentham, 173

    and constituent power, 106

    and Diderot, 160

    and king's trial, 157

    and Louis XVI, 156

    and *sans-culottes*, 160, 162

    case for war, 157

    on America, 175

    on war, 176

Britain, 57

    public debt in, 36

Brothers, Richard, 45

Burke, Edmund, 32, 34, 49, 57

    on National Guard, 145

    Reflections on the Revolution in France, 66

Cabanis, Pierre-Jean-Georges

    and Condorcet, 207

    on women, 207

Caesar, Julius, 42

Calonne, Charles-Alexandre de, 3, 52, 53,

    55, 57, 62, 87, 111

Cato, the Censor, 41

causation, 68

    and creation, 71

    and unintended consequences, 71

    problems of, 69

centralisation

    and decentralisation, 115

Chambon de Montaux, Nicolas, 182

Champs de Mars

    massacre of, 150, 162, 176

Charlemagne, 225

Chas, Jean

    and constituent power, 106

Chastellux, François-Jean, comte de, 119,

    225

Chénier, André

    on bourgeoisie, 168

Chesterfield, Philip Dormer Stanhope,

    Earl of, 40, 51, 62

    and Mably, 41

    on public debt, 40

    prediction of revolution, 40

Choiseul, Etienne-François, duc de, 67

Christ, 26, 56, 124

    and Christology, 225

Christian doctrine

    and the Fall, 26

church, 102, 115

church property. *See* property

    and *biens nationaux*, 109

    sale of, 143

citizenship
  active and passive, 135, 140, 142
  and assignat, 135
  and taxation, 141
civil war, 20, 107, 159, 164, 170, 171
  Mably on, 165
  Mercier on, 165, 172
civilisation
  concept of, 30
Claude, Jean, 26
Clavière, Etienne, 111
  and America, 175
  and *assignat*, 140
  and deficit, 156
  and emigration, 155
  on French economy, 175
Club de l'évêché
  and Jacobins, 162
Club de la sainte-chapelle
  and Feuillants, 162
clubs, *See* Jacobins
Cochin, Augustin, 217
colonies
  and empire, 136
communes, 195
Comte, Auguste, 223
Condillac, Etienne Bonnot de, 16, 203
  and language, 206
  Le commerce et le gouvernement considérés relativement l'un à l'autre, 210
  on memory and analysis, 80
  Rousseau on, 80
Condorcet, Marie-Jean-Antoine-Nicolas de Caritat, marquis de, 87, 119
  and civil war, 164
  on citizenship, 141
constituent assembly, 88
constituent power, 19, 102, 115, 131, 133, 181
  after 1789, 135
  ambiguiities of, 131

and government, 134
and historiography of French Revolution, 134
and public debt, 105
and Sieyès, 81, 103
Aubert de Vitry on, 107
defined, 132
Duport on, 136
in Aubert de Vitry, 106
in Ramsay, 104, 119
in Ramsay and Harrington, 104
in Ramsay and Hume, 118
in Sieyès, 134
Robespierre on, 138, 139, 181
Sieyès on, 135
constitution
  British, 65
  ratification of, 88
  Saint-Just on, 195
constitution, democratic
  Rousseau on, 116
consumption
  and Diderot effect, 126
Coquéau, Claude Philiberet, 182
counterfactuals, 70
Couthon, Georges, 7
credit
  public and private, 35
crisis, 29
criticism
  enlightenment, 69, 70
Croce, Benedetto, 12
Cromwell, Oliver, 9
cult of reason, 8
cybernetics, 204

debt, 115
debt-default, 19, 51
dechristianisation, Robespierre on, 193
decimation, 22
  Roman concept of, 23, 155

Declaration of the Rights of Man, 214
Declaration of the Rights of Nations, 214
decline and fall, 29, 30
deficit, 6, 7, 102
    royal, 3
Delolme, Jean-Louis, 65
democracy, 20, 73
    Rousseau on, 133
democratic constitution
    Rousseau on, 83
Der Geschlossene Handelstaat (Fichte), 185
Desmoulins, Camille, 98
despotism, Robespierre on, 193
Destutt de Tracy, Antoine-Louis-Claude
    and ideology, 207
deux cent familles, 219
Dickinson, Goldsworthy Lowes, 215
Diderot, Denis, 16, 139, 217
    and 'Diderot effect', 126
    and *genre sérieux*, 125
    and Hobbes, 131
    and Ramsay, 129
    and Rousseau on Hobbes, 129
    Essai sur les règnes de Claude et de Néron,
        128
    on commerce, 129
    on Morellet and Beccaria, 122
    on political economy, 123
    versus Rousseau, 124, 217
distribution, 37
division of labour, 82, 131
    and constituent power, 119, 120
    and occupational specialisation, 117
    and separation of powers, 117
    Sieyès on, 116
    Smith and Rousseau on, 121
droit de commune, 19, 20, 95, 140, 183, 214
    and militia, 97
    Argenson on, 96
    in 1789, 96
    interpretations of, 95

Mably on, 96
Ducos, Roger, 74
Dumas, Mathieu
    and emigration, 153
Dupont de Nemours, Pierre-Samuel, 72,
    87, 182, 205
Duport, Adrien, 100, 153, 165, 184
    and *assignat*, 141
    and constituernt power, 114
    and sale of church property, 110
    on *assignat*, 113
    on constituent power, 136

économie populaire, 185
elections
    of 1791, 162
electoral system
    versus property system, 218
eligibility
    for election, 140
emigration
    and empire, 135, 155, 172
    and French finances, 143
    French, 22
émigrés
    as outlaws, 155
    property of, 172
empire
    and emigration, 135, 172
    and slavery, 152, 174
    French, 22
    loss of, 143
    Napoleonic, 7
Enfantin, Prosper, 215
enlightenment, 15, 16, 18
    and The Enlightenment, 14, 18, 19, 50,
        204
    concepts of, 14, 15, 20, 34
    Condillac and Diderot on, 16
    Diderot on, 16
    end of, 204

equality, 184, 217
   versus inequality, 217
Essay on the Constitution of England (1776).
     See Delolme
Essay on the Right of Property in Land
     (Ogilvie), 182
estates, 3
Estates-General, 5, 51
   composition of, 5
   in Memorandum of Princes (1788), 92
   Mably on, 44
Évêché club, 182
events
   and causation, 69
   ordinary and extraordinary, 68
events, significant, 20

facticity, 71, 226
   Fichte on, 224
Fall, the, 15, 61
fashion's empire
   and Diderot effect, 126
federalism, 184
fédéré, 184
Fénelon, François de Salignac de la
     Mothe, 15, 16, 56, 62, 107, 192, 218
   Adventures of Telemachus, 56
Festival of the Federation, 52
fête de la fédération, 143, 178, 183
Feuillants, 100, 132, 136
   and abolition of noble titles, 101
   and end of the Old Regime, 101
   and Girondins, 156
   failuire of, 149
   politics of, 100
   secession of, 150, 153, 162
Fichte, Johann Gottlieb, 71, 185
   and historicity, 221
finance, French, 32
finance, public
   and international capital markets, 91

financial crisis 1788, 5
France
   state of, 63
Franklin, Benjamin, 108
Frederick II (of Prussia)
   as patriot king, 91
freemasonry, 15
French Revolution
   and enlightenment, 18
   historiography of, 22, 33, 38, 50, 204,
     215, 216, 219, 220, 223, 226
Frossard, Benjamin Sigismond
   on slavery, 174
Furet, François, 216
   and historiography of French
     Revolution, 135

Gasquet, Hyacinthe de, 64
Gauchet, Marcel, 216
general will, 73, 84, 133
   and particular wills, 85
general will, Saint-Just on, 196
Geoffrin, Louise de
   and *culottes*, 127
   and *sans-culottes*, 164
Gilbert, Nicolas
   and *sans-culottes*, 160
Gillies, John
   on Frederck II of Prussia, 91
Girondins, 100, 128
   and Feuillants, 132
   and Jacobin club, 165
   and *sans-culottes*, 161
glory
   in Hobbes, 129, 130
Gorsas, Antoine-Joseph, 225
   and Feuillant-Jacobin split, 167
   and Pétion, 169
   and *sans-culottes*, 165, 169
   and satire, 165
   as *sans-culotte*, 170

Gorsas, Antoine-Joseph (cont.)
  Mais! Qu'est-ce qu'un sans-culotte?, 177
  on bourgeoisie, 168
  on *sans-culottes*, 178
government
  and rule, 86
  and sovereignty, 115, 133
  constitution of, 88
  hereditary, versus elected, 87
  in Rousseau, 84
  in Sieyès, 86
  representative, 86
  revolutionary, 186–90, 194, 214
  Rousseau and Sieyès on, 78
Gracchi, 41
grace
  and the Fall, 61
gradated promotion
  and Rousseau, 143
  Barnave on, 108
  Rousseau on, 82
  Sieyès and, 99
grande nation
  and *civitas maxima*, 96
grande peur (Great Fear), 98, 143
Great Elector
  Sieyès on, 79
Grégoire, Henri, 214
Groethuysen, Bernard
  and *esprit bourgeois*, 124
Grotius, Hugo, 18, 60
Grouchy, Sophie de
  on Adam Smith, 207
Guibert, 49
Guibert, Jacques-Antoine-Hyppolite,
    comte de
  on revolution, 46
Gustavus III, of Sweden, 29

Harrington, James, 20, 106
  and Rutledge, 107

and constituent power, 104
  and Hume, 76
  and Joseph Saige, 146
  and Sieyès, 75
  on property and power, 116
Hauriou, Maurice, 218
Hebrew republic, 165
Hegel, Georg Wilhelm Friedrich, 2, 117,
    221, 223
Heidegger, Martin, 10, 13, 223
Helvétius, Claude-Adrien, 16, 17, 87
  and Brissot, 129
  on sociability, 129
Henri IV
  as patriot king, 57
history
  and facticity, 221
  and historiography of French
    Revolution, 220
  as comparative history, 13
  as contemporary history, 12
  Fichte on, 223
Hobbes, Thomas, 18
  and sociability, 129
  intellectual legacy, 130
Holbach, Pierre-Paul Thiry, baron d'
  Théologie portative, 60
Holbach, Pierre-Paul Thiry, baron d', 16,
    119
Holy Alliance, 218
honnêtes gens
  and *sans-culottes*, 160
Hume, David, 37, 57, 219
  and concept of constituent power, 103
  and Diderot, 119
  and Harrington, 76
  and Ramsay, 103
  and standard of taste, 126
  Idea of a Perfect Commonwealth, 76
  moral theory, 123
  on public debt, 38, 47

ideas
  and events, 225
  and historiography, 221
  as events, 50
  as evidence, 11, 50
ideology, 16, 203
imagination
  Rousseau and Condillac
    on, 205
inequality, 65, 107
insurrection
  10 August 1792, 20
  Parisian, 6
Israel, 58

Jacobin club, 7, 59, 94, 100
  disintegration of, 165
Jansenism, 61
Jaume, Lucien, 216
Jefferson, Thomas, 48, 49, 181, 207
Jellinek, Georg, 218
justice, 37, 217

Kant, Immanuel, 15
  and Rousseau, 130
king's party
  versus queen's party, 93
kings
  in ancient Israel, 58
Koselleck, Reinhart, 135

Labriola, Antonio, 216
Lafayette, Marie-Josephe-Paul-Yves-Roche
  Gilbert du Motier, marquis de, 65,
  108, 145, 149, 150, 174, 177
Lameth brothers, Alexandre, Charles and
  Théodore de, 100
Lameth, Charles de, 110, 153, 165
  on sale of *biens nationaux*, 110
land
  in Physiocracy, 37

language
  origin of, 206
Lask, Emil, 223
Law, John, 112, 185
  and *assignat*, 113
law, living, 215
Le Chapelier law
  and petitions, 150
Le Chapelier, René-Guy, 152
Lebrun, Charles-François, 212
  La voix du citoyen, 212
Lebrun, Pons-Denis-Ecouchard (also
  known as 'Pindar' Lebrun), 52, 53, 55
legislator, 133
  in Rousseau, 83, 133, 134
legislature
  bicameral, 147
Leibniz, Gottfried Wilhelm, 16
  and Condillac, 206
levée en masse, 7
leveller, 225
Liberté, Egalité, Fraternité
  and Robespierre, 142
life-peerage
  Barnave and, 139
Locke, John, 18, 62, 106
  and religion of the magistrate, 103, 105
Longwy, battle of, 180
Lotze, Hermann, 223
Louis XIV, 53, 60
Louis XV, 4, 53, 67, 68, 171
Louis XVI, 3, 9, 20, 24, 25, 28, 52, 79, 99,
  132, 145, 147, 151, 154, 163, 177,
  180
  and Estates-General, 92
  and Henri IV, 56
  and Mirabeau, 153
  and street demonstration of
    20 June 1792, 163
  as patriot king, 53, 55, 225
  coronation of, 68

Louis XVI (cont.)
  execution of, 68
  flight of, 70
  Robespierre on, 56
Louis XVIII, 218
Lukacs, Georgy, 223
luxury, 116
  and Diderot effect, 126

Mably, Gabriel Bonnot de, 39, 41, 49, 51,
    62, 87, 107, 192, 203, *See* also
    Condillac
  and managed revolution, 42
  and modern monarchy, 43
  and revolution, 41, 48
  and the politics of necessity, 42
  De la législation, ou principes des lois, 51
  Des droits et des devoirs du citoyen, 41,
    170
  Le droit public de l'Europe, 210
  Observations sur l'histoire de France, 96
  on Charlemagne, 208
  on civil war, 107, 170
  on Roman republic, 41
Machiavelli, 60, 195
macrobiotics, 204
Madison and Washington
  compared to Necker and Lafayette,
    66
majority rule
  in Sieyès and Rousseau, 85
Mallet du Pan, Jacques-Pierre, 33, 34, 93,
    138
Maréchal, Sylvain
  Le jugement dernier des rois, 59
Marie Antoinette, 20, 25, 132, 147
  and cake, 25
  and diamond necklace affair, 90
  as patron, 160
market
  versus the state, 37

Marseillaise
  and Rouget de Lisle, 178
Marseille, 64
Marx, Karl, 9
Maupeou coup, 4, 21, 32, 53, 89, 91, 97
maximum, 193
Mazzei, Filippo, 87
Mendelssohn, Moses, 221
Menou, Jacques-François
  and church property, 110
mercantile system, 29
Mercier, Louis-Sébastien, 107, 185
  and Brissot, 160
  and civil war, 164
  Fragments de politique et d'histoire, 171
  L'an 2440, rêve s'il en fut jamais, 171
  Notions claires sur les gouvernments,
    171
  on civil war, 171
Metternich, Klemens Wenzen, von, 218
militias. *See* National Guard
milliard des émigrés, 219
Milton, John, 27
  on revolt, 26
Ministry of the Hundred Hours, 6
Mirabeau, Honoré Gabriel de Riqueti,
    comte de, 27, 29, 74, 99, 137, 165
  death of, 139
  and bicameral legislature, 147
  and royal court, 147
  on assignat, 112
  on emigration, 153
Mirabeau, Victor Riqueti, marquis de, 29,
    30, 36, 39, 107
  and Rousseau, 79
  on election and inheritance, 79
Miranda, Francisco
  and Brissot, 176
mixed system, 65
moi (self)
  in Rousseau, 131

Molière
  in Gorsas, 166
Monarchiens, 65, 143, 165
monarchy
  and reform. *See* also Mably
  Montesquieu on, 36
money, 185, 186
  concepts of, 35
money as a sign
  versus money as a value, 35
Montesquieu, Charles-Louis de Secondat,
    baron de, 18, 19, 36, 37, 38
  and *Samuel*, 59
  and veil over liberty, 154
  History of the Troglodytes, 59
  on public debt, 36
  The Spirit of Laws, 22, 73
Montlosier, comte de, 24
morality, 217
Morellet, André, 87, 119
  translation of Beccaria, 121
Mounier, Jean-Joseph, 65, 143,
    165

narratives
  and events, 69
nation
  in Sieyès, 86
National Guard, 101, 102, 143, 215
  and army, 136
  and Barnave, 149
  and citizenship, 140, 141
  and *droit de commune*, 98
  and Lafayette, 145
  composition of, 135, 141
  Robespierre on, 142
natural disasters
  and theocracy, 124
natural jurisprudence, 18
necessity
  politics of, 217

Necker, Jacques, 5, 65, 97, 165, 186
  and Bailly and Lafayette, 108
  and Caisse d'Escompte, 109
needs
  in Rousseau, 130
net product
  in Physiocracy, 37
Netherlands, United Provinces
  conflict in, 88
  Prussian invastion, 89
nobility
  abolition of titles, June 1790, 138
  and Restoration, 218
  and second chamber, 146
nobility, French, 65
Notables, Assembly of, 3, 4, 52, 53,
    87, 99

offices
  venal, 63
Ogilvie, William, 112, 182
Old Regime, 50
outlaw, 23
  medieval concept of, 23

Paine, Tom, 62
  Common Sense, 62
  debate with Sieyès, 146
Paris
  Sieyès on administration of, 144
Parlements, 4, 44, 45, 49, 51
Pastoret, Charles-Emmanuel-Joseph-
    Pierre
  and veil over liberty, 154
patriot coalition, 143
  membership of, 165
patriot king, 49, 57, 71
  and Calonne, 52
  and Louis XVI, 91
  concept of, 62
patriotism, 53, 56

Pennsylvania
  legislature of, 66
perfectibilité
  in Rousseau, 15
Pétion, 180
Pétion Jérôme
  on Parisian sugar riots, 168
Pétion, Jérôme, 177, 178, 182
  and *assignat*, 113
  and *sans-culottes*, 159
  as mayor of Paris, 163
Pétiot, Joseph, 64
phenomenology, 2
Physiocracy, 29, 36, 65
  and taxation, 39
Pilnitz Declaration, 154, 175
Pitt, William (the elder), 175
political economy
  different versions of, 35
  Rousseau and Diderot on, 123
political theology, 28, 62
  Jansenist, 61
polyarchy
  Sieyès on, 146
poverty, 64
priestcraft, 17
property, 36, 182–3, 192
  and *assignat*, 112
  and citizenship, 87
  and possession, in Rousseau, 84
  in Restoration, 219
  of church, 99, 109
property system, 218
Provence, comte de, 154
Providence, 192
  Robespierre and, 190–3
Prudhomme, Louis-Marie
  on National Guard, 141
public credit, 19, 185
public debt, 34
  assessments of, 38

in modern historiography, 34
Pufendorf, Samuel, 18, 60, 183

Quesnay, François, 36

Racine, Jean
  in Gorsas, 166
Ramsay, Allan, 82, 114, 116
  and constituent power, 103, 113, 132, 133, 135, 136
  and Diderot, 121
  and Jean Chas, 105
  and religion of the magistrate, 105
  Essay on the Constitution of England, 103
  on Beccaria, 121
  on social contract, 122
Ramsay, Andrew Michael, 15
Ramsay, James (vicar of Teston, Kent)
  and slavery, 174
ranks, system of
  Ramsay on, 122
Raynal, Guillaume-Thomas, 16, 28, 119, 173
  and civil war, 164
realization
  and Condillac, 16
  in Leibniz, 206
Recherches philosophiques sur le droit de propriété considéré dans la nature (Brissot), 182
reform
  visions of, 54
religion, 17
religion of the magistrate, 19, 103, 105
  in Ramsay, 105
representation, 197
  in Sieyès, 134
representative government
  principle of, 73
representative government, Robespierre on, 193

representative system, 71, 116
ré-privé
    and absolute government, 86
ré-privé versus *ré-publique*, 63
republic, first French, 7
    Hebrew, 19
ré-publique,
    in Sieyès, 86
Restoration, 51
ré-total
    and democratic government, 86
revolt
    and the Fall, 26
    defined, 26
    versus revolution, 24, 28, 31
revolution
    concept of, 24, 25
    eighteenth-century concepts
        of, 27
    Mably on, 43
    predictions of, 44, 45, 49, 51
    versus revolt, 24, 26
revolution, 10 August 1792, 180
revolution, American, 30
revolution, Danish, 28
Revolution, Glorious of 1688, 180
revolution, managed
    see Mably, 45
revolution, Swedish, 30
Rickert, Heinrich, 220
riots
    Parisian sugar riots, 167
Robespierre, 184
Robespierre, Maximilien, 7, 21, 23, 27, 49,
        56, 57, 100, 177, 182, 184, 198, 214,
        225
    and citizenship, 139
    and constituent power, 138
    and elections to Legislative Assembly,
        137
    and Jacobin club, 179

    and liberty, equality and fraternity, 142
    and patriot king, 55
    and *sans-culottes*, 177
    on Brissot and *sans-culottes*, 161
    on constituent power, 137
    on Rousseau, 137
    on *sans-culottes*, 177
Robinson Crusoe
    in Rousseau, 130
Rochefoucauld-Liancourt, duc de la, 24
Roederer, Pierre-Louis, 75
    on Terror, 188
Roman law, 95
Rome
    and French monarchy, 60
Rouget de Lisle
    and *Marseillaise*, 178
Rousseau, Jean-Jacques, 15, 16, 49, 185,
        193, 197, 217, 221
    and ancient slavery, 81
    and cake, 25
    and Condillac, 80
    and Diderot, 129
    and elected aristocracy, 81, 99
    and elections, 135
    and gradated promotion, 99
    and Harrington, 76
    and Hobbes, 130, 131
    and Hume, 76
    and legislator, 119
    and *normal Volk* in Fichte, 222
    and Sieyès, 74, 76, 78, 85, 93, 116, 225
    and social contract, 116
    Cabanis on, 207
    Confessions, 76
    *Considerations on the Government of
        Poland*, 47, 77
    Discourse on the Origin of Inequality,
        15
    Emile, 47, 80
    in Aubert de Vitry, 107

Rousseau, Jean-Jacques (cont.)
  Letters from the Mountain, 83, 115, 116
  on *amour-propre*, 129
  on citizenship, 139
  on democracy, 83
  on democratic constitution, 83
  on division of labour, 120
  on election versus inheritance, 78
  on emigration, 154
  on imagination, 206
  on militias, 142
  on pity and animals, 80
  on Poland, 78
  on *Samuel*, 60
  on sovereignty and government, 85
  on Third Estate, 77
  overlap with Sieyès, 81
  Pliny in, 79
  predictions of revolution, 47
  Social Contract, 77, 84, 85, 120
  versus Diderot, 217
Rutledge, James (or Jacques)
  and Mme Geoffrin, 160
  Le Bureau d'esprit, 107

Saige, Joseph
  Catéchisme du citoyen, 146
Saint Paul, and charity, 183
Saint-Just, Louis-Antoine, 7, 21, 68, 177, 194
  on work, 198
Saint-Simon, Claude-Henri de, 215, 223
salons, 20
  and *sans-culottes*, 165
Samuel
  and kings, 225
  God's warning to, 58, 61
  Mercier on, 172
Samuel, Bk.1, ch. 8, 58
San-Domingo
  insurrection in, 176

sans-culotte ministry, 159, 179, 180
  and Girondins, 163
sans-culottes, 8, 20, 21, 59, 108, 127, 158, 184, 185
  against patronage, 150
  and 20 June 1792, 163
  and disintegration of patriot coalition, 165
  and Girondins, 159, 177
  and Gorsas, 167
  and *honnêtes gens*, 159
  and republican government, 177
  and Robespierre, 177
  as symbols of French republic, 177
  emergence of, 162
  identities of, 225
satire, 107, 165
  and Gorsas, 165
  and *sans-culottes*, 198
Scheffer, Carl Fredrik, 29
Schmitt, Carl, 28
  and Sieyès, 81
science sociale
  in Sieyès, 85
Ségur, Philippe-Henri, marquis de
  and army reform, 89
Seneca
  in Diderot, 126
Sidney, Algernon
  in Mercier, 171
Sieyès, Emmanuel-Joseph, 49, 63, 72, 87, 94, 98, 102, 115, 183, 192, 225
  and Aubert de Vitry, 106
  and bicameral legislature, 75
  and constituent power, 132, 134
  and constitution of Paris, 144
  and crisis of 1787, 92
  and Diderot's followers, 119
  and division of labour, 75
  and electism, 135
  and Harrington, 75

and Hobbes, 73
and Hume, 116
and Jean Chas, 106
and Paine, 79
and reform, 93
and representative system, 81
and Rousseau, 72, 76, 79, 80, 94, 160
and slavery, 81
and Third Estate, 77
and Tom Paine, 146
Barnave on, 72
biography, 74
characterisations of his thought, 72
on Adam Smith, 117
on citizenship, 139
on Condillac, 80
on constituent power, 133
on democracy, 134
on division of labour, 117, 131
on legislature, 139
on monarchy versus polyarchy, 79
on representation, 197
on Terror, 188
on Third Estate, 78
on work, 199
pamphlets by, 74
*Quelques idées de constitution applicable à
    la ville de Paris, en juillet 1789*, 143
Views of the executive means, 118
*Vues sur les moyens d'exécution dont les
    représentants de France pourront disposer
    en 1789*, 86
What is the Third Estate?, 74, 92, 118
slaves
    after 1789, 152
Smith, Adam, 57, 119
    and constituent power, 104
sociability, 72
    democratic, Furet on, 135
sociability, unsocial
    and history, 131

in Kant and Rousseau, 130
social contract
    in Rousseau, 131
social science, 204, 205, See *science
    sociale*
    and law of nature, 205
    and political economy, 205
socialism, 183
Société des amis des noirs, 165
    Brissot and, 174
Society of Friends of the Constitution
    or Jacobin club, 165
sociology
    and Comte, 223
sovereignty
    and constituent power, 132, 134
    and government, 63, 133
    and legitimation, 86, 115
    as legitimating power, 84
    democratic, 85
    in Rousseau, 84
    of nation, 88
Stanhope
    see Chesterfield, 43
state of France
    assessments of, 67
state of grace
    and state of nature, 61
state of nature
    and state of grace, 61
states
    in Jellinek, 218
statue of liberty, veiled, 23
Steuart, Sir James, 112
    and public debt, 46
    on revolution, 46, 47
Suard, Jean-Baptiste-Antoine, 119
Sully, Maximilien de Béthune, duc de, 33
Supreme Being
    festival of, 18
suspects, law of, 184

technology, 204
Terray, Joseph Marie, 32
Terror, 7
   and predictions of revolution, 45
   Tallien, Jean-Lambert, on, 188
theocracy
   and political economy, 123
Theophilanthropy, 8
Third Estate
   Rousseau and Sieyès on, 77
   Sieyès on, 93
Thouret, Jacques-Guillaume,
     96
   and constitution of Legislative
     Assembly, 137
Townsend, Joseph (rector of Pewsey)
   Bentham on, 173
trade
   and utility, 174
   based on luxury versus on economy,
     36
Turgot, Anne-Robert-Jacques, 87, 116,
     119
   Mémoire sur les municipalités, 88

United States of America, 7, 15
Universalism, 15
utilitarianism, 17
   and Brissot, 173
   Bentham on, 173

Varennes, flight to, 20, 21, 70, 132, 138,
     148, 149, 151, 153, 162, 198
veil, over liberty
   Montesquieu on, 22, 153
Venturi, Franco
   on Boulanger, 125
Verdun, battle of, 180
Versailles, 63
Versailles, march on, 5 October 1789,
     108, 145

Vertot, René, 27
Vico, Giambattista
   and Boulanger, 123
virtue, 17, 56
   bourgeois versus noble, 125
   Diderot on, 17
Voltaire, François Arouet, *dit*, 18, 35, 37,
     49, 62
   and *Henriade*, 57
   Le pauvre diable, 170
   on public debt, 36
   Saul, 59

Walsh, Robert
   and predictions of revolution,
     47
   on revolution, 45
war, 7
   and French finances, 176
   and public debt, 29, 38
   and *sans-culotte* ministry, 163
   Brissot on, 157
   French declaration of, 20 April 1792,
     159
war veterans, 215, 220
Washington, George, 9, 66, 108
   Barnave on, 148
Waterloo
   battle of, 7, 9, 34, 219
wealth
   and virtue, 64
Weber, Max, 216, 218
Williams, David, 112
Windelband, Wilhelm, 220
Wolff, Christian, 221
Wordsworth, William, 31,
     93
work, 198

Young, Arthur, 31, 34
   and bankruptcy, 31

For EU product safety concerns, contact us at Calle de José Abascal, 56–1°, 28003 Madrid, Spain or eugpsr@cambridge.org.